AN ETHNOGRAPHY OF HUNGER

AN ETHNOGRAPHY OF HUNGER

Politics, Subsistence, and the Unpredictable Grace of the Sun

Kristin D. Phillips

Indiana University Press

This book is a publication of

Indiana University Press
Office of Scholarly Publishing
Herman B Wells Library 350
1320 East 10th Street
Bloomington, Indiana 47405 USA

iupress.indiana.edu

Library of Congress Cataloging-in-Publication Data

Names: Phillips, Kristin, author.
Title: An ethnography of hunger : politics, subsistence, and the
    unpredictable grace of the sun / Kristin Phillips.
Description: Bloomington : Indiana University Press, 2018. | Series: Framing
    the global book series | Includes bibliographical references and index. |
    Identifiers: LCCN 2018013046 (print) | LCCN 2018025310 (ebook) | ISBN
    9780253038401 (e-book) | ISBN 9780253038364 (hardback : alk. paper) | ISBN
    9780253038371 (pbk. : alk. paper)
Subjects: LCSH: Subsistence economy—Tanzania. | Food security—Social
    aspects—Tanzania. | Food security—Political aspects—Tanzania.
Classification: LCC HC885.Z9 (ebook) | LCC HC885.Z9 P61593 2018 (print) | DDC
    339.46096782—dc23
LC record available at https://lccn.loc.gov/2018013046

1 2 3 4 5   23 22 21 20 19 18

To Jim, Burke, and Marcus

Contents

Preface

In your text, treat Africa as if it were one country. It is hot and dusty with
rolling grasslands and huge herds of animals and tall, thin people who are
starving.... Don't get bogged down with precise descriptions. Africa is big:
fifty-four countries, 900 million people who are too busy starving and dying
and warring and emigrating to read your book.... Among your characters
you must always include The Starving African, who wanders the refugee camp
nearly naked, and waits for the benevolence of the West. Her children have flies
on their eyelids and pot bellies, and her breasts are flat and empty. She must
look utterly helpless. She can have no past, no history; such diversions ruin the
dramatic moment. Moans are good. She must never say anything about herself
in the dialogue except to speak of her (unspeakable) suffering.

    Binyavanga Wainaina, *How to Write about Africa*

6-Day Visit to Rural African Village Completely Transforms Woman's
Facebook Profile Picture

    2014 headline from satirical newspaper *The Onion*

Trenchant critiques of the Global North's representations of the African
continent mark our new millennium. Often articulated as satire, such critiques—
of literature, film, travelogues, Western media, academic and aid-industry publications, and more recently, social media—poke fun at projected ideas of "Africa"
as utterly primitive, desperately hungry, hopelessly broken, or wholly unspoilt.
Such pervasive (yet contradictory) images highlight the personal insecurities,
political and economic agendas, superficiality, and what Stephen Ellis (2011)
aptly referred to as a singular "unoriginality" that undergirds so many representations of African contexts to Western publics today. Tongue-in-cheek, these
satires present readers with the most hackneyed and effective tropes they might
employ to reduce Africa to a single country, and a billion Africans' lives to—what
Chimamanda Ngozi Adichie (2009) calls—a "single story."

    A 2012 article in the satirical newspaper *The Onion* mocks the way in which
media depictions render "Africa" not merely a site of death, dearth, and disaster,
but itself the explanation for them:

Africa, which affects upwards of 40 million new residents annually, has only
grown more deadly over the years. According to WHO figures, many of the
afflicted die from Africa or Africa-related complications before they even

reach the age of 5. In addition to the staggering number of deaths attributable to the persistent, destructive Africa, roughly 1 billion individuals are now said to be living with the highly lethal continent, and for most there is little hope of recovery.... Additionally, graphic images of violent military crackdowns, vicious border disputes, and outright slaughter confirm that large parts of Egypt, Sudan, and Somalia have once again collapsed into full-scale Africa.[1]

When "Africa" itself is made the agent of communicable disease, dearth, natural disaster, and even war—then who needs an understanding of history, politics, culture, the global economy, or even science to explain what goes on inside its fifty-plus countries? In these depictions of Africa ridiculed by the *Onion* piece, Africa has become the empty, yet only, explanation for itself.

Hunger (and in particular *rural* hunger) is very much a part of this single story about Africa—that simultaneously constructs and asserts African deficiency, passivity, timelessness, and victimhood on the one hand, and Western righteousness, modernity, heroism, labor, and beneficence on the other. That hunger is part and parcel of this single story makes writing an ethnography about hunger in Tanzania a project fraught with the risk of reproducing this unimaginative and problematic repertoire of ideas. Yet, just as there is not a single story of "Africa," there is no single story of hunger. Just as there are many faces of "Africa," there are many faces of hunger. And just as the continent we call Africa has many interwoven pasts, many interlocking presents, and many possible futures, so hunger has its diverse roots, manifestations, and trajectories. Through contextualizing and historicizing hunger in one district of rural central Tanzania—where seasonal food crises *undermine*, more than they kill—this book aims to contradict some of the stereotypes. It underscores that African hunger is not a natural fact. It is not ahistorical or unchanging. It does not neutralize human agency. It is neither universally manifested nor uniformly experienced. The book seeks to *complicate* other stereotypical ideas—to give quintessential images a past and a present, a history and a context, confirmation and qualification. To paraphrase Adichie, the problem with many stereotypes is not necessarily that they are not true, but that they are incomplete.

Hunger, if understood from the dictionary definition to be a severe lack of food, is not easy to study ethnographically. If hunger is indeed the absence of food, the non-act of not eating, the reduction of body mass, the interminable wait for assistance, then it is no wonder that so many media outlets resort to the universal sign for hunger, that cliché of international telecasts—the bloated child, the blank-faced mother, the fly on the face, the outstretched hands. As if a lack of food or water eliminated the need for labor and effort and human interaction, instead of exponentially increasing it. As if deprivation, in its eons of history, actually had the power to interrupt time, halt action, cease sociality, or stop life. It is telling, as Alex de Waal has written, that "English definitions of famine ... leave the affected people as agents out of the causal scheme altogether.... These are essentially conceptions we could only apply to other people's societies: if a famine were to strike our own, it would be conceptualized in a different way, probably as a time of dearth, but also as a heroic struggle against the destruction of our way of life" (de Waal 1989, 32).

The idea of this book then, is to examine hunger in the Singida region of rural central Tanzania, as if in relief, by attending to the concepts of food, power, and sociality with which hunger is in relation and opposition. It resists the erasure of life and agency from chronically food-insecure communities (all too often the hallmark of hunger images that are produced in the West) even as it refuses to deny hunger and suffering (which is a tendency of attempts to provide more agentive accounts). By studying subsistence and its politics, I aim to emphasize hunger in this book to the same extent that rural Singidans do, to throw hunger into relief in order to acknowledge its very materiality, the life force it infuses, and the interactions and affiliations between people, their environment, and their government that it shapes. For it is indeed a pattern of relationships, events, structures, discourses, and practices that organizes access to food and fundamentally shapes people's labor, language, politics, and lives.

* * *

I did not go to Singida to study hunger; I landed in this rural central Tanzanian region to investigate the relationship between poverty, rural development, and participatory processes. I wanted to assess how people in Singida—a remote part of Tanzania characterized by its poverty but also by its economic similarity to so many other parts of Tanzania—were positioned to engage, influence and access the state in the age of "participatory development." I was particularly interested in the way that global and national initiatives to increase "community participation" in the design, planning, and implementation of rural development projects involved rural people and incorporated their perspectives, resources, and labor. But living in rural Singida between 2004 and 2006—a period that spanned the 2005 presidential elections in Tanzania and a major drought and food crisis affecting most of East Africa—I encountered a lot of "noise" in my study of rural development.

Now, many social scientific approaches to studying poverty and politics are driven by the quest to distinguish causes and consequences from mere coincidences. Ethnographic methods, on the other hand, allow a wider frame, inviting new characters and unanticipated plots to enter the story. Like history, ethnography presents the opportunity to research, think, and write "symphonically"— "demonstrating relationships between and among processes social scientists often separate" (Crais 2011, 29). So as the 2005 election activity became more frenzied, economic conditions more ominous, participatory development projects more coercive, and the stakes of my own relationships with villagers much higher, the interconnectedness of food, politics, and development became impossible to leave at the margins of my research. The co-incidence of these key events, amid the menacing steady march of state participatory development projects that placed incessant demands on villagers for "contributions" (that is, labor and money, or *michango*), raised questions about political subjectivity in rural Singida that required a much wider lens than I had originally planned. Why did villagers go on strike *against* development projects? Why did the 2005 elections yield virtually unanimous support for the ruling party amid economic conditions that seemed to be worsening, rather than improving? And why, amid so much labor and sacrifice to get by and "build the nation," did rural people so often accept and reproduce narratives of rural dependency? In spite of all the hype about *development*, my inquiries highlighted *subsistence* as the key project and central paradox of everyday life in Singida.

One of the singular, valuable, and most humbling aspects of long-term fieldwork is that history happens as you go. The political and economic landscape I set out to theorize after finishing nearly two years of field research in 2006 was both the same and different than the ones I encountered on return trips to Tanzania in 2007, 2010, 2011, 2012, 2013, and 2014. The concentric cycles of scarcity and plenty whittled into people's lives by the election cycle, years of food crisis, and the annual agricultural cycle were always strikingly discernible. But development was also evident. This included a new government health clinic, a new village office (finally distinct from the ruling party office), and more students studying at the secondary level than ever before. Yet this changing landscape also raised new questions. Why, despite these improvements, did people's sense of precarity remain unchanged? Following so many years of a seeming blind faith in the ruling party, how did a rights-talking opposition candidate suddenly win the Singida East parliamentary seat in 2010? And why, despite this leader's fulfillment of many promises, had some people become disillusioned with him by 2014? Reckoning with political and economic change discourages facile interpretations and predictions. The theoretical frame I offer in this book, *subsistence citizenship*, represents the unanticipated fruit of this decade of research among these shifting winds of political change. It is a frame that proposes to make sense of the enduring storyline of rural life in Singida: how the everyday project of subsistence shapes rural people's engagement with the state, with contemporary democratic structures and processes, and with each other.

Studying these social, political, environmental, and economic fields of subsistence turned out to be inescapable, for I was thrust into them during the course of my fieldwork. Like many anthropologists who have gone far from home for their research, I encountered starkly different cultural, language, and technological contexts than those in which I had grown up, and I began my fieldwork in a state of extreme dependence on those around me. Even though I showed up thirty years old, preparing to be married, knowing Swahili, and having lived previously in East Africa (though mainly in hostels where I purchased food, and water was in steady supply if not also running), I was in many respects for my Nyaturu neighbors still a child who needed to be taught the most basic norms of social intercourse and guidelines for human survival in a rural area: to speak, to greet, to walk, to host, to not catch my skirt on fire as I cooked, to wash my clothes without using a village's worth of water, and so on. I also received instruction on many things my own children learned in pre-school (formally and informally): how to be a girl or a boy, how to respect your elders, how to be a friend, how to disagree, how to share, how to keep, and how to stand your ground. The human universal is that we all learn these lessons. The cultural particular is the forms we are taught. Living in rural Singida involved, above all else, many earnest but fumbling attempts on my part to be a person—in the Nyaturu sense.

Yet this state of dependence early in my fieldwork was buttressed by the foreign currency of my research stipend and the white skin that signaled expertise, wealth, and empathy in a region that rarely received white visitors who were not missionaries, donors, or technical specialists like agronomists or engineers. So my dependence was a tremendously privileged one that opened doors, invited tribute, and attracted many friends. These friends included both disinterested ones and those seeking material help. My days were taken up with interviewing, writing fieldnotes, hiking to far-flung hamlets down in the valley, or traveling by *daladala* mini-bus to attend meetings in neighboring villages. But notwithstanding these critical research activities, my central anthropological project (and challenge) was to know how to appropriately feel compassion (*kuona huruma*—a Swahili expression my Nyaturu friends used with strong material implications), and honor obligations and debts—particularly in the rural community that hosted me, protected me, and provided me with the research material that would make me a living long into the future. I struggled to walk the line between honoring my relationships and commodifying them, between being human and becoming unhuman, between loosening the grip on privilege and power and simply reproducing it—slips that have both human consequences and also ones for research.

With regard to reciprocity in my formal relationships with interviewees, I tried to follow the general advice I had received in my graduate training in anthropology.[2] But living on my own in a room in the village office (what I have often likened to camping in a garage), I didn't just drop in to the village to neatly extract knowledge and leave. I was a part of it, and I desperately needed the people around me—for their security, their mutual aid, their advice, and their company. When the Reverend Dr. Howard Olson (a Lutheran missionary and linguist who lived among the Nyaturu in the 1950s and 60s) first arrived in Singida his neighbor Gwao came to him and greeted him with the following words, "When your fire goes out you can get embers from me, and when my fire goes out I will get coals from you" (Olson 2002, 133). As riddled as village relationships are in Singida with the usual neighborly tensions, competition, and gossip, there is no more apt metaphor for what it means to be part of a rural community in Singida.

So the longer I lived in Langilanga village, and the more I became threaded into its social and economic fabric, the more my friendships and relationships came to be interwoven with expectations of material support, and even long-term patronage. As a middle-class American, accustomed to performing socio-economic equality—even where it does not exist—and of using the market to create the most temporary economic relationships, I was instinctively uncomfortable with this. Schooled in critical anthropology on patronage as the backbone of "bad-faith" economies, I was even more uneasy. In his recent book, James Ferguson (2015) sheds some light on this "discomfort with dependence" felt by many from the Global North who encounter requests for patronage: "The long, noble history of antislavery and anticolonial struggles makes it easy ... for us to equate human dignity and value with autonomy and independence. A will to dependence therefore seems sad—even shameful. In this optic, dependence is a kind of bondage, a life in chains—the very opposite of freedom" (143).

Living in a Singida village, I found, mandated a very different approach to economic relationships: an explicit acknowledgement of wealth differences between friends and acquaintances that set the tone of future interactions and transactions. Dependence was indeed actively—sometimes even cheerfully—sought and cultivated not only by the poor with the rich, but also by the rich with the richer. Among the women I knew, the principles of reciprocity were always in effect, but often along uneven lines of resources. Where cash was needed, labor would be returned. Where labor was desired, the assurance of future assistance was granted. I saw economically diverse groups of women using local patronage relationships to get by, but also to "humanize" the market—to make lives and a community out of unequal opportunities and asymmetrical fortunes. I came to see this barefaced and unabashed material interconnection, so foreign to my own cultural conditioning, to be as much an index of *economic intimacy*, as it was of dependency. Such intimacy allowed for, demanded, and even rendered obligatory reciprocal relations between rich and poor.[3]

In this social and economic context I often assisted with medical fees for a sick child ($5), purchased eggs I did not need for a few hundred shillings (10 or 20 cents), bought charcoal only from the neediest women ($3.50), and responded to requests for small loans for food ($2) that I knew well would not be returned. While most of the loans went unpaid, at harvest time, like other wealthier families in the village, I was overwhelmed with gifts of fresh maize and pumpkins, peanuts and cowpeas, and, once, a mutant sweet potato as big as my head. Yet I lived in a village of 2000 people, and like others in the village who often helped dependent kin, my resources also had their limits, and so it was not every day and certainly not in every instance that I could assist. This, I came to find, was also essential. Both my assistance, and its limitations, familiarized me and human- ized me to people in Langilanga. But my intimacy was a practiced one, never second nature, and always somewhat awkwardly performed. And while I came to be certain that I should share, and I did share, sharing always reflected, rather than rectified, the inequality of our positions. Hence, this new role of patron was extremely uncomfortable, even distressing, throughout my research. And it was only as I was packing up to leave Singida in May 2006 that I fully recognized the gendered and social role I had acquired when two friends lamented before me that their "husband" was leaving them.

But, what I also came to learn is that this moral landscape of patronage, reciprocity, and mutual support is as contested as it is pervasive, as political as it moral, and as fluctuating as it is persistent. The aim of this book then is to trace the spatial, historical, and temporal contours of this moral geography in this paradoxical age of markets and rights. It is to show how these conditions of rural life in Singida—driven by cycles of scarcity and plenty, unpredictability, anxiety, and unbearably high stakes—profoundly shape not only the experience and outcomes of rural fieldwork, but also the politics of identity, belonging, and claims-making. These politics—born of economic, environmental, and political precarity in a time of immense inequality—I call "subsistence citizenship."

Notes

1. "Tens of thousands dead in ongoing Africa" (*The Onion*, May 16, 2012).
2. A rough sketch of my approach to material relationships with research participants is the following: I generally did not pay people for initial interviews. On a first visit I always offered to take a photograph of interviewees and/or their family and return a copy to them. This was almost universally accepted. If invited for a second research visit (a decision based on mutual interest), I always brought a gift of some material value (usually sugar and soap). In a few cases, where the knowledge I acquired was specialized, I paid cash. Otherwise, I reserved cash payments and gifts for contributions to community projects that would benefit all or much of the community. When people I had previously interviewed came to me for assistance (for food, health clinic fees, or other urgent needs) I made it a priority to always give what I could. With requests for school fee assistance however (usually reaching into the hundreds of dollars) I could rarely oblige.
3. Related to this point, Aaron Ansell (2014) has coined the phrase "intimate hierarchy" to refer to "local political alliances mediated by exchange" that imply a "posture of moral equality within the context of material hierarchy" (8).

Acknowledgments

I INCURRED COUNTLESS personal and intellectual debts during the decade that this book was in the making. First and foremost, I thank the village leaders, officials, families, and elders who hosted me in Singida. I am particularly grateful to Yusuphu Ramadhani for his leadership, welcome, and insights into rural political culture; to Celestin Yunde and Iddi Mnyau for their support for the project; to Verena Silvery for opening her home, heart, and perspectives to me during her work as a research assistant; and to Zena Saidi for being a wonderful and constant friend, confidant, host, and neighbor. I also offer many thanks to NyaEda, NyaMusa, NyaSalome, Juliana Severini, NyaJuli, Francisca Telespori, Nyalamek, Nyalamek, NyaAugustino, Mzee Rajabu, Mzee Severini, Wilson Saidi, Shabani Rajabu, Augustino Lamek, Ruben Lamek, Rajabu Omari, Sister Mary McNulty, Sister Rosemarie Steinbach, and the many others who enriched my stay in rural Singida with companionship, cooperation, debate, and laughter.

At the Singida Rural District and Regional Offices, Everest Mnaranara, Amasi Joseph, Joseph Sabore, Richard David Mtilimbania, Erasto Sima, Joram Njiku, and Patrick Mdachi answered my many questions and facilitated access to communities and archives. Rev. Naftali Ngughu blessed me with his warmth, Nyaturu instruction and research assistance; Rev. Dr. Peter A.S. Kijanga shared his kind collegiality and research insights into all things Nyaturu. Richard Viner, Robert Backstrom and Sister Scolastica granted me spaces in town to recharge my batteries and spirits as needed. In Singida Town, Simon Idabu, Edith Leonard Suih, Mangi Saidi, Mzee Abdallah Mtonga, Lissu Mwanga (Bosi), Mzee Saidi, Abdallah, Masumbuko, and many others nourished me with their friendship, endless curiosity, and profound insights into Singida's place in the nation and the world. A number of friends and interlocutors in Singida did not live to see this book published; some died long before their time. Matthias Mwiko of HAPA taught me much of what I know about participation in Singida. Esther warmed me with her kindness. Mzee Iddi was my favorite person to come across on the cattle path. Mzee Omari's pluck and persistence taught me quite a bit about the moral economy and the redistribution of resources in rural Singida.

For research clearance, I am grateful to the Tanzania Commission for Science and Technology and to Professor George Malekela for his collegiality and support. Colleagues at eight archives aided me in accessing the exceptionally rich historical record on the Nyaturu and on Singida District. At the Tanzania National Archives, Moshi Omari Mwinyimvua tirelessly sought out the files I needed and, more recently, Director Charles Magaya facilitated the permissions process with ease and friendliness. I also thank Adam Minakowski, Jake Homiak, and Daisy Njoku at the National Anthropological Archives of the Smithsonian Institution; Joel Thoreson at the Archives of the Evangelical Lutheran Church in America; Father Marcel Boivin at the White Fathers Archives in Dar es Salaam; and staff at the Archives of the School of Oriental and African Studies, the British National Archives, and the Singida Regional and District Archives.

Individuals in Tanzania's vibrant non-governmental networks—Joseph Kisanji, Marjorie Mbilinyi, and Rakesh Rajani—contributed much to my understanding of Tanzanian political culture. Rakesh's insights were particularly powerful and I thank him for continuing to challenge me along the way. Members of Parliament (MPs) from Singida Mohammed Dewji, Tundu Lissu, Mohamed Missanga, and Lazaro Nyalandu were very gracious over the years. As a political personality, MP Tundu Lissu is even larger in life than I have been able to render him in the pages of this book and I am grateful for the chance to access his charisma and critiques. The Hon. Juma Mwapachu has been a charming and wise interlocutor, offering his rich historical perspective on Tanzanian governance. Prior to his passing, the late Dr. Howard Olson generously responded to my inquiries about his many years of missionary work in Singida.

These years of Tanzanian fieldwork were enriched by the insights and support of friends and research colleagues, in particular Steinur Bell, Beth Bishop, Paul Bjerk, Lowell Brower, Natalie Bourdon, Diana Carvalho, David Colvin, Erin Dean, Iddi Haji, Andy Eisenberg, Caitlin Enright, Steve Fabian, Laura Fair, Howard Frederick, Cassie Hays, Dorothy Hodgson, Simon Ihonde, Thabit Jacob, Dorothea John, Susi Keefe, Sean Kirby, Matthew Knisley, Aikande Kwayu, Enock Makupa, Mwelu Mkilya, Tonya Muro, Amy Nichols-Belo, Patricia Piechowski, Andreana Prichard, Kate Raum, Ryan Ronnenberg, Mangi Saidi, Wilson Shailla, Sarah Smiley, Gasiano Sumbai, Jimmy Trask, Andrew Williams, and the families of Clement Kwayu, Elikana Ngogo, and Mzee Kingu.

This book owes much to those who engaged me and my ideas in their earliest iterations. I am greatly indebted to Rosalind Andreas, John Jeep, and Robert Nash for their early faith, support, and mentoring. At the University of Wisconsin-Madison and in subsequent years Amy Stambach worked with me from the ground up, apprenticing me in research, modeling conceptual rigor, yet keeping the reins loose so I could make my own way. Sharon Hutchinson pushed me to balance scholarly precision in anthropology and African Studies with the pursuit of social and political commitments. Others left lasting intellectual imprints through their teaching, conversations, and feedback: Michael Apple, Katherine Bowie, Ken George, Magdalena Hauner, Charles Hirschkind, Nancy Kendall, Dan Magaziner, Paul Nadasdy, Kirin Narayan, Adam Nelson, Frank Salomon, Jen Sandler, Michael Schatzberg, Fran Schrag, Katrina Thompson, Aili Tripp, and Neil Whitehead. A two-year writing fellowship at the Carter G.

Woodson Institute for African-American and African Studies at the University of Virginia offered a stimulating environment for thinking across disciplinary and geographic boundaries. I thank Deborah McDowell, Cynthia Hoehler-Fatton, the community of fellows at the Woodson Institute, and colleagues in UVA's Department of Anthropology for their friendship and critical engagement with my work: Ira Bashkow, Yarimar Bonilla, Ellen Contini-Morava, Deirdre Cooper Owens, Robert Fatton, Roquinaldo Ferreira, Bukky Gbadegesin, Adam Harr, Jason Hickel, Nathan Hedges, Brandi Hughes, Arsalan Khan, Adria LaViolette, Joe Miller, Amy Nichols-Belo, Marlon Ross, Holly Singh, David Strohl, Clare Terni, and Thabiti Willis.

During my three years teaching at Michigan State University, it was my privilege to be surrounded by great minds and wonderful people in the Center for African Studies and the College of Education. It was consistently a learning experience to sit at a table with James Pritchett. John Metzler deepened my appreciation for the field of African Studies. Jack Schwille was a dynamic and engaged mentor. Laura Fair, Deo Ngonyani, Bre Grace, Josh Grace, Amy Jamison, John Bonnell, and Betsy Ferrer Okello enriched my time at MSU and also my knowledge of East Africa. For their support along the way, I am also thankful to Beth Drexler, Kiki Edozie, Anne Ferguson, Rob Glew, Gretchen Neisler, Jeff Riedinger, Diane Ruonavaara, Chantal Tetreault, Chris Wheeler, Suzanne Wilson, and Peter Youngs.

At Emory University, Bobbi Patterson has continually graced me and our whole family with her mentorship, friendship, keen insights, and kindness. In their separate ways, Clifton Crais and Pamela Scully each breathed new life into this project at its nascent stages of re-conceptualization. I cannot thank Clifton enough for his always timely and sound advice, his close reading of multiple drafts, and his intellectual leadership and mentorship in the Institute of African Studies (IAS). I am grateful to colleagues in IAS, the Department of Anthropology, the Masters in Development Practice program, and elsewhere at Emory for welcoming me into the fold and for their collegiality, stimulation, and personal and professional support: Peter Little, David Nugent, Peggy Barlett, Peter Brown, Jenny Chio, Rick Doner, Susan Gagliardi, Aubrey Graham, Anna Grimshaw, Melissa Hackman, Nadine Kaslow, Bruce Knauft, Kristin Mann, Lora McDonald, Chikako Ozawa da Silva, Michael Peletz, Carla Roncoli, Bradd Shore, Sydney Silverstein, Liv Nilsson Stutz, Mandy Suhr-Sytsma, Nathan Suhr-Sytsma, Ana Teixeira, Jessica Thompson, Debra Vidali, Mari Webel, and Deans Carla Freeman and Lisa Tedesco. I cannot name all the Emory students who have touched my thinking by sharing with me their experiences and analyses, but I extend to them my gratitude.

Invitations and opportunities to present this research in various locales resulted in fruitful conversations and a sharpening of my analytical frames. Specifically, I am grateful to my hosts at Cornell University's Institute for African Development (IAD); University of Pennsylvania's Graduate School of Education; Oxford University's Department of Education; the University of Western Australia; Emory University's Program in Development Studies, Institute of African Studies, and Department of Anthropology; Michigan State University's Center for African Studies, the Center for Gender in Global Context, and Center for the Advanced Study of International Development; the Carter G. Woodson Institute at the University of Virginia, the Department of Anthropology at the New College of Florida; Hakielimu, and annual meetings of the American Anthropological Association, the African Studies Association, and the Comparative and International Education Society. In these and other settings, I have gleaned much from the commentary and insights of N'Dri Assie-Lumumba, Arjun Appadurai, Monisha Bajaj, Brenda Chalfin, Mike Degani, Alex de Waal, Husseina Dinani, Doug Fallon, Martin Forsey, Marie-Aude Fouéré, Kathy Hall, Holly Hanson, Angelique Haugerud, Rylan Higgins, Jim Hoesterey, David Hughes, George Paul Meiu, Greg Maddox, Zachariah Mampilly, Mike McGovern, David Mills, Lioba Moshi, Karen Mundy, Muna Ndulo, Alwiya Omar, David Post, James Pritchett, Katie Rhine, Joel Samoff, Leander Schneider, Martin Schoenhals, James H. Smith, Deborah Thomas, Fran Vavrus, Maria Vesperi, Marcus Watson, Brad Weiss, and Stanton Wortham.

This manuscript would not be what it is without the direct and critical engagement of colleagues in the past three years. Clifton Crais read the entire draft several times and was instrumental to its re-shaping. Leander Schneider's comments on the penultimate draft lent a much-needed critical eye to the latter half of the manuscript. Jen Sandler's unmistakable imprint on chapter 6 made this a better book. Melissa Hackman could not have been a better in-town writing partner and friend in this process, providing me with regular deadlines, warm breakfasts in the cold abyss of writing, and insightful feedback. Across the miles, Kara Moskowitz regularly provided feedback on chapters, lending me her remarkable analytical clarity and careful attention to evidence. Omolade Adunbi, Paul Bjerk, Lowell Brower, Erin Dean, Peter A.S. Kijanga, Aikande Kwayu, Peter Little, David Nugent, and Sydney Silverstein each read and provided important feedback on portions of the manuscript, lending me fresh insights and perspectives on my data. Katie Van Heest read an early draft of the manuscript and offered writing tutelage and publishing advice. At Indiana University Press, Dee Mortensen's careful insights and wise counsel saw me through the review process. I am deeply appreciative of her backing and assistance. Jennika Baines took on the project when it joined the Mellon-sponsored Framing the Global series and was wonderful to work with. Stephanie Smith's assistance and insights during the production process were invaluable. The comments and suggestions of two reviewers challenged me to reorganize the manuscript and think carefully about its frames. Though still far from perfect, it has no doubt been strengthened by their engagement. All errors and mis-interpretations remain, of course, my own.

For financial support of this project, I am thankful to the Fulbright-Hays Program for Doctoral Dissertation Research (DDRA); the Spencer Foundation, the Fulbright-Hays Group Project Abroad for the Advanced Study of KiSwahili; the Foreign Language and Area Studies (FLAS) fellowship program, and the Scott Kloeck-Jenson research fund at the University of Wisconsin-Madison. At the University of Virginia, a two-year fellowship at the Carter G. Woodson Institute for African-American and African Studies supported writing. At Michigan State University, the Center for International Studies and Programs funded trips to Tanzania in 2010, 2011, 2012, and 2013 for additional research. Support from the Department of Anthropology and the Institute of African Studies at Emory University helped to fund additional research trips and the Center for Faculty Development and Excellence funded editorial support. Subvention funds from Emory College and Laney Graduate School supported the publication of color images in the book. A Mellon Foundation grant to Indiana University Press for its series Framing the Global supported some of the book's production costs.

Some chapters contain material previously published elsewhere and are reprinted here with permission. Portions of chapter 4 appeared in *African Studies Review* 52(1): 23–45 and portions of chapter 6 appeared in *PoLAR: Political and Legal Anthropology Review* 33(2): 109–132 and in the 2015 volume *Remembering Nyerere: History, Memory, Legacy*, edited by Marie-Aude Fouéré, (Dar es Salaam: Mkuki na Nyota Press). I also thank Walter Bgoya of Mkuki na Nyota Press for his support. An earlier version of chapter 5 appeared in *Comparative Education Review* 57(4): 637–661. The version of the Prayer to the Sun reprinted in chapter 2 was originally published in the 1967 article "Praising the Sun" by Marguerite Jellicoe, Philip Puja, and Jeremiah Sombi (*Transition* 31: 27–31). I am grateful to the incredibly talented and politically provocative artist David Chikoko who gave permission to reprint his cartoon. Megan Slemons in Emory's Center for Digital Scholarship produced the maps of Singida and Tanzania.

In the course of this project, important friendships grew and sustained me. Thank you especially to Erin Dean, and to Jen Sandler, Amy Nichols-Belo, Jacqueline Brown Scott, and Angela Wagner for supporting, advising, inspiring, and balancing me over the years. I am also grateful to Omolade Adunbi, Lowell Brower, Laura Fair, Melissa Hackman, Dinah Hannaford, Matthew Knisley, Aikande Kwayu, Sydney Silverstein, Wilson Shailla, and to the "village" in Atlanta that supports our family: Sheena and Prem Kandiah, Cassie and Brad Strawn, Eric and Ping Moore, and our community at the Episcopal Church of the Epiphany.

My parents (Bette Phillips-Hershey, Richard and Karen Phillips, and Bob Hershey), the Lance family (Wendy, Jay, Jack, Anna, Oliver, and Theodore), and my late grandmother Mrs. Gertrude Hanson each supported and nourished me, inspired me with their separate paths, and grounded me in steadfast love and support. My mother Bette, in particular, encouraged me from an early age to learn and grow in relation to new people, ideas, and places. Jim Hanson, Liz Lavine, and Bob and Carol Phillips have always been there for me. The Hoesterey family—large and loving—has given me new insight into family support and the ties that bind us together.

Sharing this journey with Jim Hoesterey has been a tremendous gift. I am thankful for his intuitive counsel, his sense of humor and perspective, his irreverence, and his exuberant love of life. In essence, this project and our life together were conceived alongside each other, nurtured and developed on three continents, eventually yielding our two impossibly beautiful and spirited boys—Burke and Marcus—and now this book.

Becoming a mother halfway through this project left nothing in my life untouched or unaltered, including my subjective orientation to the themes of this book: unpredictability, precarity, and the beauty and vulnerability of a life lived in relation with others. It is the women and men I knew in Singida who have taught me the most about living so exposed, about remaining open to the world, connecting rather than disconnecting, when it all seems too precious to bear. I am grateful to them for sharing with me their experiences, insights, and ideas— at times amid staggering hardship—and I remain deeply in their debt.

Note on Language and Translation

Swahili is the national language of Tanzania and bridges linguistic divides between Tanzania's 110 diverse ethnic language populations. In much of rural Singida KiNyaturu (also known as KiRimi) is the first language spoken at home, though children begin speaking Swahili as soon as they enter school around age six or seven, if not much earlier. Prior to beginning research, I had studied Swahili through the advanced level (that included two summers in Tanzania). Upon my arrival in Singida, I studied KiNyaturu for three months, both independently with the aid of a phonology and morphology of KiNyaturu produced by linguist and missionary Rev. Dr. Howard Olson (1964), as well as formally with a retired Nyaturu Lutheran minister—Mchungaji Naftali Ngughu—who had spent many years assisting with the translation of the Bible from English into KiNyaturu.

I conducted the lion's share of this research in KiSwahili, aided in rural areas by a research assistant—Verena Silvery—who was fluent in both KiSwahili and KiNyaturu. In the few cases where research participants spoke only KiNyaturu (mostly elder women), Ms. Silvery translated between KiNyaturu and KiSwahili, though I knew enough KiNyaturu to roughly follow what my interlocutors were saying. Nearly all the interviews were recorded, and Ms. Silvery transcribed them. Translations from Swahili into English are my own.

In this book I provide translations of particularly apt quotes or important concepts or phrasings. These translations are in the KiSwahili, unless otherwise noted with a "Ny." for KiNyaturu.

AN ETHNOGRAPHY OF HUNGER

Introduction

Subsistence Citizenship

THE 2006 HUNGER in the Singida region of central Tanzania was neither sudden nor surprising. Worse, it had been long anticipated—since the annual rains had failed eleven months earlier and the young maize had withered in the sun (see plate 1). The sorghum crop had been heartier, but the harvest had still only produced a third of "Langilanga" village's food requirements.[1] Villagers had sold some of this meager harvest to pay off debts and the mandated contributions to development projects. But by January 2006, food had run thin in household stores, and to exacerbate conditions, the 2006 rains were late. In the best case, if it started raining now, the lean weeks would stretch into aching months before the first pumpkins would be ready to pick.

Like many of his neighbors, Baba Saidi appeared to me smaller in January 2006 than the last time I had seen him. Baba Saidi was a Muslim man who lived near the road in Langilanga. He was Chairman of this village—the highest elected office—and was husband to one wife and, at the time, father to five small children. His family was eating, he told me: they cooked *ugali* and wild greens once a day, and let the children eat the *ikhokho* (Ny. reheated leftovers) in the evening. They could (and likely would) sell a chicken or a goat to purchase food—but the price of sorghum and maize had skyrocketed, while the value of the livestock that they traded dropped to a third of its normal value. Investors in the village who had bought grain cheaply at harvest-time and could later resell high made a huge profit, but for cash-poor villagers, a sale meant compromising the future to hardly make a dent in their hunger. Other households without livestock for sale or children to attract NGO food aid were much worse off, Baba Saidi observed. Government food aid would come, he noted. But when? How much? And for whom?

As the drought dragged on into February, village women woke at three in the morning to draw water from the sometimes-trickling well. The poorest of the village poor—widows without land or cattle—struggled to eke a living out of the environment: eating wild fruit, borrowing from neighbors, walking the eight miles to Singida town and back to find a buyer for the wild greens they had picked so they could buy a bit of grain for their children. People pressured wealthier kin, village leaders, and the families of elected officials for food assistance for these poorer neighbors: "They are living on wild fruit"; "She is eating grass"; "Where is the food aid?" Opportunities for day labor had disappeared entirely, with even wealthy families tightly cinching their belts. People remarked constantly on the sun's anger, and prayed for its unpredictable grace. As one young man noted, "There is no assistance in these days, no opportunities for day labor to be found. Now is hunger. People fear the sun, this sun of drought. Their hands are deep in their pockets. The young men have fled to the cities. They are afraid of this sun."

The waiting, Baba Saidi remarked, was its own form of hell. To drive this point home he told me a story that had been circulating in the village as of late.

> So while God was Creator of the world, he noted that: Now I have created this Man. How can I persuade him to believe in me? And God asked Man: "Man, who are you? And who am I?" And Man responded: "You are you and I am me." And God was very upset at this response because, of all the creatures he had created, never had one answered him like that before. He decided, "I will give Man the punishment of one hundred years of hell." After the one hundred years of hell, God asked Man again: "Man, who are you and who am I?" And Man answered: "I am me and you are you." And God thought, "This Man ... why does he say this? Wait, I will sentence him to another one hundred years of hell." And after yet another one hundred years, He asked him once again, "Who are you and who am I?" And again, Man answered, "You are you and I am me." And God thought, "How can this be? How can this punishment not be enough for him? So He said, "Fine. Let me try another punishment." And this time He gave Man the punishment of hunger, a great hunger of one hundred years. And Man was sick with hunger for one hundred years, during which he suffered and shriveled up with exhaustion. And then Man was called again and asked, "Who are you and who am I?" And Man answered, "You are Almighty God, and I am your Creation." At this, Almighty God was very happy, for He saw that Man now believed in him.

Baba Saidi had heard this story of hell and hunger from a local imam. To many rural Singidans it circulated as a story of faith and of coming to God, made intelligible through invoking the power of hunger. To me however, it was a story of the suffering of hunger, made intelligible through invoking the specter of hell. God, in this tale, wields hunger as a weapon that brings about the truest suffering and produces the ultimate humility.

Hell, the story asserts, has nothing on hunger in propelling human action, taming conceit, forging bonds, and sparking faith. And indeed, the entanglements of food, farming, faith, hunger, and power were highlighted again and again during my decade of research in rural Tanzania. For the story's heavenly leveraging of hunger to elicit faith was not unlike the earthly leveraging of hunger and its relief to confer legitimacy on the contemporary organization of economic and political life in rural Tanzania. Indeed, the historical and social experience of hunger exerts a powerful influence on the way rural people wake up each day to engage life, God, resources, opportunities, and each other. The lived experience of hunger breaks people of their arrogance. It puts them in relation with a higher order and it asserts order among human beings themselves. In anticipation of hunger, and in the throes of it, people cast wide webs of connection, obligation, and pressure—to God, to the powerful, and to each other. Through acts of both conflict and cooperation, and through networks of both inequality and interdependence, hunger brings people to each other; it brings people to God; and—as this book goes on to argue—it brings them to their government.

* * *

Eventually, it did rain. Within days of the first drops, the Singida landscape turned from brown to green—*chanikiwiti*—green, the color of heaven. Surrounded now by auspicious sprouts of maize and sorghum, the mood of the village lifted, even though it would still be months before Singidans' hunger would be healed. Skyward eyes turned to earth as people weeded, cultivated, and planted sweet potatoes. And as grain stores continued to dwindle and food prices continued to skyrocket, the government further delayed on its promises for relief food—what the Nyaturu refer to as *ufoni* (Ny.), or the "healing" of their hunger.

Throughout February (Ny. *mweri munti*, or the "month of hardship"), Singidans struggled to safeguard their food supply, secure relations with political patrons, and communicate their food deficits by participating in village surveys. The tone of this claims-making—both to individual patrons and to village government leaders—was conciliatory: conflict was minimized, patrons' egos stroked, favors begged, relationships recalled, and obligations invoked.

But it did not take long for the most wealthy and well-connected of the village to flee the flood of claims: *"Amesafiri"* ("He has taken a trip") became the inevitable greeting the hungry received when they knocked on the doors of cattle-owners, businessmen, and ward officials. And it soon became evident that as aid trickled down through national and district bureaucracies, rural Singidans' right to food threatened to be "eaten" by officials, diverted to other communities, or funneled narrowly to target only the very poorest citizens. At this threshold of subsistence, tensions came to a climax when the young men of Langilanga village went on strike, announcing that until their "right to food" had arrived they would refuse to "build the nation"—that is, to participate in village development projects. The men's threat to not participate imperiled the village's progress in constructing teacher housing, repairing school latrines that had collapsed in the previous year's rains, and digging a deep-water well. All of these projects would come to an abrupt halt without community labor. In the face of such a powerful threat to its primary locus of legitimacy—development—and this rupture in political relationships, the village leadership quietly agreed to evenly distribute the food aid they had received from the government across the village population, rather than targeting the poorest households.

The issues raised in this particular case of the politics of subsistence reflect recurrent tensions that emerged during the two years of ethnographic fieldwork I conducted in Singida (2004–2007) and during five shorter research visits between 2010 and 2014. In the context of deciding what crops to farm, who to vote for, which children to educate, how much labor and money to contribute to community development, and which food and livestock to keep, consume, or sell, Singida villagers regularly faced questions related to the terms of, and prospects for, their biological persistence. As they negotiated challenges to subsistence, they contemplated the most effective mode of political claims-making, gauged the strength of their relationships, weighed the risks and benefits of political revolt, and asserted the autonomy of their labor and access to its fruits—often under the most trying of circumstances. In these projects for survival, they alternately enlisted and evaded state structures and state agents, engaging in a politics of subsistence that sought to prompt, resist or redirect redistributive efforts.

And yet the mass of villagers who succeeded in staking claims on food aid in this case ultimately did so at the expense of the poorest households who suffered the most severe hunger. For the limited food aid that eventually arrived (a mere 128 sacks of grain in the face of a shortage of 5276 sacks) came to be distributed among the entire village population, not just the government's intended targets (the poorest of the poor). And indeed the moral economy of the poor—those reciprocal links between the haves and the have-nots that temper inequality—is all too often articulated at odds with those who need it most.

These conditions of rural life in Singida—with its volatile cycles of scarcity and plenty and the disquieting spectre of suffering that looms—profoundly shape the political engagement of rural Tanzanians with key contemporary democratic forms like electoral politics, participatory development, and humanitarian aid. I call this very historically particular form of political engagement, born in the context of widening wealth disparities, the globalization of markets and human rights, and intensifying economic and environmental challenges, "subsistence citizenship." This subsistence citizenship refers not to a deficient, unsuccessful, or ineffective citizenship, but rather to a particular relationship between smallholder farmers and the twenty-first century state that is both constituted and constrained by the project of meeting basic needs.

Subsistence citizenship, I go on to demonstrate in this book, bears distinctive temporal and spatial attributes, characterized by seasonality in relation to water and food supply; strategic code-switching and code-mixing of market, patronage, and rights-based idioms of resource distribution; ebbs and flows of political attention and engagement in relation to election cycles and dearth; and unpredictability in terms of the climate, market, and government aid. It is also marked by governments' political opportunism in the face of disaster, the high stakes of rural dependency on food aid, and the invisibility of rural governance that permits coercion without repercussion. In the context of such palpable and embodied constraints on political agency, and a national political culture that refuses (and vilifies) claims-making for sub-national or regional development, rural people in Singida region have tended to employ a softer advocacy. They engage widely circulating moral idioms centering on ideas about food, feeding, and family even as they simultaneously, and increasingly, individualize their efforts for material improvement and resist demands on their labor, time, and resources for village development initiatives.

These subsistence politics provoke vital questions for the projects of development and democracy in Africa. First, how do people in agrarian communities in Africa experience intensifying challenges to subsistence? Second, in the context of these constraints on political agency, how do rural Tanzanians understand, analyze, and negotiate the rights and obligations of citizenship? And finally, how does the everyday project of subsistence—with its cycles of dearth and bounty, its volatility, and the magnitude of its stakes—shape rural people's engagement with key contemporary democratic forms like electoral politics, participatory development, and humanitarian aid? Driven by these questions, this book chronicles the practice and paradox of rural citizenship in twenty-first century Tanzania.

The analysis of subsistence citizenship makes distinctive contributions to the anthropological and African Studies literatures on hunger, agrarian politics, environmental studies, and development.[2] First, it ethnographically represents and theorizes the *banality of hunger* for rural subsistence farmers. Hunger, for most people in the world today, does not resemble the spectacular suffering in 1980s Ethiopia etched indelibly into American popular culture by Michael Jackson and Lionel Richie's charity song "We Are the World." Nor is it represented by the haunting famine of the Ik people in Uganda chronicled by Colin Turnbull (1972), or the constant and chronic hunger so poignantly portrayed by Nancy Scheper-Hughes (1992) in northeast Brazil. In rural Tanzania, people live with hunger far more than they die from hunger. Hunger is seasonal and episodic but regular and rhythmic. Hunger in Singida haunts; it waxes and wanes. Hunger is usually eventually satiated, but always anticipated. Hunger is a mnemonic (what Parker Shipton [1990]) has called a hitching-post for history): structuring time, marking memory, and periodizing the past. Hunger, for the Nyaturu-speakers living in Singida, orients time, space, and action, lingering as a specter in everyday life, language, lore and politics.

Thus, despite all the daily hype about *development* by international aid organizations, national politicians, and the village elite, it is *subsistence* and the management of risk that for many rural villagers is the key project of everyday life. The concepts of subsistence and development, while certainly related, invite different understandings of the stakes of social, political, and economic change. In rural Singida, development centers on the progressive will to improve (Li 2007), to seek a better life, to recreate self and society, sacrificing the now for an easier, healthier, more sustainable or more fulfilled life later. Subsistence, less ambitious and more essential, aims at sustaining life in the face of mounting unpredictability and increasingly precarious livelihood. In a context of increasing competition for resources, both projects require continuing adaptation of life skills and strategies. While in theory development initiatives depend upon and contribute to subsistence, this book shows how with a lack of careful consideration for the precarity of the rural poor, some forms of development can just as easily threaten subsistence.

As an anthropologist, I hone in on the individual threads that constitute this story of subsistence and development in Tanzania, relating micro-level histories and the narratives of individuals, families, and communities. At this level, it is not difficult to care and connect, in the human sense. But it is also important to not miss the story's more global significance and the way that the political, social, economic, and environmental threads that constitute this story—"processes situated deep inside the national" (Sassen 2014, ix)—stretch far beyond the rocks of Singida and the borders of Tanzania to constitute other, similar stories in far-away places. For such tensions between subsistence and development are hardly unique to rural central Tanzania.

For example, in 2014, an op-ed in the *New York Times* described a recent Nigerian gubernatorial election in Ekiti State that pitted Kayode Fayemi—a pro-democracy incumbent with a solid record of administration and focus on infrastructural development—against Ayo Fayose—a former governor who had been impeached based on apparent corrupt practices and human rights violations.[3] Fayemi waged a political campaign to convince his rural constituents that big projects like roads would improve their economic futures by making it easier to get their products to market. Fayose, on the other hand, went on the campaign trail with massive quantities of Thai rice (with his name embossed on the sacks) that he distributed to hungry voters. Fayose won. In the editorial, the author asserted: "The tactic, hugely successful, points to the challenge that faces all "developing" countries: how to negotiate a compromise between the immediate demands of an impoverished, mostly illiterate populace, and the urgent need for capital projects that will lift them out of poverty. Hungry people will always be susceptible to immediate inducements of the kind offered by politicians like Mr. Fayose" (Maja-Pearce 2014).

In the Nigerian press, Fayose's campaign tactic came to be known as a focus on "stomach infrastructure" (in contrast to promises to develop "physical infrastructure").[4] Proponents of stomach infrastructure in Nigeria argued that development cannot happen on empty stomachs, while critics saw it as purchasing votes at the expense of what was really needed for long-term economic development (schools, hospitals, and roads, for example). Such debates speak to the pervasiveness of subsistence politics, in which physical suffering is seen to forge a particular kind of political subjectivity and to shape political action. At the same time it also reveals the binary and oppositional terms through which such politics are frequently understood and analyzed: corruption against justice; development against subsistence; the body against the mind; long-term good against short-term gain; personal benefit against public good; rural ignorance against cosmopolitan understanding. Like these political commentators, I highlight the political and economic dilemmas such politics present, by understanding how people create lives on the margins and do so in situations of great constraint, exclusion, marginality and inequality (Peters 2004). But voters' choices to engage in the politics of stomach infrastructure, I argue, may also arise from knowing, social conditioning, creativity, deliberation, historical experience, tactic, or collective praxis, in addition to being produced by faulty understanding, crisis, or corruption.[5] The political modalities of rural Tanzanians, like those of everyone everywhere, are born of history, society, and human creativity, as well as of biological need.

The frame that this story develops—subsistence citizenship—thus lends both clarifying and destabilizing insights to the global politics of hunger and distribution. For the reality of hunger exists not simply within the everyday lives of people who suffer from it, but within the structures of meaning in the places where food's distribution and availability is organized—on national and international markets and in the boardrooms and ballrooms where policies, alliances, and decisions are made. The inability of your average lawmaker, businessman, tourist, or voter to grasp the experience of chronic food insecurity is as much a part of the actuality of hunger as its insidious normality for those who live it day in and day out.[6] The success of efforts to alleviate hunger in rural Tanzania and beyond will depend on all of our grasp of the banality of hunger and its implications for politics, participation, and citizenship.

And yet as we work to comprehend the global lessons of this Singidan story for (what James Scott calls) our schemes to improve the human condition, let us not forget the human, the historical, and the particular. For Nyaturu people in Singida have long persisted, worked, prayed, migrated, loved, fought, intermingled, danced, transgressed, and reproduced amid ecological hardship and material uncertainty (Iliffe 1979; Jellicoe 1969, 1978; Schneider 1970; 1982; Von Sick 1915). So to reduce Singida—the setting of this research—to just a place of predominantly poor rural people, would be to miss most of the story. To paraphrase Adichie (2009), it would flatten Singidans' experience and overlook the many other stories that have formed them. People in Singida—like all of us—wake up to their own histories and ways of seeing and being in the world and they make lives with the technologies, material resources, social relationships, interpretive frames and collective histories at hand. A second—and no less important—aim of this book then is to describe these Singidan lifeworlds and their shifting sands: to understand how people in Singida make do, make meaning, and carry on.

The Social Project of Subsistence: Materiality, Subjectivity, Politics

Scholars, activists, and development planners have largely displaced "subsistence" as an explicit goal of poverty alleviation. In earlier decades subsistence referred to the production of enough food to meet caloric requirements and to furnish a replacement fund of seed and other agricultural inputs. Today conversations in social science theory, human rights, and development practice are broader in time, scale, and ambition. We rarely talk of simple reproduction, that is, base physiological survival from year to year. Instead we add concerns about malnourishment to those of undernourishment. We use concepts like "livelihood," "capabilities," and "resilience" instead of "subsistence" to signal our interest not just in the physical but in the social, economic, environmental, and political dimensions of well-being too. Such choices draw attention to the expanded time-scale of development goals and the desire to sustain both people and the natural resource base long into the future.[7] In this broader, more long-term, and more qualitative understanding of well-being, access to a cell phone—as much as to a hand hoe—becomes a vital instrument to make it from day to day.

In centering my analysis on subsistence, it is important to not reduce well-being to the satisfaction of material wants or to undo the considerable intellectual and practical work that has been done to expand notions of poverty and livelihood to include the perspectives of those most challenged by them. In his exquisite *Life within Limits: Well-being in a World of Want*, anthropologist and poet Michael Jackson notes,

> In understanding what it means to be well we must therefore take into account not only what we need as a bare minimum to survive but what we need for our lives to be worthwhile—for we do not live by bread alone, and well-being is never simply the satisfaction of biological needs, the possession of primary goods, or the attainment of personal fulfillment and happiness. Nor is it a matter of adaptation, since getting what we want invariably leads us to conceive new wants, as if satisfaction is always a matter of possessing more than we have, even when we appear to have everything we could possibly wish for (2011, 60).

If Jackson's profoundly empathetic contribution is to highlight the human universality of material want and to draw connections between its experience by rich and poor alike, my project—alternately—is to draw sharper distinctions between these experiences, to understand what want *does* at the threshold of subsistence, that it *does not* do in less precarious circumstances. So as we fruitfully broaden and nuance conversations about what it takes to get by, this book argues that we should not lose sight of the very specific space in which physical persistence is insecure, and of what happens in this space that shapes political forms, social experience, and human economies. It is not enough to look simply at physiological life and death. But nor should we forget the materiality of poverty.

The material referent of subsistence is the broad and indeterminate but precarious threshold between physical persistence and death. Subsistence, understood in this way, has a base, raw, fundamentally material character that is substantively experienced by individuals and groups alongside their everyday pursuit of well-being and human connection. Subsistence is an art in Singida, one that is continually shaped and re-worked by old and new tastes, habits, histories, environments, and economic opportunities. Subsistence is also a science in Singida, built on understandings of minimal intake, protein deficiency, and nutritional need gleaned from everyday life as well as from school curricula, mission interventions, and school feeding program supplements.

There is also a local science of starvation in Singida, one grounded on local historical and empirical data from periods of widespread hunger in between the times of plenty when people have all the ugali, beans, wild greens, fruits, and occasionally even meat to satiate them. This commonsense in Singida reminds people if they try to survive on sweet potatoes alone, they will swell with kwashiorkor (a form of severe protein deficiency); that while a sauce of wild greens and okra (*mlenda*) does nothing to fill the belly, it is a necessary part of their diet; and that there are famine foods from which one can eke calories and protein from the environment in the leanest of times: cow's blood, flour ground from certain thorns, and wild fruits. Singidans use these principles to identify and communicate the early signs of severe crisis: "She has started to swell"; "They are eating grass"; and "They are living on *zambarau* [a small purple wild fruit that comes into season in the worst of the hunger months]" were three of the most commonly referenced euphemisms for starvation used in Singida in the first decade of the new millennium.

Subsistence, Subjectivity, and the State

Beyond its lived physical manifestations, the project of subsistence also has enduring effects on historical subjectivity, as a rich literature in agrarian studies, political science and anthropology attests. That is, as a daily labor and a central social project, subsistence exerts a powerful influence on the way people wake up each day to engage life, resources, opportunities, and each other. English historian and economist R.H. Tawney once wrote of this precarious existential position of smallholder farming populations as "that of a man standing permanently up to the neck in water, so that even a ripple is sufficient to drown him" (Tawney 1966, 77).

James Scott (1976) theorized this experience of precarity and associated risk aversion as a "subsistence ethic" that was born of the commercialization of agriculture and systems of tenancy and taxation that destabilized agrarian incomes. This subsistence ethic governed community norms of entitlement to make a living from village resources, consensus about reciprocity, and patterns of patron-client relations, with the peasant's test for rebellion "more likely to be 'What is left?' than 'How much is taken?'" (7). Scott thus marks exploitation in relative and subjective terms as the tipping point at which clients experience demands by patrons as threats to subsistence. He credits smallholder farmers with the agency to change, noting their tendency to "plunge ahead" with new techniques or technologies when these present little risk to subsistence. Rebellion occurs only after long-term and persistent threats to subsistence, when the "safety-first" principle breaks down. As we will see in chapter 6, for the risk-averse—those "up to the neck in water"—social and political upheavals are often a "last gasp" (26).

Other developments in agrarian studies and anthropology have challenged us to complicate our understandings of agrarian politics, for neither rural people, nor their governments, can be painted with a broad brush. In the first place, as Eric Wolf (1966) noted, there is not a single homogenous peasantry. Accordingly, peasants have not just one trait, but many. In the quest to characterize and understand rural politics, "peasants" have often come out as a culture with a personality: looking alternately excessively noble, rational, stubbornly adherent to tradition, subjugated, or rebellious (see Glassman 1995 and Olivier de Sardan 1999 for particularly apt critiques). Much scholarship on peasant communities has either valorized as superior the peasantry's moral order, or hyper-emphasized its rationality. Rather than seeing subsistence as an "ethic" upheld by some but not others, economies as more or less moral, or individuals as solidly "inside" or "outside" these ethical communities, I instead try to understand how socially experienced and materially conditioned ideas about morality drive human experience and action, often in diverse and unanticipated ways.

One must also be careful of drawing sharp distinctions—in temperament, motivation, appetite or honor—between peasants and their governments. In the analysis of political and economic issues in Africa, Mike McGovern (2011) has suggested, "we tend to exonerate 'the people' … [yet] the assumptions underlying this distinction leave some key questions unanswered, one being, where does the terrible elite come from, if not the people" (173). A study of rural African political subjectivity must keep in mind that like peasantries, "states" too are internally heterogeneous, complex, and often contradictory institutions that are constituted of individuals and groups that have diverse connections to the people they govern (Askew 2002; Berman & Lonsdale 1992; Berry 1993). A sidelong view of the rural "state" in Tanzania reveals that the state that regularly frets about the rains and the food supply is not necessarily the same state that adjudicates domestic altercations, that ceremoniously stops by the village during campaign season, or that seems constantly to be "eating" development resources.

Recent work has characterized the state-and-society relationship in many African countries as one marked not by the binary terms of resistance, subjugation, or collaboration, but rather by complicity, conviviality, and illicit cohabitation (Edmondson 2007; Mbembe 2001; Nyamnjoh 2002; Smith 2007; Werbner 2002).

These terms speak aptly to the *ambivalence* with which state and non-state agents engage each other in rural contexts on issues of subsistence and development. In rural Tanzania, there is not only an art of governance and an art to not being governed (as Scott 2009 has shown), but also an art to being governed, and an art to not governing. On both sides of the state/society relationship there exists a tension between the longing to capture and the desire to escape; to exert power and to skirt intimacy; to entice into an obligation and to evade reciprocal demands. Physical remoteness serves as an obstacle *and* a buffer to *both* those who rule and those who are ruled. "Subsistence," then, is one dynamic terrain on which one can observe how "state" and "society" emerge as particular, connected entities.

Hunger and the Politics of Representation

Beyond its inscription on bodies and subjectivities, subsistence is also operative in the political realm. As Josué de Castro wrote in 1952, "Hunger is the most degrading of adversities; it demonstrates the inability of existing culture to satisfy the most fundamental necessities, and it always implies society's guilt" (58). Media attention has brought hunger's condemnation of society into our own homes. Butterly and Shepherd (2010) argue that media coverage has produced a "new paradigm of the biology and politics of starvation" that governs both conscience and politics: that is, one in which "we know" (4). Knowing and its attendant moral imperative for action are the key drivers of the contemporary politics of hunger.

In this way—and particularly for those who face less spectacular stages of hunger that require convincing potential benefactors of impending crisis—*subsistence is an inherently political question*, subject to conflicts over representation, communication, and interpretation. These politics have direct effects on both redistributive efforts and the political legitimacy of local and national leadership, which often frames itself in the predominant paternalist discourse of the feeding father. As Michael Schatzberg has noted of many sub-Saharan African political contexts, "if the father nourishes and nurtures, he has the right to rule ... and the right to 'eat'" (2001, 150). The representation of well-being, therefore, is a site of intense struggle, because of its concomitant implications for political legitimacy. For example, during a 2003 food crisis two people died in a Singida village. When their bodies arrived for examination at the hospital, doctors concluded and announced on national radio that two people in Singida had died of hunger. I was told that regional government medical officials arrived promptly thereafter to perform autopsies and immediately had national radio announcing that "No one has died of hunger in Singida."[8] Such tensions over representation speak directly to the social and political shame that hunger produces.

In this age of humanitarian crises where people tend to look blankly past chronic malnutrition, but see the image of the wasting child as evidence of total social breakdown, the threshold of subsistence reveals the threshold between market and rights. It is at this threshold that food may cease to be a commodity, subject to laws of supply, demand, and property; it may become a right, governed by entirely different norms and rules of distribution. Following Richard Wilson's (2006) call to attend to the "social life of rights," this analysis highlights the impermanence and conditionality of rights. In light of food's "rights potential"— I show—one of the most effective weapons of the weak in the struggle to access resources is *the threat not to subsist*, for it is the threat of death from starvation that triggers redistribution in the name of rights. In this way, statements by villagers or village leadership that "They are starting to eat grass" or "She is starting to swell" become political propositions as much as direct observations. (Local government administrators refer to such public threats not to subsist as *kulia njaa*, or "to cry hunger.") The threshold of subsistence is therefore inherently political: a rich rhetorical space of often frenzied activity to perform or deny suffering—as well as to endure it—in order to prompt, resist, and/or redirect redistributive efforts.

An anthropology of subsistence that takes seriously hunger's materiality, subjectivity *and* politics must start, as we will in chapter 1, with the "existential conditions of the rural producers" (Watts 1983, 105) and with recognizing the significance of a threshold of subsistence at which point understandings of political legitimacy—that which is politically thinkable and politically un-thinkable—dramatically shift.[9] It must acknowledge the heterogeneity, unboundedness, contradictions, complexity, and complicity of states, rural communities and their ethical domains. It must take seriously the broad discursive strategies, in addition to the broad social networks, used by both rural people and the state to negotiate the distribution of entitlements, obligations, and political authority. It must not reduce rural people's lives to a succession of crises and a series of dependencies. But it must take seriously how rural people and states experience crisis and dependency, and use discourses of crisis and dependency as they go about their everyday pursuit of well-being. Finally it must take into account how the threshold of subsistence—those weeks, months, or years, where physical persistence is called into question—has also offered colonial and postcolonial states unparalleled opportunity to wield power, enforce dependencies, or implement large-scale state schemes. For it is at the threshold of subsistence where states and non-state agents alike practice a politics of precarity to pursue their own ends. This book highlights the human significance of these struggles.

"The Sound of Someone Eating Creates Envy": Inequality and Citizenship in Tanzania

If neither hunger nor subsistence is experienced uniformly across time and space, then we must consider the particular historical conjuncture that frames this subsistence citizenship in rural Tanzania. When I once asked a group of elders in rural Singida what had happened to the president's promise to deliver mosquito nets to all pregnant and nursing mothers in Tanzania, one responded: "My friend, those promises aren't meant for us. Singida's still Tanganyika. Dar es Salaam ... now that's in Tanzania." Through discursively situating rural Singida in the colonial mainland territory of Tanganyika, and locating Dar es Salaam, a national urban center, in the modern nation-state of Tanzania, this elder alluded to rural Singidans' sense of being disconnected from the course of time, history, and economic change, and pointed to the persistent challenges rural Tanzanians face in accessing resources for development from the state.

Continuities aside for the moment, there is no question that, in the last 30 years, Tanzania has undergone two concurrent sea changes in its political economy. The first—economic liberalization—was launched in 1985 when President Julius Nyerere stepped down from the presidency, closing a twenty-year post-independence era of Tanzanian socialism and self-reliance (or *ujamaa*). This was neoliberalism in the "African" sense (Ferguson 2010)—the opening of Tanzania's economy to international markets, foreign debt, and austerity programs and the privatization of state industries and social services. The second transition—political liberalization—was undertaken in 1992 with the declaration of a multiparty system and the ostensible dissolution of state-party power, formerly concentrated in the *Chama cha Mapinduzi* or "Party of the Revolution" (CCM) and its antecedents (TANU and ASP) during the single party era from 1965 to 1992.[10]

In Tanzania, there is no doubt that economic liberalization has had tangible effects on everyday life. Indeed, the rapidly sprouting skyline of Dar es Salaam provides a potent visual testament to the rosy "Africa Rising" story of dramatic economic growth in Tanzania. Yet in many places across the Global South, this growth has been accompanied by a vastly uneven distribution of wealth across space and population and—in Tanzania—even an *increase* in what analysts call "lived poverty" (Dulani, Mattes, & Logan 2013). The other structural transition— political liberalization—has remained incomplete, still resulting in landslide electoral victories for CCM and its continued monopolization of parliamentary seats in the five multiparty general elections held since 1995 (though the 2010 and 2015 elections showed significant gains by the opposition). For many political commentators, *too little* has changed in Tanzania. While many analysts cite ideological conservatism for CCM's continued strength, particularly among rural voters, it is important to note that CCM has remained structurally embedded in the Tanzanian state in a way that allows it to effectively *occupy* it—by monopolizing, to the best of its ability, state structures, resources, and political discourses to reproduce its own power (Makulilo 2012; Phillips 2010; 2015).

The conjuncture of these two tidal shifts in Tanzania's political economy— that have adhered political power to capital and capital to political power— serves as a backdrop for national debates about (1) the distribution of wealth, infrastructure and resources across spaces and populations, and (2) the distribution of power (between the ruling party and the opposition, government and citizen, center and periphery, the mainland and the isles). Such debates are reflected in the recent upsurge in popular concern about corruption and *ufisadi*, or "white collar crime" (Lofchie 2014), as well as in escalating protests by local and regional groups over the terms of state and transnational exploitation of natural resources (Balile 2013; Mampilly 2013).

Despite a rapid influx of development funding toward the Millennium Development Goals in the first decade of the new millennium, official statistics reveal considerable disparities in economic development, particularly between rural and urban areas. Rural Tanzanians are disproportionately more likely to live below both the food poverty line and the basic needs poverty line. They are less likely to have access to schools, health facilities, transportation, telecommunications, electricity, banks, safe water sources, employment and trade opportunities, and micro-credit finance programs. And they are more likely to be malnourished, undereducated or illiterate, or to die of malaria or diarrheal diseases (United Republic of Tanzania 2010). Though urban poverty certainly exists, is growing at alarming rates, and is itself not unconnected to some of the undesirable conditions of rural life, many analysts argue that poverty in Tanzania, and food poverty in particular, remains an overwhelmingly rural issue—with 84 percent of the poor population living in rural areas (United Republic of Tanzania 2013) and the rural poor living deeper in poverty than the poor of Dar es Salaam and other urban areas. (National Panel Survey 2010/11; United Republic of Tanzania 2012).

Tanzania is not unique for its differentiated terrain of citizenship. In the new millennium, the pressures of environmental destruction, population growth, and increased consumer demand have prompted many states to deliberate how entitlements and responsibilities should be distributed among their populations. Such a differentiated citizenship, Holston argues that "uses social differences that are *not* the basis of national membership—primarily differences of education, property, race, gender, and occupation—to distribute different treatment to different categories of citizens. It thereby generates a gradation of rights among them, in which most rights are available only to particular kinds of citizens and exercised as the privilege of particular social categories" (2008, 7). This "unsettled" citizenship (Holston 2008, xiii), from a functionalist perspective, becomes one way that the state and its subjects deal with scarcity of labor and resources for economic development amid sky-high expectations (cf. Pallotti 2008).

Tanzania is a unique historical context in which to study the terrain of citizenship, for it has long been noted for its lack of ethnicization and regionalization of politics and wealth distribution (Lofchie 2014). Indeed, the dominant political discourse in Tanzania—that of a peaceful nationalism that decries both regionalism and tribalism—has remained remarkably constant. For this, Tanzanians thank "Father of the Nation" Julius Nyerere who at independence united over 110 ethnic groups with the East African trade language of Swahili; peacefully instituted two decades of relative economic egalitarianism with policies of Tanzanian socialism, self-reliance, and villagization (Bjerk 2015); and constitutionally and legally forbid the political instrumentalization of ethnicity or regionalism. This national unity and relative peace has marked Tanzania as an exception among many of its East African neighbors and other African states where ethnicity has dominated the political discourse since independence. A commitment to peace and nation remains today an essential part of Tanzanian identity.

What is not often noted however is just how important the *denial* of ethnicity and regionalism is in Tanzanian politics. For this narrative of peace and nation has also been mobilized by the ruling party to claim a monopoly on peace—by insisting that multiparty politics and opposition parties themselves threaten to tear at the fabric of a carefully woven nation (Phillips 2010; 2015). Indeed, vilifying sub-national claims has become a primary technique of governance in Tanzania (Makulilo 2012; 2014; Phillips 2015). When ruling party candidates point to Angola, Burundi, and Liberia as foreshadowing what will happen when multiparty politics enters the country (TEMCO 2011), they pit nationalism against democracy to get votes. When the government accuses southern Tanzanians who protested in 2013 over natural gas extraction of *majimbo*-ism or "regionalism," they deny outright the capacity of those who live on the margins to question the terms in which "national" resources are distributed across spaces and populations. And when regions, districts, villages, and wards are the recognized units of governance, development, and the measurement of poverty, but are eschewed as the appropriate units of political action, identity, or mobilization, it becomes exceedingly difficult to challenge the spatial dimensions of socioeconomic disparities. Nationalism, indeed, "works" in Tanzania, but at what cost, and to whom?[11]

Others interested in this question in Tanzania (Aminzade 2013; Brennan 2012; Edmondson 2007; Kaiser 1996) have referenced or described racial exclusions, in particular of the South Asian population in Tanzania. Dorothy Hodgson (2001) has demonstrated how images of Maasai (the ethnic exception in Tanzania) as "primitive" and "conservative" have been used to justify excessively harsh state interventions, land grabs of wildlife- and water-rich areas, and the direction of national resources to more "progressive" and politically powerful groups.[12] My focus on the Nyaturu of rural Singida—who have been less charismatic in their ethnic expression since independence and less the target of state intervention and land appropriation than the Maasai—calls for attention to the instrumentalization of *spatial* identities (rather than racial or ethnic ones) as a key organizing principle for statecraft and socioeconomic exclusion.

I argue that in Tanzania processes of the state and citizenship take place within a social field that allots rights, responsibilities, and resources partly in accordance with a distinction between city and village. This is a slippery social field: on one hand, the political narrative of the farming rural citizen has been pivotal to Tanzanian nationalist discourse since independence, and indeed as others (Brennan 2012; Schneider 2014) have persuasively argued, has been used to politically exclude racial minorities and the urban working class. And yet widely circulating ideas about the "natural marginality" of rural people (based on their physical location, seemingly discontinuous temporality, and presumed deficient merit) have also conditioned development planning, minimized rural "needs," and rationalized a lack of accountability of the state to poor and rural populations (cf. Das & Poole 2004:17). As one interlocutor noted, "only the villager can starve." As I go on to describe in chapter 5, forced contributions and mandated labor requirements (*michango*) in Singida were widely perceived to be "only possible in the village."

Such differentiation, I argue, is often justified with the political narratives of participation and self-reliance that suggest that those Tanzanians who already have access to schools, hospitals, food security and water are those who have already "participated" while the rural poor are those who have not yet done their part to "build the nation" (*kujenga taifa*). Through such narratives, and the extractive and unregulated taxation they have legitimated in rural Singida, the responsibility for building the nation radiates out from political centers, disproportionately burdening some of the poorest and most rural populations. But—as we will see—such exploitation has its limits at the threshold of subsistence, when the "safety first" principle breaks down and there is precious little left to lose.

Code-Switching Citizenship: Rights and Patronage as Discourses of Claims-Making

So it is not only the *conditions* of life that vary across rural and urban spaces, but also *citizenship* itself, which I understand in this book as the highly spatialized, temporalized, and culturally elaborated processes for negotiating the ostensibly shared rights, privileges, and obligations of national belonging. It was January 2006, and after my first year of rural fieldwork in Singida, I had just arrived in the Dar es Salaam office of a well-known Tanzanian activist and NGO director. He was a celebrity in Tanzania's political circles, notorious at that time for calling out the government on empty promises, unimplemented policies, and contradictory practices. It was my first interview with him, and despite the warm welcome from the receptionist and the lively and homey décor of the well-furnished Dar es Salaam office, I was self-consciously on my best behavior. I had just offered him my most respectful Swahili greeting when he regarded me wearily and said, "Oh, please … don't *shikamoo* me." The shikamoo is Lesson One of every Swahili text (though used mainly in Tanzania, not in Kenya and Uganda), most of which refer to its early usage as a slave's greeting to his or her master. At some point, it slid into widespread usage as a greeting of a child or young person to his elder. Over time, the shikamoo has also become a borrowed greeting in many of Tanzania's 110 vernacular languages, including the Bantu Nyaturu language of Singida, where I had been living for the past year and a half. The director took a deep breath and explained clearly, if not a bit impatiently: "I'm the last person you want to say shikamoo to. I am famous for hating the shikamoo. I met Mwalimu Nyerere [Tanzania's first president] some years ago, and it created a scandal when I would not shikamoo him. His aides were shocked. They couldn't understand my reasons. They couldn't understand that as much as I respected him, that I don't believe we should lower ourselves before our leaders, like I don't think you should lower yourself before me. This is one of the many problems with our country." Though many foreign agencies discourage expatriate workers from using the shikamoo (in part because of its tendency to undo bureaucratic hierarchies), I had spent the last year in Tanzania cultivating my downcast eyes and my barely whispered shKAmo. I had watched it transform my social and professional interactions in government offices, in rural households, on the cattle path. As a foreign, unmarried, and childless woman, this shikamoo had offered me the relational ground on which I could initially stand in Singida's villages, where to walk with presumption is contemptuous (*kuwa na dharau*), and to be contemptuous is the greatest social transgression.

What this NGO director was lamenting however was the way an ethic of *obligation* tends to override an ethic of *rights* in many social, political, and institutional relationships in Tanzania, and particularly in the prototype of Tanzanian social life—the village. He was protesting the shikamoo as a performance in Judith Butler's sense[13]—that through saying, "I hold your feet" (as some have literally translated shikamoo), young and lower-status Tanzanians were left, politically and economically, "holding feet," that is, catering to the whims of an outmoded gerontocracy, or worse—a self-serving ruling elite. What struck me in this exchange was not so much the argument for more democratic interaction (important in itself), but rather the abrupt reminder of a contested moral geography in Tanzania—in which the value of an idiom of "rights" versus that of "obligations" varies considerably (though not absolutely) from cities to villages, from homes to offices, from season to season, and across people and moments.

The view from rural Singida, which this book affords, highlights the complexity of this terrain of claims-making. In rural Singida, a moral economy of patronage that links the rich and the poor has tempered pre-conquest inequalities, mitigated the colonial reconfiguration of property and authority, and has mediated and moderated the growing disparities of contemporary globalization. Yet while patronage relationships have been central to the subsistence and security of rural populations in Singida, one must not *over*estimate or idealize the redistribution that occurs through clientelistic relationships. In Tanzania's postcolonial and postsocialist eras it is democracy, and in particular rights-based approaches, that have been lauded for their potential to mediate the politics of re-distribution and create more equitable access to resources. Yet rights discourses too have their limitations. As many have argued from both the left and the right ends of the political spectrum, rights are not a particularly compelling or effective means for regulating the distribution of economic goods and services (like education, work, food, housing, and water) in market economies (Branco 2009; Shivji 1996). Put simply, why should people or institutions give something away for free, when they could be paid for it (in market terms) or receive some other benefit in kind (in a patron-client relationship)? What incentive or accountability is there for one to fulfill the "duty" that one bears?

An anecdote related by James Ferguson in his (2015) *Give a Man a Fish*, portrays this dilemma of economic rights. He describes a day-long housing rights workshop in Cape Town organized by an NGO in a poor urban neighborhood. After several hours of the workshop, an older gentleman raised his hand from the back of the room and stood to speak: "I'm afraid there has been some mistake here. All I have heard about today is that I have the right to a house … But … I don't want the right to a house … I want a *house*" (48; quote excerpted). The gentleman's comment spotlights what Paul Farmer and Nicole Gastineau have also observed, that "rights attributed on paper are of little value when the existing political and social structures do not afford all individuals the ability to enjoy these rights, let alone defend them" (2009, 152).

For rural Singidans, the charge and the tone of these two forms of claims-making—rights and patronage—is both the same and different. Many rural Singidans—cognizant of the gradations of political membership described above—tend to perceive a *risk of rights* in relation to the security of paternalism as a discourse of claims-making for the rural poor. Ferguson (2015) has argued that patronage relationships constitute *social inequalities*, as opposed to *asocial* ones. The significance of this characterization is clear in Singida, where patronage claims ask people to make good on an established relationship, referencing both a past and a future of cooperation, interconnection, and mutual assistance. When successful, patronage claims satisfy present needs and promise to secure a fruitful future. But when patronage claims fail (such that their refusal implies a denial or an abdication of the relationship), then rights claims emerge on the political horizon as a last resort.

Rights, in Tanzania and elsewhere, are grounded on a notion of membership (to a nation, a state, and/or a species). Rights discourses are often wielded in ways that self-consciously render *social* relationships irrelevant, even problematic, implying what I call *asocial equalities*—normative assertions about equal opportunity and distribution that, in the village at least, are cast adrift from the relationships through which they might actually be realized. And indeed, Singidans see such invocations of rights as risky, principally because (as one neighbor told me) "rights refuse relationships"; that is, their depersonalized discourse detaches claims from mutual obligations forged over time, potentially even permanently rupturing those relationships that have sustained people—even minimally—in the past. Moreover, as Katherine Verdery and Caroline Humphrey have pointed out, "rights terminology creates only one kind of person, who has or does not have rights" (2004, 16). Such a concept is hardly robust enough to deal with the gradations of identity, affiliation, and responsibility in relation to resources that are so characteristic in conditions of scarcity (described in chapter 3). Patronage, on the other hand, has been valued in Singida precisely for its effectiveness in capturing the state and its resources through more enduring moral connections to those in power. Rights thus become most viable as a form of claims-making in rural Singida precisely at the threshold of subsistence, as a "last-gasp" (Scott 1976), when there is virtually nothing left to lose. But it is essential to note that in rural Singida, *neither* rights *nor* patronage serve as catchall idioms of economic accountability. It is not that Singidans are opting for patronage relationships *over* democratic forms, or vice versa. Rather, each mode of claims-making has its season. To be sure, it is the political code-switching and code-mixing that is the hallmark of subsistence citizenship that allows rural Singidans to capture as much of the state and subsistence as they do.

Plan of the Book

The following chapters expand on the interlinkages between subsistence and citizenship. The first part of the book lays out the ethnographic and historical frames for understanding the banality of hunger and struggles for subsistence in contemporary Tanzania. Chapter 1 introduces the social and material landscape of subsistence and livelihood in one hamlet of a rural Singida village. It narrates the everyday lives and situated perspectives of the kin, clan, and neighbors of an elder woman, NyaConstantino, and describes the pulse of the annual agricultural cycle and the labor that brings food into being.

This quest for subsistence in Singida has never been a project to be taken for granted. The Nyaturu oral traditions, archival and secondary sources, and oral histories that I review in chapter 2 trace the history of famine and food politics in Singida. Through the enduring cultural idiom of "the sun's unpredictable grace," these sources suggest major shifts in ideas about political membership, authority, development, entitlement and obligation as they relate to the project of subsistence. They also speak to the long history of precarity and its politics in the governance of rural Singida. Taxation, labor mandates, and the political use of food aid have all left their mark on the moral and material terrain of political engagement. The chapter affords the opportunity to contemplate how generations of food insecurity make persons, construct worldviews, forge identities, and drive history.

The second part of the book considers the social life of food and the politics of claims-making in Singida. Chapter 3 traces the social life cycle of the subsistence grains used to make the staple Nyaturu food ugali—bulrush millet, sorghum, and maize—and illuminates how grains travel and transform between four phases of their social life: social entitlement, commodity, gift, and aid. It is food's capacity to hold many contiguous meanings—and people's ability to make use of these to pursue life and livelihood—that allows food to transcend fixed codes of distribution and to follow unpredicted paths. This chapter lays the foundation for analyzing various political discourses of distribution and redistribution (market, rights, and patronage) in chapters 4, 5, and 6.

Chapter 4 extends this analysis to describe how Singida villagers accessed food aid by invoking narratives of crisis and paternal obligation to stake claims on state resources. But when food aid failed to materialize from the state, villagers countered the government's seeming paternal neglect and abandonment with a threat to no longer participate in (i.e., labor for) development projects. This filial rebellion threatened not only the material achievement of district government development goals (and accordingly the livelihood of district officials who were evaluated on those outcomes), but—through a withdrawal of filial loyalty—also endangered the narrative of the political family on which the CCM-led government so substantially relies. The chapter highlights the creative energy of both citizens and state in these politics of subsistence that seek to prompt, resist, and/or redirect redistributive efforts. It also highlights the political code-switching and code-mixing between the idioms of rights and patronage that villagers employ.

Together, the final two chapters trace a period of significant political change in the Singida East voting constituency when its residents were pushed to the threshold of subsistence between 2005 and 2010. Chapter 5 examines contradictions between the official narrative of rural development as the primary mandate of the Tanzanian state, and the state's abdication of that role in Singida through "participatory" development initiatives that increasingly shifted the burden of labor and cost for development squarely onto rural Singidans. These participatory politics distributed rights and obligations according to people's spatial relation to existing development infrastructures, the market value of their labor, and their fulfillment of responsibilities in return for rights. Such "unsettled" citizenship (Holston 2008) pushed many rural Singidans to the threshold of subsistence between 2005 and 2010. Yet it also enabled the government to deal with a scarcity of labor and resources amid sky-high expectations of development.

Chapter 6 chronicles the electoral swing to the opposition party that took place when Tundu Lissu contested in and won the 2010 Singida East parliamentary elections. It frames this shift in political loyalties as a kind of peasant rebellion against a regime that threatened subsistence. In relating these political events and their aftermath, I consider how Singidans are debating the terms of a subsistence ethic that has heretofore privileged paternalistic politics over rights-based ones. I argue that for rural Singidans, rights are seen as risky because rights "refuse relationships." Paternalism, on the other hand, is valued precisely for its effectiveness in capturing the state and its resources—at least for subsistence, if not for development—through moral connections to those in power. This, I maintain, is not conservatism on the part of rural populations, but a perceptive read of a political and economic context that does little to address the question of how economic rights are to be secured, and by whom.

The conclusion draws on scenes from Malian filmmaker Abderrahmane Sissako's *La Vie sur Terre* to suggest a broader relevance of the notion of subsistence citizenship beyond Tanzania. People all over the world bring ideas and expectations about belonging, membership, entitlement, obligation, and patterns of interaction and distribution from the mode and context of their livelihood to their political preferences and practices. The citizenship of those who, year after year, live at or near the threshold of subsistence bears the same distinctive temporal and spatial attributes as their livelihoods: seasonality, ebbs and flows of attention and engagement, unpredictability, and a heavy reliance on reciprocity and mutual assistance. As the food supply has its seasons, so does citizenship.

Notes

1. At the request of research participants, I have changed the names of people and villages within Singida District to protect confidentiality. Langilanga is the Nyaturu word for "sorghum," the staple crop of Singidans. The name I gave another village, "Suna," is a wild fruit. Personal and geographical attributes are accurate. In cases where people went by Christian names, I assigned them another commonly used Christian name. I did the same for both Muslim names and Nyaturu names. With information from village surveys, the executive director for Langilanga's four-village ward wrote to the Singida Rural District Agricultural Officer in June 2005 (in anticipation of a 2006 famine) to estimate the following food shortage: Expected harvest for 2005: 2176 sacks; Shortage: 5276 sacks; Percent of food needs met by farming: 29.2%; Total food needed for 2005–6: 7452 sacks; Shortage: 5276 sacks; Total aid received by Langilanga villagers in 2006: 128 sacks. Author translation.

2. On hunger, see for example Ansell 2014; Cliggett 2005; Crais 2011; de Waal 1989; 1997; Vaughan 2007; Watts 1983. On rural politics, see Berry 1993; Das & Poole 2004; Haugerud 1995; Li 2007; 2014; Scott 1976; 1985. On development, see Olivier de Sardan 2005; Englund 2006; Ferguson 2006; 2010; Smith 2008.

3. Adewale Maja-Pearce, "Thai Rice and Nigerian Politics" (*New York Times*, 27 July 2014). http://www.nytimes.com/2014/07/08/opinion/adewale-maja-pearce-thai-rice-and -nigerian-politics.html?_r=0.

4. Gabriel Chioma, "Stomach Infrastructure: The Newest Vocabulary in Nigeria's Political Dictionary" (*Vanguard*, 27 March 2015). http://www.vanguardngr.com/2015/03 /stomach-infrastructure-the-newest-vocabulary-in-nigerias-political-dictionary/; Brian

Obara, "A Debate Ranges in Nigeria about 'Stomach Infrastructure'" (*This is Africa*, 14 June 2016) https://thisisafrica.me/a-debate-rages-in-nigeria-about-stomach-infrastructure/; Yaqoub Popoola, "Nigeria: Fayose Explains Stomach Infrastructure Concept" (*Daily Independent*, 27 October 2014) http://allafrica.com/stories/201410271875.html.

5. See Makhulu et al. (2010) for a provocative discussion of the limitations of crisis narratives about Africa.

6. I offer my thanks to Paul Bjerk for our exchange about this point.

7. On "livelihood," see Chambers & Conway 1992; on "capabilities," see Sen 1981; 1999a; 1999b; 2009; and on "well-being," see Jackson 2011; Mathews & Izquierdo 2009.

8. Interview with Irish mission priest; August 15, 2005; Singida Rural District.

9. I borrow this understanding of political legitimacy from Michael Schatzberg (2001).

10. CCM was born in 1977 with the union of the mainland's Tanganyika African National Union (TANU) Party and Zanzibar's Afro-Shirazi Party (ASP).

11. Laura Edmondson, in her 2007 book on performance and politics in Tanzania, also raises this question.

12. Igoe (2006) has argued that in the nonprofit and activist sphere, Maasai tend to dominate at the expense of less visible ethnic minorities. At the same time, there is no doubt that land appropriation from the Maasai is ongoing (Hodgson 2017).

13. "That reiterative power of discourse to produce the phenomena that it regulates and constrains" (Butler 1993, 2).

PART I: THE FRAMES OF SUBSISTENCE: COSMOLOGY, ETHNOGRAPHY, HISTORY

1 Hunger in Relief

Village Life and Livelihood

All the rocks in Singida were once meat. People were eating them all the time. But they were also given the law by the elders that they should never put salt on the meat. One day, a person decided to put salt on the meat, even though he had been told many times not to. He didn't believe it. He thought that he was doing a good thing, but kumbe!, he broke the command. On that day, all the meat turned to rocks, and there was not so much to eat.

The Story of How all the Rocks in Singida Were Once Meat.
Told by Mama Rosalia, 2005

LET US BEGIN then with the social and material landscape of Singida region. Singida region, home to over a million residents, sprawls in Tanzania's heartland, 700 kilometers northwest of Tanzania's commercial center, Dar es Salaam, and 330 kilometers northwest of the nation's capital Dodoma (see map 1.1). Three of Singida's six administrative units—Singida Town, Singida Rural District, and Ikungi district—constitute *Urimi*, the land of the Nyaturu—an ethnic group also known as the "Turu" or "Rimi." Singida Town is the administrative and trading nucleus of the region, and draws workers and professionals from the other districts of Singida. Like most of urban Tanzania, Singida Town has become a lively Swahili market town of many tongues, with migrants from northwestern Tanzania, Swahili traders from the coast, and a few Asian, Omani, and Somali families running many of the interregional food and clothing trade, bus companies, restaurants, and internet cafes.

Singida Town is a crossroads, marking the intersection of recently paved inter-city routes to Dodoma, Arusha, and Mwanza. It boasts a regional hospital, several private clinics and banks, a post office, a plethora of mosques and churches, a bus stand and a range of guesthouses and eating establishments that serve both local patrons and the many traders and truckers who pass through town. But just outside the small grid of dirt alleys that surround the intersection of these tarmacked roads, the land of the Nyaturu begins, stretching out into a thick ring around Singida Town.[1] The peri-urban villages of Singida Municipality graduate into the increasingly rural villages of Singida Rural District and Ikungi District,

Figure 1.1. Singida landscape.
Photo by author, 2005.

which are home to three loosely defined Nyaturu language sub-groups: the Wahi (to the south and west); the Wirwana (to the north) and the WaNyamunging'anyi (to the east).

Boarding a *daladala* mini-bus in Singida Town, one can journey out the Arusha road, past a rundown government secondary school and through the grand natural gates formed by two large boulders emblazoned with painted condom and laundry detergent advertisements. The road is lined with modern houses of cement brick and corrugated iron roofs, small shops with signs sponsored by soda and beer companies, and a fancy new *hoteli* serving grilled meat and beer. As the mini-bus climbs out of the large valley that houses Singida Town and its two large salt-water lakes, Singidani and Kindai, the bus ascends to what will eventually drop dramatically into the escarpment of the Great Rift Valley and—beyond Singida's borders—to the foothills of Mount Hanang. Evidence of electrical wiring has vanished.

The landscape is alternately monotonous and majestic, with broad expanses of barren brown (in the dry season) or bright green (in the short rainy months) farmland interrupted by thickets of thorny brush and striking rock outcroppings upon which cellular phone antennas or water tanks may perch. As the bus

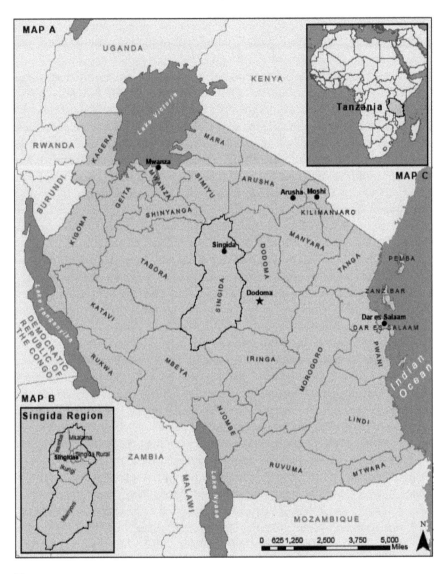

Map 1.1.
Map A: Map of mainland Tanzania with regions and key cities (as of 2015);
Map B: Map of Singida Region showing districts and Singida Municipality (as of 2017);
Map C: Map of African continent showing Tanzania's location.
Maps produced by Megan Slemon, Emory Center for Digital Scholarship, Emory
University, 2017.

climbs, modern houses become fewer and further between and in their stead one sees the *nyumba za kienyeji* (traditional houses) of the Nyaturu—the low long rectangular mud-brick structures with grass and mud roofs (see plate 2).

About ten kilometers out of town the bus reaches a crossroads from which one can glimpse a spectacular view of the escarpment and Great Rift Valley below, and the intersection of the borders of four villages. The intersection hosts a festive weekly livestock, food, and clothing market (see plate 3) and a more permanent settlement of small shops, beer clubs, and a small mosque. The grid of intersecting roads offers vehicle routes to surprisingly distinct eco-systems and linguistic and social environments in Singida. And between these roads lie an intricate network of cattle and human footpaths that carve their way through farms, forests and thornbrush. These paths circumvent the rock outcroppings to connect village centers and the hundreds of interior sub-villages (*vitongoji*, or hamlets) to transportation networks, medical facilities, schools, water sources, and each other.

The villages, even in this small corner of Singida, are each distinct from one another. There are villages that lie along the road, and so have already "received a bit of the light of development," and villages that lie "inside" well beyond the networks of public transportation. There are peri-urban villages (those lying within the boundaries of the Municipality) and rural villages (those located in Singida Rural District). In addition some villages have "given birth to" (*vimezaa*) other villages, as in the case of the village I call "Suna"—a village whose mission-constructed school served an area that has since been divided into four villages that now have primary schools of their own. Suna village is the "the elder" (*mzee*) of its offspring which, its residents assert, has mixed implications. Suna is the seat of the ward (four-village) government, the first of the four villages to get electricity, the site of a mission secondary school, and since 2007, the site of a government secondary school constructed for the four villages. Yet many in Suna consider their village as much *kikongwe* (a term also used for the elderly but with the connotation of infirmity) as *mzee* (the respected elder). Their school buildings are dilapidated and the village government is perceived to be entrenched and ineffective in contrast with its offspring "Langilanga" village's youthful energy and motivated leadership. These distinctions between villages have material implications. "Elder" Suna is seen to be the proper center for continuing development for the ward (the new secondary school should be where there is electricity, where its teachers may find housing); but youthful Langilanga, whose citizens are much less burnt out on their government, has received more opportunities for participatory pilot projects. The two interior villages of the ward receive food aid well in advance of Suna and Langilanga, whose residents—living along the road—are presumed to have better access to other forms of assistance, mobility, and support.

In contrast to the perceptions of many urban Tanzanians, tourists, and members of the foreign aid establishment, *kijijini* (the space of the village) as lived by the people of Singida, is a vastly differentiated space. Within a village, people compare spaces of good farmland and bad, heavy and poor rains, wildlife habitats and people habitats, *madukani* ("the shops") and *mbugani* ("the grasslands"), *barabarani* ("on the road) and *bondeni* ("in the valley"), kin settlements and road settlements, Lutheran, Muslim, and Roman Catholic hamlets, and places where amenities like wells, shops, transport possibilities, the school, church, and drinking clubs may be found reasonably nearby, and, alternately, places in which there is a lack thereof. In spite of these clear oppositions, not everyone experiences these spaces in the same way. For as Ching and Creed note, "almost any inhabited place can be experienced as either rural or urban" (1997, 13). A daughter-in-law from Arusha city in northern Tanzania who visits her husband's family in their homestead near the shops of the Singida roadside village of Langilanga, struggles with the drudgery of "the life of the village" (*maisha ya kjijini*). Meanwhile the head teacher's wife who has married there from a more isolated area is still acclimating to the exciting business opportunities (she brews beer) but the loose morals of "life on the road," where drinkers from outlying homesteads and hamlets gather to mingle and flirt.

And yet there are experiences and perspectives that connect rural populations in Singida unrelated to whether people are rich or poor, roadside or inside, central or marginal to Singida's social and economic life. The pulse of the annual cycle's wet and dry seasons drives an agricultural, social, political and economic calendar that, regardless of one's relative socioeconomic position, oxygenates rural lives and infuses the shared air that they breathe. To better grasp these situated and yet inextricably connected perspectives of village life, let us meet one extended family in rural Singida.

NyaConstantino's House

NyaConstantino, "the mother of Constantino," is squat and strong, though she is small and now in her sixties. She lives down in one of the deep dips along the escarpment that lead to the steep drop into the Rift Valley. The round face that she shares with her younger son, Petro, bears all the features of a good gossip, with expressions that shift quickly from shrewd assessment, to dramatic pause, to warm raucous laughter. My first visit to her home, it seemed, was good cause for all three, though she soon settled into the latter, for like the Nyaturu saying goes, "strangers are sent by the sun."

The language she speaks is the language of the elder women—the last and least of the Nyaturu to be "nationalized," to use the Tanzanian political parlance. Her words—a loose hybrid of Swahili vocabulary plugged into a river of Nyaturu words—flowed over me as I, still in my early months in Singida, tried in vain to isolate and identify them. She was equally mystified by my own Swahili, with its foreign cadence, coastal constructions, formal grammar, and absence of Nyaturu-isms, which I would eventually incorporate into my own speech. In future meetings I was often accompanied by a friend and research assistant who could bridge lingering linguistic gaps. But in this first chance encounter, we—as people are bound to—just made do.

Her children have estimated that NyaConstantino was born sometime around 1940. She herself doesn't know the year, she explains, because there was little opportunity at the time for girls to study, and little interest among their parents to educate them. There was much work to do at home in these farming and herding communities, and girls like NyaConstantino married young and left to join their husbands' families.

By the 1940s Evangelical Lutheran missionaries from the midwestern United States and European Roman Catholic missionaries had carved out separate zones of influence in rural Singida with the intent of converting Singidans and stem-ming the tide of Islam. NyaConstantino's parents converted to Christianity and from her early childhood she attended the tiny Lutheran Church in her natal vil-lage, which lay on the main road from Dodoma to Singida, approximately 15 kilo-meters from Langilanga. She would not live there many years. As was common in the 1950s, she married before she had begun to menstruate. She moved to the forests of the valley hamlet in Langilanga (see plate 4) to join her husband's fam-ily, but in accordance with custom, returned home for ritual instruction at sev-eral points in her life and maintained strong bonds, especially with her mother and brothers.

NyaConstantino gave birth to seven children, of which four are still living. Her husband died more than ten years ago, and she now enjoys the status of *mukhikuu* (Ny.), an elder woman whose sons have married and settled on lineage lands and whose wives now help her and defer to her as they manage their family affairs. Anthropologist Harold Schneider, who lived among the Nyaturu from 1959 to 1960, noted that "the ultimate position of success for a woman is to have sons and be head of a rich house, or even a homestead, after her husband dies, so that it is unnecessary for her to be inherited by a brother of her dead husband. In this status she has the greatest amount of freedom available to a woman" (1970, 126). Times have changed over the last five decades: religious and state authori-ties provide some protection against wife inheritance where it is not wanted. But now homesteads are evaluated less by their riches than by their ability to with-stand crisis (the social security of cattle having long since collapsed). Moreover, able-bodied sons and daughters increasingly migrate away from the infirm to the promise and prestige of the cities. The concern of the old women of villages is less a question of freedom than one of potential neglect. Who shall cook and farm for me, when my strength fails? Who shall pay for me to see a doctor, when I am ill? Who shall fix my roof, when the rains come? And who shall feed me, when food is scarce? Indeed, the few extreme cases of adult starvation in Singida that lead to fatality are in nearly every case elderly women who have been socially stranded by widowhood and real or functional childlessness (cf. Cliggett 2005).

As is customary, NyaConstantino shares her original homestead with her youngest son Petro and his tall, angular wife, NyaLukas. NyaConstantino's eldest child, Constantino, lives in a neighboring homestead with his own wife and five children. With two grown sons "at home" who have wives and sons of their own, NyaConstantino will be looked after in her old age, so long as her sons' households continue to thrive. Both her well-being and her precarity are securely hitched to theirs.

NyaConstantino finds social protection not only in her children but also in her local role as midwife for the hamlet. Prior to independence, her husband had been a doctor in a local clinic and taught her how to deliver babies, since trained nurses were too few. Over the last five decades she has delivered many babies in her hamlet, and while unpaid for this work, she is "remembered" (i.e., provided with material assistance) when times are difficult for her.

NyaConstantino is most animated when surrounded by her age-mates, passing the deep plastic cup of thick lukewarm sorghum beer that locals call the *chai ya wazee* (the "tea" or "breakfast" of the elders). Such occasions take place weekly in the dry and early wet season when her daughter-in-law hosts a beer party to convert some of her harvest into cash, and more often when other young women in the hamlet brew and host. The drinkers, young and old, gather in mid-morning after a first round of cultivation or other seasonal work. Some return home to work further, others loiter—singing, celebrating, flirting. Such behavior among young people is frowned on though the Catholic Church has proven more tolerant than the Lutherans, Muslims, and Pentecostal Christians. Even NyaConstantino and the elder peers with whom she shares a cup lament drunkenness among young people, who have not yet earned their right to beer through a lifetime of hard work. But as an "old woman of the old ways," even though a Lutheran, NyaConstantino is beyond sanction and beyond self-reproach. She laughs, quarrels, sings, and stumbles home to sleep.

Petro, NyaConstantino's last-born child, was born in 1967, the year of President Nyerere's Arusha Declaration of Ujamaa, or Tanzanian Socialism. He spent his first eight years "at home" on lineage land in the valley hamlet, but in 1975 NyaConstantino and her family found themselves forced to "villagize"—to move to a neighboring settlement along the road as part of Nyerere's *operesheni ni mitaa* (Ny. "operation villagization"). They were allocated a small plot of land from another family's farm to which they moved their dismantled house. Livestock accompanied them, but their farm remained in the valley hamlet. Much of their valley hamlet land was re-possessed by the village government and designated as communal ujamaa farmland, upon which villagers would contribute labor to produce a communal store of grain for food-scarce times and cash crops to be sold to fund village development projects.

NyaConstantino and her husband moved their homestead, children, and livestock early in the resettlement period, hoping to claim a decent village plot along the road. The government had promised paved roads, running water, electricity, schools, clinics, and other services that would be much easier to provide if only Tanzania's population were not so widely dispersed. Those who dragged their feet at the resettlement mandate in Langilanga soon found a troop of village primary school students (some from their own hamlet and homesteads) at their door, wielding axes and hoes. Under the direction of their head teacher, the students systematically dismantled the homesteads of stragglers, who had no choice but to re-construct them in their accorded plot in the settlement.

No one in Langilanga remembers villagization as a happy time. NyaConstantino recalled: "Between 1975 and 1988 we were moved to the center of Langilanga for the villagization operation of Nyerere. And our land here in the forest became communal farmland for the village. It was a bad life. We lived much too close to our neighbors, our cattle were far from our farmland, and people were quarreling too much. There was witchcraft. In 1988, we returned home." By 1988, villagization had yielded none of its promised fruits: students still trekked to a school in the neighboring village; water was increasingly scarce, and certainly not "running"; electricity was a dream; the hospital lay as far as it always had; and community tensions and cattle disease raged from the years of living practically on top of each other.

During the time they lived "villagized," Petro had started and completed his seven years of primary school in neighboring Suna. As a child of the new nation of Tanzania, he learned and studied in Swahili, unlike his father who had studied in English under the British. In the new educational policy of "Education for Self-Reliance" and its ultimate goal of Universal Primary Education (UPE), primary school opportunity and enrollment mushroomed, but opportunities for secondary school decreased. By his seventh grade graduation, Petro had been educated for agricultural life.

Upon Petro's completion of primary school, his father, as a man of means, hosted a circumcision (Ny. *ngoi*) for Petro and his age-mates in the hamlet. After his circumcision, Petro—unlike some of his peers who migrated to the city to seek wage labor—remained at home, farming the land, herding and breeding his father's cattle, and building a savings through craftsmanship with which he would be able to build his own house within the family homestead and take a wife. When Petro was ready to marry, he kept his eyes peeled for the right woman. One day, when visiting one of his mother's relatives near the mission settlement ten kilometers away, he met a young woman whose face and demeanor he liked. He courted her, declared his intentions, and with confidence in her consent, his own father initiated the request for a "cat" from the house of NyaLukas's father. From there the two fathers commenced with the *matya* (Ny.), a highly ritualized occasion that centers on the determination of exogamy, the *Ukuta Yuva* or Nyaturu Prayer to the Sun, and the negotiation of bridewealth cattle.

It was NyaLukas, Petro's wife, whom I first encountered one day by chance in the *zambarau* grove as I set out to hike for the first time to the remote village hamlet that lay three kilometers down in the valley. NyaLukas was heading home from the mill several kilometers away and invited me to accompany her to her homestead, "so that I should know where she lived." From that day forward, she insists on calling me *mkwe wangu* (my daughter-in-law), to signal our forthcoming relationship when I (though thirty years old at the time and myself engaged to be married) marry her seventh-grade son, Lukas, a fourteen-year-old who becomes so embarrassed by his mother's teasing that over the course of the next three years of coming and going from his house, I never actually see his face.

NyaLukas's easy laughter belies the hardship of her life in one of the most remote parts of Langilanga village, far from the road and its economic opportunities, from clean water, and from the school and health care. She has one other son who is three years old, and, when I first make her acquaintance in the zambarau grove, she is expecting a third child, who is actually her fifth because two others have already been "taken by God"—one died in infancy and the other as a toddler. Such tragedies are not uncommon: in rural Tanzania 8.5 percent of babies will die in infancy, and 13.8 percent by the time they have reached five years of age (National Bureau of Statistics and ORC Macro 2005).

NyaLukas lives here in Langilanga because she is married to Petro. As a woman by Nyaturu custom, she has no claim on the lineage land of her father, which has been divided among her brothers. Under Tanzanian national law however, she does have a right to land and property—a right that she, God willing, will not pursue unless some future calamity leaves her widowed, childless, divorced, or otherwise severed from her subsistence. Because her husband is the youngest son, they have built their own house within his parents' compound, and it is (nominally) his (though in reality her) responsibility to look after his mother in her old age.

The homestead Petro and NyaLukas share with NyaConstantino is typical, if not a bit small. In Singida more than half of homes have roofs constructed of mud and grass or leaves (United Republic of Tanzania 2015) and in 2012 only 10 percent of Singida households had access to electricity. In NyaLukas' homestead, two mud-brick houses with mud and grass roofs sit in an L-shape that becomes a completely circular homestead with a natural fence of high euphorbia shrubs. The fence contains a gate consisting of a series of loose poles that are moved, one by one, depending on the size of the guest or livestock entering the homestead. The long (original) house of NyaConstantino and Mzee Lukas contains

Figure 1.2. Visitor outside a Nyaturu homestead.
Photo by author, 2006.

Figure 1.3. Corral and house of a Nyaturu homestead.
Photo by author, 2006.

two rooms: the door opens into a sitting room in which people congregate when there are guests. Off to the side is an inner room in which NyaConstantino sleeps and stores her grain. NyaLukas shares the second house, similarly constructed, with Petro and the two (later four) children. It is in the sitting room of this house that NyaLukas cooks over a fire that nestles in an impression in the dirt floor between three cooking stones. The houses are dark (with just a small window or two in each room), low (so that one must constantly bend as one walks), and smoky, from the cooking fires.

A fenced corral for the large livestock lies inside the homestead fence (see fig. 1.3). Small livestock (sheep, goats, and chickens) who are vulnerable to predators roam the house and courtyard by day, and sleep inside the house by night. Each morning the top layer of the dirt floor that has been soiled by animals, children, and cooking debris (husks, pits, skins, and so forth) is swept out into the courtyard, to reveal the clean dirt surface underneath.

Petro and NyaLukas, like most rural Singidans, farm and herd. They grow a variety of crops, including the sorghum, maize, beans, and pumpkins that they (and most of their neighbors) consume on a daily (and seasonal) basis, as well as finger millet, which they sell to local traders who transport it to large urban centers in Tanzania. Finger millet is grown almost entirely for export and people use it to make *uji*—a thin breakfast porridge. The intensive labor involved in producing finger millet fetches it a relatively high price on the national food market so it is a key income-generating crop. Unlike their neighbors who live "on the road," Petro and NyaLukas have plenty of land to harvest. It is only the finite manure to fertilize the land and the heavy labor it takes to cultivate and guard the crop from the many pests and predators in this isolated part of the village (baboons, wild pigs, leopards, and birds) that limits what they can produce.

Petro and NyaLukas keep goats, sheep, chickens, and five cattle that they have borrowed from a wealthy relative of NyaLukas whose natal village lies approximately 12 kilometers away. *Uriha* (Ny. "cattle-loaning") has typically occurred between wealthy men and their poorer relations, though its practice is rapidly declining. Given the practice of housing large animals in the corral in order to collect their manure and keeping calves, sheep, goat, and chickens inside the house (where they are safe from predators) at night, the largest households can rarely manage more than 30 cattle. Men can however own many more cattle (in Schneider's day up to 1000) through the practice of uriha, in which an owner will loan his livestock to other (poorer) people within or even outside his own village. Schneider noted advantages to uriha that remain salient today (1970). In the first place, the owner distributes his animals far and wide, which protects his overall wealth from the devastating effects of localized livestock epidemics, droughts, or theft. But the practice also allows him to possess large numbers of animals while to some extent hiding his wealth, thus improving his position in market transactions as well as allowing him to avoid "the envy and hatred of the less well-to-do—a very important consideration to Turu" (Schneider 1970, 68). In exchange for the labor of keeping the cattle, NyaLukas and Petro reap the benefits of the milk to nourish their children and manure for fertilizing their fields. Each time I visit I am offered not only ugali and vegetables, but *maya*—the thin yogurt of fermented cow's milk that has become a rare treat since the decline of keeping cattle in Singida.

Petro is also an adept craftsman—he specializes in manufacturing *miinga*, the long thick beehives carved from tree trunks that some Langilanga residents use to harvest honey, a regional specialty of Singida. He makes and sells (for the equivalent of US$2 in 2005) the standard rope and tree-pole beds on which many Nyaturu sleep, a cowskin (or sometimes a foam mattress) cushioning their bodies against the taut scratchy rope. These items he sells at the Saturday cattle market. And he decorates the traditional *dahwa* gourds used to offer gifts of flour by burning designs into the dried vessels. This art is no longer lucrative however, given the shift in food storage to the weathered (though durable) synthetic sacks in which food aid is distributed. In addition to her weekly brew of sorghum beer for sale from her house (of which her husband and mother-in-law liberally partake), NyaLukas also fries dough into donuts (*maandazi*) to sell at the cattle market.

Figure 1.4. An elder Nyaturu man herds his cattle in rural Singida.
Photo by author, 2006.

Despite their close cooperation, co-habitation, and interdependency, NyaLukas and NyaConstantino keep the economies of their households separate. The small livestock that they keep belong to their individual "houses" within the homestead. They each cultivate their own land and store their own food, though it is NyaLukas who does most of the cooking. For NyaConstantino, this is a matter of self-reliance—that she may not feel herself too dependent on the goodwill of her children. For NyaLukas, careful accounting is the only way she may put money aside for the needs of her children—notebooks, school uniforms, school contributions, and, most significantly, medical fees. NyaLukas, NyaConstantino, and Petro are each counted as adults in the village census, and are each responsible for the mandated individual "contributions" to village development projects or other government operational funds. When they cannot or do not pay, village officers seize chickens, goats or sheep whose value often exceeds what they owe.

NyaConstantino and NyaLukas seem to share a genuine affinity for each other, not always the case in relationships between mothers- and daughters-in-law in Singida. It is likely that their relationship has evolved from its early days, when it was left to NyaConstantino and her daughter (Petro's sister) to socialize

NyaLukas into the ways of her new village and their patriline. Though formal *imaa* ceremonies for women are virtually defunct now in Singida (see Phillips 2009), expectations for respect and deference (*utii*) by daughters-in-law for their new families have changed little in rural areas, and much of the traditional hazing occurs when young brides relocate to their husbands' families.

Despite this intensive cooperation and a seemingly genuine mutual affinity for each other, I quickly learned that household economic relationships remained complex and riddled with tension. On my many visits to their homesteads, I often brought gifts like sugar or cloth, and soon learned that I must myself divide it not only between NyaLukas and her sister-in-law's homesteads, but also between the "houses" within the homesteads (between NyaLukas, wife of Petro, and Petro's mother, for example) or one woman or the other would inevitably co-opt it all into her own stockpile. This applied even to the relationship between NyaLukas and Petro, who, though of the same "house," often had different priorities in how their money would be spent.

NyaLukas and Petro are considered "regular people" according to Singida's relative socioeconomic measures, in which the average income was less than eight dollars per month in 2005 (the median income for Singida was half that— demonstrating that a small percentage of wealthier households skew the average quite considerably). In village terms they are not poor. They are a *baba na mama* household—one with an able-bodied father and mother who can share in the heavy labor of subsistence. They have access to land and access to cattle and can therefore cultivate much of their household food needs. They have no "wealth" of their own, however—that is, cattle that they may breed and sell. They are well-respected in the community (brewing and drinking aside, perhaps), and in 2006 Petro came to be elected head of the hamlet—a job that offers no salary, but brings one into the village government circles through which one gains status and a certain degree of influence. When contributions are mandated or their children need school supplies, they may sell a goat, or several, depending on the amount required. It is only the hope of "development"—the serious capital it takes to purchase sheet iron or fire bricks for a modern house, or to educate one's children at the secondary level—that remains out of their reach. Their life is difficult; at times, even grueling. In 2014 NyaLukas told me that when hailstorms came and ravaged the grain seedlings they had worked so hard to plant and sprout, the families in their hamlet just sat and cried: "Two weeks, we just sat and cried. We just sat. And then we got up and planted again." But when a good harvest is yielded they thank God that they are among the fortunate ones, and pray that they will remain so: "*munya njaa atiuhekwa*" (Ny. "he who is hungry is not laughed at") for, as most Nyaturu know well, it may be one's own turn tomorrow.

NyaConstantino's eldest son Constantino, now in his late-forties, lives in a neighboring homestead to Petro's with his own family. In contrast to his mother and younger brother, he is tall, lean, and mild, with a soft laugh. His wife has a similar disposition and reserve, and despite the poverty of their surroundings, a certain quiet gentility underlies both their easy manners. She is pregnant with her ninth child when I meet her. Constantino and his wife have already acquired a bit of "development": one of the two houses in their homestead is a "modern house" constructed of mud bricks and sheet metal that will not disintegrate in the rainy season and built high so that one may stand inside it. In 2005, two of their children were attending the divisional government secondary school. Constantino treks down the remainder of the Rift Valley escarpment several times a week into a neighboring settlement to conduct trade between the two surprisingly contrasting ecosystems over which the two villages sprawl. In addition, they herd their own cattle and farm their own acreage.

The families of Constantino and Petro, along with some of their other neighboring kin, cooperate in many aspects of their rather insular lives. Constantino and Petro are part of the same herding cooperative, in which they and their sons take turns taking their small herds out for grazing and water. The two NyaLukases (both families have first sons named Lukas, after their paternal grandfather) fetch water and do their washing together. When one of the men must travel, the other keeps an eye on his brother's homestead and family. Their children grow up as "siblings" within the patriline, hike the three kilometers out of the valley together to school, and call each other's parents "mother" and "father." With clan and non-kin neighbors in the valley, the families share the governance of their sub-village or hamlet (*kitongoji*), swap gossip, and participate in the weddings, funerals, and religious festivities of their Catholic, Muslim, and Pentecostal neighbors. When desperate moments call for desperate measures, as in early 2006 when the rains had "refused completely," the elders of the hamlet, regardless of their religious affiliations, convene to sacrifice a sheep at the main clan's rain shrine in accordance with local hamlet custom.

As leader of his hamlet, Petro is at the frontline of the village government. When a meeting is called, a contribution demanded, or food aid has arrived, the village executive director writes letters to the hamlet leader who passes on the news to their cell leaders (a party office that divided hamlets into ten-household units during one-party rule). But Petro's main responsibility is to "know his people," mediate conflicts, and prevent crises. When a couple argues, the wife may choose to stay with the women of the hamlet leader's house if she fears to return home or if her husband needs to sleep off a binge. If the hamlet receives a traveler who needs a place to spend the night, he is sent to the house of the hamlet leader, who will record his arrival and offer him food and shelter. And when hunger looms, the hamlet and cell leaders monitor the state of households, calculate annual food deficiencies in anticipation of hunger, and report to the village government. Before conditions become dire, the village sends these calculations up to the ward and district to communicate the need for food aid. During hunger, hamlet and cell leaders also provide moral leadership, reminding people to share, to guard their food and to not brew too much beer. "Hunger," I was often told in rural Singida, "is the work of the government."

"O Dry Season Give Me a Garden, the Rainy Season Will Reveal Those Who Want to Work": Food, Labor, and the Annual Cycle

> The answer is we're in a trap we don't have seasons on our map.
> Our disciplines aren't trained to see the range of seasonality.
>
> Robert Chambers

In rural Singida, dearth and plenty cycle with the seasons. The food supply, like the agricultural labor that produces it, is seasonal and episodic, but regular and rhythmic. It is these concentric cycles of scarcity and plenty, rain, heat, and wind, work and prayer that are whittled into people's lives by the earth's daily rotation around the sun, the annual agricultural calendar, and years of food crisis that mark time, organize labor, and produce particular ways of seeing, acting, and being in the world.

NyaConstantino's deceased husband, like many elder men I spoke with in my early days in Singida, would have remembered the days when it was not the Gregorian calendar but the appearance of the Pleiades (or Seven Sisters Constellation) in the night sky and the Magellanic cloud visible on the horizon that signaled coming rains and the time to begin cultivation. Regardless of how the annual cycle has been marked and anticipated, Singida, since its early inhabitance, has been a land of two seasons: *ng'i a kitiku* (Ny. literally, the "country of rain") and *ng'i a chwi* (Ny. the "country of dry"). A visitor to Singida will find the idea inherent in these translations, that the land is transformed into an entirely different space when the rains fall, not at all far-fetched. Indeed, anthropologist Marguerite Jellicoe eloquently depicted the practically overnight transformation when the rains cease; when the patches of lush grass and the blue and yellow flowers under the leafy *miombo* trees wither and die, "and once again nothing is left but a bare expanse of sand which sometimes it is hard to believe could produce so much as a blade of grass" (1978, 7) (see plates 5 and 6).

For this reason food production (mainly for subsistence but also grown for export) is necessarily condensed into a short four months of rain between December and March that tends to total between 500 and 600 millimeters. This unforgiving environment structures the annual cycle of work to the extent that most rural Singidans continue to orient their sense of time to the daily cycle of the sun and the annual cycle of food production. In a land with few watches or clocks, where the length of the day is generally consistent across the year, people regularly make appointments through referencing the position of the sun, saying "we will meet when the sun is like this" and holding their arm to demonstrate the angle of the sun to the earth.² Likewise, lunar months are associated with particular stages of cultivation of their staple foods: millet, sorghum, and more recently, maize. Though the residents of this area have long embraced the Gregorian calendar in order to integrate the school, fiscal, and political year with these agricultural-cosmological conceptions of time, people still reference the latter in everyday conversation. In recalling an earlier visit from a guest, or trying to date a debate held at a particular village meeting, people will say "ah, yes, I remember now ... that was the time of the threshing of sorghum" or "when we were eating pumpkins and fresh maize" far more than they will refer to the time as August or June.

Given that food production relies on a short rainy season between December and March, labor during this period is high stakes and highly intensive. Despite a slow diversification in livelihood (more and more, villages are populated with a range of technical experts—teachers, livestock officers, carpenters, tailors, Peace Corps volunteers, traders, nurses, local political leaders, and the occasional foreign anthropologist) and in spite of the fact that farmers fall at the bottom of the social hierarchy of livings, agricultural and pastoral labor trumps all other work. To better situate the temporality of precarity and the interconnection of weather, labor, politics, health, faith, and farming, a normative description of the annual cycle of village events and engagements provides a useful backdrop.

At the end of October or beginning of November, the "signs of rain" (*dalili za mvua*) begin to appear in the dark clouds that gather over the land in the late afternoon. Though winds often sweep these early clouds away, they signal that rains are coming soon, and Nyalukas, aided by Petro when he is available, begins some of her hardest work of the year—tilling the crusty sun-baked earth by hand hoe to prepare for planting. Though agricultural work was typically the domain of women in early colonial reports on the Nyaturu, a decline in pastoralism (understood to be the work of men) due to rampant cattle disease and the rise of cash crop production have resulted in male participation in most parts of the cultivation process.

Sometime in mid-November with the promise of the new rains, when the wells are at their driest and scarcely a blade of grass remains on the dry landscape, the new agricultural year begins with "the month of the weak cows" (Ny. *mweri yiuna ng'ombe*). As patchy rains begin, vegetation turns green, and cattle, goats, and sheep fatten with the new grass. By the next month, that of the "flowering millet" (Ny. *mweri munkinde*), the millet is nearly six inches high. The short rains continue. Wild spinach and *mlenda* leaves are widely available and women pick them in abundance to both eat and dry for consumption in "summer" (i.e., the dry months). By this time, if not much earlier, last year's food reserves begin to run out, and people must buy grain at increasingly elevating prices. In December, or "the month of the dragging and hauling" or "first culti-vation" (Ny. *mweri mnkukuta*), the millet is one to two feet high. School ends for the year and Nyalukas's schoolchildren—who now have six weeks of vacation—help at home with cultivation and the additional planting of peanuts, cowpeas, and cassava. It is in these early months of rain—lasting until the last rains in April—that the incidence of malaria and its related deaths spike, as mosquitoes breed in the now-wet marshlands and other depressions where water collects on the hard earth.

In January, Lukas and his siblings return to school while their parents plant potatoes, and may even begin to harvest beans. Rains cease and the community is at the height of its predictions about the harvest, its prayers for rain, and its lack of food. Truant schoolchildren can be found in the *zambarau* grove, stuff-ing themselves with the watery purple fruit or pilfering *lade* or other semi-wild fruits from farms bordering the school. Grain stores are jealously guarded and opportunities for day labor are virtually non-existent or, when available, only in exchange for the smallest bowl of grain. This is the time when people "fear the sun," as they hunker down until the coming harvest can be relied upon.

By February, "the month of hardship" (Ny. *mweri munti*), the long rains begin and it is time for the second cultivation. NyaLukas and Petro anxiously await the maturity of the first fresh maize, beans, and pumpkins. Heads begin to appear on the millet and people breathe a sigh of relief. In *mweri muhatu* (Ny. "the month of plenty") that spans March and April, hunger ends for the year as the family begins to eat two meals a day again with assurance, consuming maize on the cob, a variety of pumpkins and gourds boiled with a local ground salt or the loveliest *makande* of the year made with fresh beans and fresh maize. In past years at this time, people would note that the Pleiades had dipped below the horizon and would remark that the stars had fallen to the earth to be found as the sticky substance on millet heads (Jellicoe 1978). The triumph of once again having food is mitigated by the endless battle to keep the mud roofs intact and latrines from collapsing in the heavy rain storms. The repair of roofs is a constant labor for Petro and Constantino in these days. Day labor slowly becomes available again for the landless, as people loosen the grip on their dwindling resources, and once again outsource some of their agricultural work.

By May, in "the month of fixing roofs" (Ny. *mweri mnkhanda tope*), the whole family harvests maize, but it must be dried before it can be ground into flour. They strip the husks down and then tie them to a drying branch above the house. After drying, the maize cobs are taken down, stripped of their ker-nels, and the dry cobs are put aside for use as cooking fuel. The grain is stored away in tattered grey gunny sacks from years past bearing the bold blue emblems of food aid organizations. NyaLukas begins cooking ugali with beans, *mlenda*, spinach, and *dagaa*, the small dried fish available for purchase at local shops. The family also begins to harvest and eat boiled cowpeas and peanuts. Summer—the country of the dry weather—has begun.

In June, "the month of harvesting millet" (Ny. *mweri matinanga*), millet, sorghum, and late-planted maize are ready for harvest. During a one-month school vacation Lukas is once again available to help with the heavy labor of harvesting. This work must be completed quickly, especially in the less populated areas of the valley and the bush where birds, baboons, wild pigs, and leopards threaten successful crops. In the valley hamlet a rotating team of guards—Petro, Constantino, and their older sons—patrol the farms at night, armed with bow and arrow to chase off these artful pests. The school vacation also signals the time for male circumcision, when Lukas and his age-mates (generally between ages 12 and 15) have time to heal from the cutting before returning to school, and before the even more intensive labor of July and August. June is also the time of heavy winds and harsh cold that last until August, where nighttime temperatures can drop as low as 40 degrees Fahrenheit and fierce winds howl up from the Great Rift Valley.

Finally, it is in these first few months of summer that most of the work of "building the nation" (*kujenga taifa*) occurs in Langilanga village: the construction and repair of the village office, school classrooms, teacher housing, and latrines, the construction of the cattle watering place, and the digging of the deep water well. Three reasons explain this: first, there is a desperate attempt to make bricks (both fired and sun-dried) "before the water runs out"; second, the mandated financial contributions required to carry out such projects (though they are partly supported by the local and national government) can only be obtained during the period in which people once again have food and their fists have loosened in their pockets; and finally, the main labor force for such projects, who are generally males between 20 and 40, is once again well-nourished and willing to work.

In July and August, NyaLukas and Petro harvest finger millet (which they sell as a cash crop), and take on the heavy work of threshing (Ny. *mapipita*) both millet and sorghum before its storage, grinding and consumption or sale. Threshing occurs on cleared ground smeared with cow dung that dries to create a hard, smooth surface. (More well-off families like school-teachers may have a permanent round cement threshing floor). The grain is dried on the open surface and then beaten or whipped with a long pliable stick to separate the grain seeds from the rest of its stalk. People with no farms can easily find day labor during this period in exchange for food or money, and households host work parties, where workers come with the expectation of food and beer. On July 7th, Tanzania celebrates Sabasaba (7/7), the Day of the Farmers. Government workers in Singida Town celebrate the holiday with a day off work during the busiest and most grueling work month of the year for Singida villagers.

By August, the work of food production is complete. In July and August, many people sell some of their harvest (as grain, or processed as beer) in order to get money to pay off past debts, school fees, local mandated development "contributions" or to purchase new school uniforms for their children. Even though grain at this time of year fetches extremely low prices, many choose to cash their crop in early to make necessary annual purchases before the grain can be used up by needy relations, traded by a thirsty husband, or seized by people to whom one is indebted.

The work and weather of September, October and November become indistinguishable in this driest of times. Cattle and other livestock must be taken further and further away to find water and food. Food shortages begin (earlier and earlier each year, it seems) and prices for grain begin to rise. The now dried and bare grain stalks are trampled down and cut. Some are put away to use as cooking fuel, while other stalks are burned and used to fertilize the next finger millet crop, or to line *matuta*, the terraced rows of earth on which sorghum, millet, maize, and beans grow. Petro spreads what little manure he has collected in these cattle-poor times on the sandy earth. With "signs of the rain" and the assurance from NyaConstanino that "the funeral of the rain is on the bed of the ground" (Ny. *nkuya a mbua urii fang'i*—that is, those dark clouds cannot hang up there forever), people once again plant their farms. And with one eye skyward and the other on their dwindling food supply, NyaConstantino's family waits and prays for rain.

"God is One and Faith is One. Religion is like Multipartyism"

NyaConstantino and her children identify as Lutheran. More Lutherans live in this northern hamlet of Langilanga than any other, for American Lutherans settled this hamlet in the early part of the twentieth century. To the south of Langilanga is a Roman Catholic mission and church, so the southern hamlets are dense with villagers who identify as "RC." To the west lies the district administrative border with the Municipality of Singida (Singida Mjini), where many Muslims live. The northwestern corner of Langilanga village lies at the crossroads of two unpaved inter-city routes. At this crossroads, there is a mosque of the Wahabi sect. The crossroads mosque is known as the mosque of *siasa kali* ("harsh politics") said to be brought here by "people from the outside" or "Arabs." The crossroads hosts the weekly cattle market for which people come from surrounding villages and divisions to trade each Saturday. Those who reside at the crossroads are also seen to be outsiders who have settled there for its economic opportunities. Inter-city buses pass twice daily along this route and so the intersection provides ripe opportunities for selling seasonal produce through car windows: bananas, peanuts (boiled or roasted), guava fruits, tomatoes, and cowpeas. This largely Muslim (even though mainly Nyaturu) trading population is seen to be "not from here." Mistrust on both sides leaves the crossroads population somewhat marginalized from the rest of Langilanga.

The crossroads population aside, there is intensive cooperation and cohabitation among people of different religions in Langilanga, and conversion from one world religion or denomination to another is not uncommon. While the majority of people in Langilanga are Roman Catholic, Langilanga's chairman, head teacher, and many of the hamlet leaders are Muslim. Many people told me they preferred a Muslim leader who did not drink alcohol, because he would more trustworthy, not someone of "many words." One extended family I knew in the valley hamlet was particularly diverse. Mzee Luciani was an elder and kin to NyaConstantino's husband. He was born "pagan," worshipping the Creator (*Mulunda*) through the ancestors as his own ancestors had done. He married a girl, whom I knew as NyaAgnes, from a Muslim family and decided they would both become Roman Catholic. She converted and studied on her own, eventually teaching him to pray so they could both be baptized and married at the church. When Mzee Luciani was in his forties he became very ill. His head would swirl, other days his arm would ache. No doctor or healer could make him better. After spending a lot of money at the hospital, he finally went to the Pentecostal church and they diagnosed him with a sickness of the spirits. The Pentecostal leaders laid hands on him and he healed. He converted to Pentecostalism straightaway. NyaAgnes however declined to convert again and stayed with the Roman Catholic Church. Mzee Luciani's closest neighbor was his full brother Mzee Abduli, a widower who cared for their aged mother as well as three children of his own. Their mother never converted to Christianity or Islam, and when I met her, was herself on the way to her ancestors. Mzee Abduli converted to Islam in his youth. His young son, who was all of eighteen when I met him, had converted to Lutheranism when he was in school. Mzee Luciani explained religious tolerance in his own family, and in Langilanga more broadly, in the following way:

> God is one. And faith is one. Our aim is that we arrive in heaven. Religion is like multipartyism. We all have the same goal, and there are many ways to reach it. It's best that if a person feels himself touched, that he does not try and force anyone else. One can decide for oneself alone. We Tanzanians, we cooperate. When it is Eid the Christians go to celebrate with the Muslims and when it is Easter and Christmas, the Muslims go to celebrate with the Christians and their leaders. We are taught not to enter matters of religion. If you give a speech, you don't speak about someone's faith. You don't criticize or ruin the faith of someone else. Even if he prays at the hole in the tree, you leave the honey there. It's good to sit together and talk to him about it: "Me, I saw where you were praying. Did you see God in there?" So you can explain to him how it is. If he agrees, okay. If he refuses, you say, "Okay, go ahead. Maybe another day you will see the good in what I say." He should not sacrifice a sheep though at my door. There he would break a law. But he may do it at the free spaces, like at the hole in the tree there.

More than just tolerance, religious diversity in Singida also seems strategic. Prayers for rain and prayers for deliverance must reach God's ears through every possible route.

"The Rain has the Head of a Mad Man"

It is not very surprising to note that the annual cycle of rain and sun, physical labor and spiritual work, and dearth and plenty does not always keep to its orbit. NyaConstantino and her family are thus no strangers to hunger: between 1998 and 2014, they faced five significant food crises. Local histories, relief organizations, and national reports all detail the official history of hunger in Singida in terms of natural disasters or climate issues: grasshoppers, locusts, birds, drought, and floods that destroy crops or prevent their growth. Severe weather in 1998, known locally as "*Elamino*" (and worldwide as El Niño) brought heavy rains and flooding up to one and a half meters high, followed by a plague of pests that destroyed the entire harvest in Singida, Kondoa, and Dodoma regions. In Singida today, many people remembered *Elamino* as the worst hunger of their lifetime—when *watu wamekufa kabisa* ("people were literally dying"). Until food aid arrived, not even local elites had reserves of hoarded food to be sold at astronomical prices. In 2003, the rain "refused" completely in most areas of Singida Rural District. With government food aid, assistance from a local mission, and with a moderate crop in 2004, NyaConstantino's family had "already healed" from hunger by my arrival in Singida in October. However light rains and a reduced crop in 2005 followed by very late rains and a late harvest in 2006, meant that my last five months of long-term fieldwork occurred in a period of extreme food shortage. Drought in 2007–2008 and again in 2011–2012 once again strained the food supply.

It is important to note that other historical currents beside weather have shaped the context of vulnerability to food crisis in Singida. Rampant cattle disease struck Singida herds in the 1980s and 1990s causing many households to lose 5 to 20 percent of their stocks, and some to lose all. The perceived insecurity of this form of wealth, as well as a greater need and desire to liquidate one's stocks to pay for secondary school fees, healthcare costs, or to invest in other development, has led to a further decline of cattle herding as a primary livelihood for Singidans and of cattle-loaning (uriha) as a social security. With so little manure to fertilize the arid soil, agricultural crop yield has declined proportionately. Nowadays, without manure Nyalukas can expect three gunnysacks of grain per acre in a good year, and two in a bad one. With manure, she could expect five or six gunnysacks. The decline of cattle-keeping by smallholder farmers has without a doubt drastically impacted food production in Singida.

Shifts in the staple crops that Singidans cultivate also shape the context of vulnerability. Bulrush millet (Ny. *uvee*) and red and white sorghum (Ny. *langilanga*) have long been the grains of choice for cultivation, because of their suitability to the irregular rains and poor sandy soil of rural Singida. More recently however, people have begun to produce maize, because in a good year with regular rain, the lack of threshing required and maize's large kernels yield large quantities of food with little land and less work. If "the rain refuses" however, so does the maize, and the entire crop will be lost if the short rains of December and January are not quickly followed by the long rains of late-February and early March.

Finally, the growing scarcity of arable land is another issue in Singida. Between 2004 and 2014, the population grew from approximately 2400 to 3200. Apart from the growing crossroads population, there is little immigration into the village, but as the younger generation grows up and starts families and households of their own, family landholdings are divided ever further among descendants, leaving plots ever more insufficient for subsistence. In any event, these yearly cycles of dearth and bounty and the unpredictable and even waning success of annual harvests by NyaConstantino and her family underscore the *banality of hunger* for rural subsistence farmers in places like Singida.

NyaConstantino's world offers us a glimpse into the organization, strength, and intricacy of social relations at the village level and the context of material precarity in which these are lived. Looking out from her vantage point, it is not difficult grasp the beehive of activity and reservoir of local farming knowledge required to eke subsistence out of the Singida sun, rain, and soil. Let us now cast a glance backward to understand the emergence of statecraft in the twentieth century amid the sun's unpredictable grace.

Notes

1. Ikungi was part of Singida Rural District until 2010, when it was made its own district.
2. By 2014, the pervasiveness of cell phones had started to shift this way of marking time.

2 The Unpredictable Grace of the Sun

Cosmology, Conquest, and the Politics of Subsistence

> The prayer to the Sun places the Arimi traditional society in an endless interconnectedness.... But the contemporary Arimi generation is separated from the clear conclusions of this traditional worldview by a great mountain of boredom and disillusionment thrown up by past experience. To use Achebe's phrase, "things have fallen apart" for us all. And yet the prayer to the Sun should not only leave a nostalgic religious sentiment in the hearts and minds of Arimi people, but also an indelible social responsibility. The beauty and goodness of voluntary actions in which anyone who has caught the Sun's unpredictable "grace" willingly enhances the unity that is prescribed in the ancient African philosophy ... that of regional and global human solidarity and responsibility.
>
> > Reverend Dr. Peter A.S. Kijanga in his analysis of the Nyaturu [Arimi] Prayer to the Sun, *Ukuta Ryuva/Yuva*
>
> Men measured out their lives in famines.
>
> > John Iliffe, *A Modern History of Tanganyika*
>
> The past is brother to the present.
>
> > Nyaturu proverb

Since the earliest years into which Nyaturu oral traditions give us insight, the project of subsistence in Singida has never been taken for granted. Indeed, Nyaturu oral traditions, archival records, secondary sources, and oral histories underscore how central the precarity of subsistence has been to the worldview of people, to the politics of their engagement with outsiders, and to the emergence of statecraft and nationhood, as far back as we can see. These sources highlight the historical conjuncture of subsistence events (both boon and crisis) with political and cosmological shifts. To be sure, cosmology, politics, and subsistence have been mutually constitutive in Singidans' reflections on their past. In this chapter, I draw on a variety of primary and secondary sources to explore shifts and continuities in the ideas of political membership, authority, development, entitlement and obligation.[1] Precolonial forms of authority, I argue, shifted suddenly at colonial conquest from a local politics of charismatic leadership to a bureaucratized, depersonalized, and extractive authority laced with violence and mystified by orders and technologies from elsewhere. Before, during, and after this transition, Singidans consistently articulated their reactions to these far-reaching political transitions through an idiom of the sun's powerful but unpredictable grace—that governs the interconnection of the cosmological order, the natural world, and human action.

Through German and later British rule, a common sense would emerge that colonial military power implied that the sun's grace had been transferred to the newcomers. This transfer of authority *obligated* Nyaturu to their colonial masters, who could and would make material claims for labor and resources on the Nyaturu with acts or threats of violence. This institutionalization by the Germans of both taxation and forced labor set the tone and terms of statecraft for the British colonial and independent political regimes to come. Yet after several decades of British rule, Nyaturu populations also began to associate the bequest of the sun's grace on the British with a minimal sense of entitlement to freedom from famine for which the British should be responsible. Thus by independence, an abstract and incipient notion of *citizenship*—membership and belonging to something beyond Unyaturu—had dawned in Singida, and this conception of citizenship was integrally connected to the sun's grace and to the project of subsistence.

Yet this is not simply a story of the past, for understandings of the sun's grace continue to inflect contemporary practices of Christianity, Islam, and citizenship, particularly in the anticipation and experience of food crisis. I end this chapter ethnographically, looking at how the sun's grace is understood and talked about in contemporary life. Following the historical threads of these politics of subsistence in Singida offers the opportunity to contemplate how generations of food insecurity constructs worldviews, forges identities, and drives history. For, as the Nyaturu say, "the past is brother to the present."[2]

So why tell the story of Singida through the story of the sun? What can ideas about the sun's grace teach us about history, precarious livelihoods, and citizenship in rural Tanzania? Attending to narratives of the sun provides insight into what many rural subsistence farmers today articulate as a sense of extreme interdependence with their natural, social, and political environment. Indeed, getting by in Singida relies on a delicate and fervent attention to order—cosmological, political, environmental, and social—that drives and structures everyday life. Yet labor and hardship, as well as bounty and rest, take turns around the sun and in relation to it, alternating by day and by night, by month and by season, by cycle and year. There is a temporality and rhythm to life that follows and mimics the earth's relation to the sun, and is the underlying foundation of resilience. Hardship always awaits, but then again, so does relief.

The Sun, the Moon, and the Pleiades: Subsistence and the Nyaturu Prior to European Conquest

The Ukuta Yuva, or ritual "Prayer to the Sun" (see table 2.1), is an oral tradition that has codified Nyaturu beliefs in the cosmological and social order at least since the earliest accounts of Nyaturu custom by German colonial administrators (cf. Jellicoe 1967, 1978; Olson 2002). John Iliffe has noted that one of the most widely accepted concepts of God among Tanganyikan peoples in the western plateau and in the northeast is one that centers on the sun as divine symbol, with the word for "sun" deriving from the root -*uba* or -*uva*. Indeed, the shared cosmology centering on the movements of the sun (*Yuva*), the moon (*Mweri-Matunda*) and the Pleiades (*Kiimia*—more commonly known as the Seven Sisters constellation) whose orderly procession framed the universe as created by *Matunda* [the Creator] offered some unity and cohesion to the fluid and non-hierarchical Nyaturu society of precolonial times (1979).[3]

By all accounts, before the drastic re-organization of power effected by German and British colonization, Nyaturu peoples (also called the Turu and the Rimi) were decentralized (Von Sick 1915, 30), like many of their neighbors in eastern and southern Africa. When the Germans arrived in 1901, no chiefly system existed (Jellicoe 1969). Instead, lineages had informal elder councils who served as advisors and mediated conflict. Clusters of these lineage groups followed charismatic leaders who gained power through their leadership in battle and their support of key diviners. Cultural and linguistic distinctions between the three main dialect groups of the Nyaturu—the Wirwana, the Wahi, and the Wanyamunying'anyi—persist to the present and many variations among these groups reflect the influences of neighboring ethnic groups with whom the Nyaturu have a history of intermarriage: the Nyiramba, Nyamwezi, Iraqw, Sandawe, Barbaig (also called the Mang'ati) and Gogo of Dodoma.[4] Yet despite these loose affiliations and wide cultural and linguistic variations, Nyaturu have shared a common agropastoralist livelihood. The ethnonym most used by Nyaturu to refer to themselves when speaking KiNyaturu—"Rimi"—literally translates as "cultivators." Linguist Howard Olson noted that it was "a name believed to have been chosen by the people themselves to distinguish them from the hunting-gathering people whom they first encountered on their ... arrival in the area" (2002, 188). Alongside these deep agricultural roots, the earliest accounts of the Nyaturu show them also to be active pastoralists, with deep rivalries with the Maasai who often traveled south to raid Nyaturu cattle.

Despite the linguistic and cultural variation among those who identify as Nyaturu, the sun has been a primary religious symbol across sub-groups. Marguerite Jellicoe, a cultural anthropologist who worked as a community development officer in Singida in the early 1960s, argued compellingly that this

Ukuta Yuva
(Nyaturu Prayer to the Sun)

O SUN, Creator, you have opened. You are praised by the cock and by the morning warbler, by the male donkey and the male goat; by the eland in the forest, a wild animal grazing on the leaves of the muntumba tree. Since you went down we have seen no bad omen; we have heard no funeral cry; no one has died. Sun, you have opened well.

Now you have thrown white butter of blessing on the mountain and the baobab tree. May we all be cool. Sun, place four sticks in the west, and in the north, and in the south, and in the east. At midday pause over a homestead with ten houses, spread out your blessing there; to a homestead with only one house also send goodness. Do not burn us; do not be too hot

In the evening return safely those who have gone herding and those traveling in the forests. Take with you to the west the poisonous snakes, rhinoceroses, lions. Take with you all fevers of our people and our herds; take them to your homestead in the west, to the deep chasm of the borassus palm, and bury them there under a flat stone.

Now eat cool food in your homestead; do not eat hot food. Go take from your herd and sacrifice a black steer, a black ram and a big elephant. Put the chyme in a grain trough of heavy wood, the chyme of those three, together with a pestle of light wood and an iron bradawl. Now go to the east with your coolness, carrying the skin bracelet of an infant and the tail of a wildebeeste, breathing saliva of blessing. Scatter the chyme on all large trees, pools, forests, cattle-paths and millet fields, cleansing them.

You who are my grandmother, you who are my grandfather, Creator, our great God, give me goodness. Put the root of a tree across the path to my homestead, that no troublemaker may come. See that no sleeping child is caused to fall into the fire.

I have finished with you, Sun.

O Moon, Creator, give birth to two children, a boy and a girl. Let them grow up and marry, let them look after each other as a herdsman looks after his flocks. Bear a male calf and a female calf; a male lamb and a female lamb; a male goat and a female goat; a male donkey and a female donkey; a female chicken and a male chicken; a female puppy and a male puppy; a female kitten and a male kitten. Give to the forest many wild animals, bearing two of each, one male and one female. O Sun, you who are the Moon, even minute creatures of the earth, such as small ants, bear two also, one female and one male. For it is good that all creatures should multiply. I have finished with you, Moon.

O Kiimia, you suckle us, you are grandmother, give us food. Let my grain swell, my people increase, my flocks also. Let my homestead grow larger. Kiimia, your flower is a bride, with white beads and cowrie shells on her head and a baby-carrier on her back. Your flower is a warrior who has killed a lion. Send flowers to all sorts of millet — bulrush millet, long-headed sorghum, short-headed sorghum, red sorghum, white sorghum, pumpkins, cowpeas, sunflower, castor; crown with your flowers Kiimia. We will keep their good seeds and throw away the bad seeds. Send flowers to all trees, the figtree and the candelabra tree; let them bear fruit that we may eat. If we find that some of the fruits are bitter, we will leave them for the birds. Let there be flowers everywhere....

Table 2.1. Excerpts from the Nyaturu Prayer to the Sun, recited in Marguerite Jellicoe, Philip Puja, and Jeremiah Sombi's 1967 "Praising the Sun," published in the journal *Transition*. Reprinted with permission from Indiana University Press.

cosmology and the division of spiritual labor it sketches is deeply gendered (1978). Through associations with divining and herding, Nyaturu people render the sun masculine. It controls the cycle of time that brings good and evil, birth, health, death, danger and disease. In the morning, when cool and benevolent, the sun brings blessings. He is the prototype of the herder (who protects) and of the diviner (who brings health and prosperity). In the evening, he is the *musimbuya* (Ny.), or diviner's intermediary (who is charged with removing the dangerous objects identified by a diviner), and he shepherds all things evil and dangerous into the night sky. The moon, or Mweri-Matunda, is a grown woman who controls the cycle of birth, conception, and creation. The grandmotherly postreproductive femininity of the Pleiades constellation, or Kiimia, manages the cycle of subsistence in Singida. Her appearance in the night sky signals coming rains and the time to begin cultivation. The Pleiades produces and controls the natural and human environment—the rains, harvest, wildlife, and the powers of divining and trade—within which people flourish, flounder, feast, and starve.

In the early twentieth century Singidans recited the Prayer to the Sun (which also has verses that praise the Moon and the Pleiades) prior to three ritual events: the women's coming-of-age ritual or *imaa* (Ny.), the negotiation of bridewealth between two fathers, and the seeking of the services of a diviner (during the course of the twentieth century occurrences of all three types of events became less frequent, or, in the case of the imaa ceased almost entirely).[5] That it was these three occasions, specifically, that called for the praising of the sun is suggestive of the sun's perceived influence over sociality, spirituality, politics, economy and the natural world and the interlinkages between them. Two of the three occasions (the imaa and the negotiation of bridewealth) center on the key rituals for managing gender relations, social reproduction, generational change, and the building of affinal relations between patrilines. The third occasion, seeking the services of a diviner, was closely associated with the consolidation of power in war and accumulation of wealth in cattle through tending to the relation between forces seen and unseen, times past and present, and matters earthly and otherworldly. Ecological balance (and thus, subsistence) hung on the tending of the sun's power at these key social, political, and spiritual moments. The sun's power must be seen and fed. Well-being must be lifted up. Grace must be reciprocated.

In addition to sketching out the cosmological order of things, the Ukuta Yuva also reveals other attributes of life in rural Singida in the late-nineteenth and twentieth century. First, it alludes to some economic differentiation between households, for some people live in homesteads with ten houses, while others in only one house. Second, it underscores that life for agropastoralists in this land of two seasons has long born blessings and perils, opportunities and catastrophes, despair and hope. In the face of the ecological and political tenuousness that characterized Nyaturu life, the sun has offered security in its unwavering cyclicality as well as relief. For the sun marks the passage of time that—though it brings pain and suffering—also heals or removes it. Agriculture, and specifically the production of millet, is essential to livelihood. Yet the prayer also highlights the importance of herding for subsistence and sociality in addition to pointing to the uncertainty of its outcomes. Certainly herding, like agriculture, bore its own precarities in the late nineteenth and early twentieth centuries.[6]

Finally, it is the grace of the sun—who must be flattered and cajoled—that protects homes from dearth, disaster, disease, and invasion. It is not possible to know to whom the word "trouble-makers" refers in this iteration of the Ukuta Yuva, but the historical record suggests a number of possibilities. Slave caravans passed directly beneath Unyaturu through Kilimatinde on their way to the trans-Indian slave market in Zanzibar. Notoriously murderous explorer Henry Morton Stanley published the first written accounts of the Nyaturu in his dubious 1875 travel log *Through the Dark Continent*. And the Maasai frequently raided the cattle of the Nyaturu in the nineteenth century as a means of acquiring wealth and for young men to acquire authority. The last known Maasai raid on the Nyaturu was in 1890, just prior to the arrival of the Germans in the region.

Oral traditions documented in the late colonial period certainly support the impression that drought, pests, and hostile invasion conditioned food security and household well-being in the nineteenth century. In the fieldnotes he took in 1960, anthropologist Harold Schneider highlighted the significance of famine in the oral traditions he had collected:

> The Turu word for famine is *njaa* or "hunger." Famines are of common occurrence in this country, but what is meant by famine varies greatly. It can range all the way from localized poor production, to localized failure, to general poor production, to general failure. Apparently only the latter are real famines to the Turu and these acquire names to mark them. *Njaa kinyamakaa* or the "hunger of African foreigners" occurred before the Germans came and the name denotes the fact that these Africans (apparently also hungry) attacked the country to steal grain.... The famine of *pafa* occurred when Lisu was a small boy, the pafa being the seeds of a wild tree which were eaten. The famine of *mado* [potatoes] is claimed to have been the last general famine.... Many people are said to have died in this famine. The famine of *amurea* is another, this apparently preceding the Germans.... It is impossible to relate these names to actual famines in most cases, and in any case the names are probably localized in reference. However the general picture is fairly clear.[7]

Schneider also noted the way in which lineage and village histories were bound up in stories of famine.

> Death through starvation in bad famine years is common. There are occasional references in genealogies to such deaths, such as the death of the eldest brother Nkuniungi, of Mosi and Masaka with all his children in the

famine of amurea. Furthermore, whole villages were sometimes broken up by starvation and migration. The village that used to sit where Kinyankanga and Bumba are now was broken up by invading foreign Africans, perhaps Mangati, during famine as they looked for food. The village that used to be southwest of Ikungi was "destroyed" by famine. And the village at the rocks of Kimai was formed after the British came by people who were driven by famine from another area to the east. They found the site of a former village, perhaps also wiped out by famine.[8]

Famine, such evidence suggests, has not only been a driver of migration, identity, and settlement, but has also played a central role in conceptualizing and narrating them.

In sum then, while we cannot be certain about the specific moments of change over time, we can draw several conclusions about the social and political organization of Nyaturu peoples prior to their encounter with Europeans at the turn of the twentieth century. Nyaturu people living in Singida were agropastoralists who were fiercely protective of their kin, cattle, and territory in the face of hostile outsiders. They were non-hierarchical in their social organization, rather fluid in their identities, affiliations, and alliances, and slightly varied in their wealth. They lived their lives with a consciousness of intense (and even intensifying) ecological, political, and economic precarity. And their ritual practices—born of this consciousness and the humility it rendered—sought to keep the cosmological order in balance and to invite its grace.

"Strangers are Sent by the Sun": Conquest and the German Years (1901–1920)

> When Von Sick [*sic*] was seen entering the [Tita rain] shrine, people said, "Malayuva (the Sun) is finished"—meaning that the blessing had been removed from the people and conferred on the strangers.
>
> Marguerite Jellicoe, "The Turu Resistance Movement"

As one Singida resident recounted, the Germans entered first through Mgori, coming into Isanga by way of Mwanja Hanji, an old chief:

> When the German brought his war to Singida, the locals slaughtered a sheep to calm him down. And he settled. He sees that the people of Unyankhanya are gentle; they want peace. And so they warned him about Kifiindi, an old witchdoctor who lived at Kinku Ndang'ongo. Kifindi had the power to hurt people, to make birds fall from the trees. He could tap a stick on a hole and make a certain kind of animal, the *munyasera*, come out. The Germans went to find this fierce witchdoctor, and they killed him and his son Njiku. There the war ended in this country. And Khondeya was elevated to chief. People were gentle in Nali. And so he went on to Siuyu by way of my grandfather Malonga. He was just an ordinary man, but he gave them sheep and in return

he was given a cap and white clothes and made a chief. Malonga was ruler from Siuyu to UghaUgha.

Then the German left here and arrived at KiÑyalissu. They found one man, Mdinya, who was very fierce. They killed him and his son Itema. Then they left and entered Unyamikumbi by way of Kinene. There they received him well. They left and went to see Mwama, who was fierce and so they killed him. Then they went to Kisaki. They left there in peace and went to Kititimu. There they set up tents. From there they went to the Ifembe Rock where they found Mulale and made him chief. Then they left and built a fort where Singida Town now sits ... because they found water and the lakes. From Singida Town they went to Puma and then to Unyahati. When they arrived at Samumba village they found a very famous woman named Liti, who was very fierce. The Germans were not welcomed there. Liti kept bees and controlled them with her witchcraft. She managed to chase the German out. They said, "What are we going to do with this woman?" They even tried to attack her at night, but the bees kept them out. Finally another Nyaturu man helped the Germans to get past her. They dressed in rubber clothes and covered everything but their eyes and they killed Liti. Today we still sing of her.

So they left that area and went to Wirwana. They went to see Sima who was fierce and refused to be ruled. So they shot him. His son Salim was given the chiefdom. Then they went to see Yunga in Ilongero. He was peaceful and so they made him chief. And Igwe was also made chief. Then they went to Kinyagigi to Tati, and Tati had no ill words so he was made chief. And they returned to Mughamu and built a lookout [on what is now the Arusha road]. They were looking for the British. They stayed for three years, and in the fifth year, the British came.[9]

This history highlights the sense of arbitrariness, haphazardness, and violence of the hierarchy that the Germans so rapidly imposed in Singida and left in their wake. The qualities for which the Germans appointed chiefs included neither experience in leadership nor strength of character; on the contrary, they were selected for their ready acquiescence to German power in the face of military might. Indeed, Schneider's interlocutors in 1959 told him that the men appointed by the Germans to be chiefs were often unpopular with their neighbors.[10] This narration of Singida's history offers a sense of the tentative nature of alliance in Unyaturu and a relatively quick turnover of allegiances and alignments as a new power broker appeared on the scene.

Colonial power transformed not only the face of governance in Singida, but also its character, pitting Nyaturu technologies and cosmologies against ones from elsewhere. The Germans arrived in Singida to find—not chiefs or headmen with territories of governance—but notably fierce war leaders and ritual specialists whose position "depended on the free and always transferable 'grace' of the sun" (Jellicoe 1969, 2). When the Germans used their weapons and protective clothing to wipe out fierce resistors, kill Kifiindi (neutralizing his sticks and medicines that could summon animals from the ground and make birds tumble from the sky) and survive Liti's bees, they also invited new understandings of power and forms of legitimacy and authority.[11]

The German record offers a different elaboration and timeline of events. Bismarck laid claim to the territory that became known as German East Africa during the Berlin Conference in 1885. But he did not begin to extend German influence into the Turu, Iramba and Isanzu country until about 1901, from the Kilimatinde fort built in 1894. The Germans encountered an Unyaturu much weakened by three drought-ridden decades prior, that culminated in a severe rinderpest epidemic in 1896. The chiefs that quickly submitted to German authority during this time of conquest imposed taxation in the area, usually in the form of a hut tax of three rupees per hut. Forced labor was the alternative to paying cash—and was used to build roads and forts (Coulson 1982). Liti, according to Von Sick, only briefly frustrated German efforts to establish rule in Turu land in 1903 before she was killed during an altercation with German troops. Of greater significance were the organized rebellions of the Nyaturu, the Nyiramba, the Nyaisanzu, the Tatog, and the Mbugwe.

This was a time of growing resistance to German rule in Tanganyika. Between 1905 and 1907, Africans in the southern half of the country rebelled against German colonialism. They killed or drove out European settlers, administrators, missionaries, and even African adjutants. This uprising, known as the Maji Maji Rebellion, takes its name from the water (*maji*) distributed by a charismatic healer and leader of the rebellion to protect men against European bullets (cf. Giblin & Monson 2010). As a result of German retaliation, an estimated 75,000 people died of violence, hunger, and disease. Iliffe writes that German military engagement during these revolts was secondary to the tactics of food seizure and the destruction of crops: "'In my view,' [Captain] Wangenheim reported on 22 October, 'only hunger and want can bring about a final submission. Military actions alone will remain more or less a drop in the ocean'" (Iliffe 1979, 193). Count Gustav Adolf von Goetzen set his mind to creating a famine throughout the rebel area (Goetzen 1905, in Iliffe [1979]) while "rebels seized food from loyalists and sought safe bases in which to cultivate" (Iliffe 1979, 193). Famine was indeed a colonial technology of conquest.

The Germans did not have time or need to employ such biopower in Unyaturu. The Nyaturu revolt, which occurred shortly after Maji Maji in 1908, consisted of "unrest and riots" in Puma near the rumbling rain-shrine rock of Tita (Von Sick 1915). The widely known Tatoga rainmaker Akida Maussa (or Gidamausa) of Dongobesh is said to have led sacrifices inside Tita for the bewitchment of the Germans and the protection of the Nyaturu. The invulnerability medicine he distributed unified Iramba, Mbugwe, and Unyaturu into a multi-tribal revolt (Jellicoe 1969). The resistance collapsed after minimal fighting and Von Sick later insisted on entering the rain-shrine, but residents did not allow him to enter the inner chamber. He noted at the time that Tita "no longer sang" and later "when Von Sick was seen entering the shrine, people said, '*Malayuva* (the Sun) is finished'—meaning that the blessing had been removed from the people and conferred on the strangers" (Jellicoe 1978, 9). The sun, as powerful as ever, seemed to the Nyaturu to favor the German newcomers.

After the rebellion at Puma, the Germans used forced labor to construct a fort in 1909 between Lakes Singidani and Kindai in what is now present-day Singida town (Cory 1951). Within several years, trade with German administrators had grown, a small market had opened near the fort, and an increasing number of Nyaturu had become concentrated near there. The first decade of the twentieth century was blessed with rain, and in 1910, the Germans described Turu country as the bread basket for the surrounding regions (Von Sick 1915). In time, traders from other areas—Arabs, Tanganyikans from the Swahili coast, and Indian settlers—came to partake of the economic opportunity in the area (Jellicoe 1969). But aside from the increase in trade, the greatest shift in subsistence practices for households in Singida was the necessity for men to migrate for paid employment that would enable them to pay their taxes, and for women to assume their labor when they were away. By 1910, Singida—like Tabora, Kigoma, Ruvuma, Mtwara and Ufipa—was becoming a labor reserve for the plantations, mines, and infrastructural construction in other parts of the territory (Slater 1977, 170).

Educational opportunities did emerge in Tanganyika under German rule. Though they successfully quelled the uprisings, the Germans were fearful of further African retaliation and subsequent development policy emphasized social development. But with its peripheral location and status, Singida remained outside networks of social improvement. Instead, the government imported secondary-educated young men from the coast to be *akida* and *jumbe* (middlemen and headmen in charge of tax collection) in the interior (Coulson 1982). A single French mission, the White Fathers, settled in Singida in 1909 and attempted to save the souls of the Nyaturu with little success (colonial administrators accorded this failure to the missionaries' opposition to polygamy and divorce). With little incentive for upward mobility, and little opportunity to change their economic circumstances (beyond the more familiar means of converting surplus agricultural output into cattle), the Nyaturu seemed neither to seek nor to gain access to "improvement" during German rule.

By 1916, the tsetse fly had spread widely. But rain blessed Unyaturu during the years of German occupation, and though these years are remembered for their violence and "darkness" (*giza*—referring to the lack of world religion and development), they are also remembered for their lack of drought and famine until the onset of the Great War and the end of the German occupation of Singida. But apart from the devastation caused by the spread of tsetse fly, the two most enduring effects of the brief German tenure were (1) the structures now in place for the mobilization of labor; and (2) the hasty consolidation of new forms of political power. Through taxation managed by a newly founded system of "traditional power" (the chiefs), the Germans had "taught" Singidans "to work." Through force, and apparently with the grace of the sun, the Germans had lodged key individuals into positions of governance over their peers. This is not to argue that there had been social and economic equality in the past. Rather, power had been reorganized and reconceptualized in Unyaturu. No longer in the hands of charismatic local leaders, power was now associated with a new "big man"—a dominant European capable of summoning the rain, whose tactics in some ways mimicked those of the relentless sun.

Statecraft on a Shoestring: Subsistence, Compulsion, and Food Relief under British Rule (1919–1961)

After the German defeat in World War I and the loss of tens of thousands of African troops in the East African campaign, a newly formed League of Nations assumed control of Tanganyika territory in 1919.[12] The British Mandate signed in 1922 gave Britain "'full powers of legislation and administration' while binding her to promote 'the material and moral well-being and the social progress of the inhabitants'" (Iliffe 1979, 147). The Mandate was understood to be a temporary arrangement, for "peoples not yet able to stand by themselves under the strenuous conditions of the modern world" (Article 2 of the Covenant with the League of Nations).

What was the Tanganyika Territory to the British Empire? Iliffe writes that "Tanganyika had been Germany's most valued colony. The British wanted only to deny it to others" (261). The empire was considerably weakened following the war, and the territory offered little wealth to the British in relation to its other resource-rich colonies. Consequently, the British advocated against converting Tanganyika into a settler colony for European immigrants, and argued it should remain "primarily a Black man's country" (262) under a policy of indirect rule. And while the British continued to try to wring a surplus out of Tanganyika, the new territory also inherited the emerging shades of humanitarianism and paternalism that England was cultivating and codifying both at home (with the Poor Law amendment of 1834) and also elsewhere in its empire—particularly India (Brennan 1984; Singh 1993).

The British quickly implemented a system of indirect rule through establishing Native Authorities in the rural areas in 1926. Colonial administrators attempted to rule through the chiefs by dictating rural agriculture, taxation, and development policies (Coulson 1982, 97). And chiefs were able to harness the power of "tradition," even where these traditions were newly produced, to incorporate rural Tanganyikans into the building of empire. Speaking generally to the British colonial project in Africa, Mahmood Mamdani notes that this was a "regime that breathed life into a whole range of compulsions: forced labor, forced crops, forced sales, forced contributions, and forced removals" (1996, 22–23). Such compulsions were particularly important for colonial subjects in the labor-exporting regions like Singida, where the primary economic contribution to the territory was to provide workers to regions with cash-crop and plantation agriculture and who, far from producing a regular surplus, encountered rather regular periods of famine.

The Singida "entrusted" to the British after World War I was still recovering from the worst famine of the twentieth century for central Tanzania: known more widely by the Gogo name, "Mtunya" ("the scramble"). The famine hit Singida, Kondoa, and Dodoma regions especially hard: severe drought had exacerbated the toll taken by German requisitions of cattle, food, and labor during World War I (Brooke 1967). Maddox notes that seizure of food continued under the British during the war, with "the only change in the situation after the British occupied the region [starting in 1916] [being] the language in which the demands were made" (1990, 184). Though the British often paid for confiscated food on the spot, the threat of force was always implied. Starting in 1916, they also began to collect taxes (Iliffe 1979). But "strangers," people say, "are sent by the sun," and the transfer of the sun's grace from the Germans to the British did not—at least at first—seem to have significant effects on Singidans.

"Teaching the Turu to Work": Money, Markets, and the Commodification of Food

After these crisis years in Singida had passed, the "customary" rule of chiefs regulated the collection of taxes, agricultural development, and the mobilization of labor. For men who could not produce the money for their household's taxes, labor on colonial projects was required, though chiefs often exhausted every possible means of extracting cash before labor tickets were issued. According to the report of one British official: "When I came here in 1920, one of my first duties was to interview every Jumbe. To my question 'what are your duties as chief' the answer was too often 'If a man does not pay his tax I tie him up.' I had seen instances of this 'tying up' (the victim's arms were tied behind him with a bowstring which, as it contracted, sometimes cut through the flesh on the upper arm to the bone)."[13] This threat of violence provided a strong inducement to comply with Native Authorities' extraction of household resources. By 1934 the District Commissioner reported that pressure put on Singidans to pay their taxes had caused the number of cases of cattle theft being heard at the Native Courts to skyrocket.[14]

The British expressed frustration at the apparent lack of interest among the Nyaturu in money, markets, and agriculture for the sake of personal accumulation. It was not that the Nyaturu had no conception of wealth and its associated status; rather that wealth was acquired, exchanged, and performed through cattle, which reproduced themselves with only moderate intervention.[15] This lack of interest in money presented an obstacle to administrators, who sought not only to collect taxes from Singidans, but also to transform Singida into a profit-turning region. This frustration was manifested in the chronic colonial complaint that the Nyaturu had "not yet learned to work." The pedagogy of industry—in the perennial pursuit of tax revenue and economic growth—soon became the primary project of the district colonial regime. Specifically, the British meant for Singidans to become economically productive members of the territory. Yet the labor that the British understood to be most economically productive contrasted with the ideas of Nyaturu farmers, who emphasized the dry season spiritual work of ritual celebration and sacrifice that they considered so central to the annual cycle of production.

"Learning to work," under the British definition, required the acquisition of a very specific set of dispositions and inclinations. Most importantly, it mandated an increasing emphasis on and re-gendering of agricultural work (tradition-ally the domain of women) over pastoralism (the labor of men). Nyaturu were encouraged to embrace the value of producing an agricultural and livestock sur-plus beyond what they wanted to consume themselves and this surplus was to be desired for its exchange value, not for any symbolic associations with "wealth" (as was the existing case with livestock). Valuing the production of surplus required a willingness to shape one's livestock and agricultural practice in line with the demands of external markets, and to adopt new technologies and inputs.

By 1922, the district had devoted "especial attention" to inducing the Singida farmer "to pay more attention to his crops than hitherto." Colonial officials offered advice on planting, and "encouragement" in the form of twenty-two and a half bags of ground nut seed which were disseminated to each Jumbe in the hopes of giving "a start to what should in future be a profitable and '*Kodi-producing*' [tax-producing] crop."[16] Efficiency also demanded breeding and marketing "good butchers' beasts" rather than the small disease-resistant and drought-resistant local breeds. In 1922 a district officer congratulated himself on the growing atten-tion among the Nyaturu to the terms of the market: "the native now realizes what the butcher 'demands' and he is endeavouring to create the 'supply' in response, he incidentally benefits not a little in getting better prices."[17]

By 1929 Tanganyika felt the global shockwaves of the economic crisis and from the Depression through the Second World War this "iron fist that under-lay the velvet glove of colonialism was more perceptible than usual" (Coulson 1982, 44). Between 1930 and 1950, the colonial administration and the chiefs relied increasingly on the use of force in the implementation of agricultural development. During the Great Depression, when global and domestic prices had dropped sharply, the government did not amend the poll tax accordingly. Instead, peasants had to double and triple their efforts in order to pay taxes. A central zone District Commissioner noted in 1931,

In a year like the one under review the raising of money was rather like getting blood from a stone.... Every well, watering place, borehole or dam about the countryside helped ten, twenty, fifty, or a hundred men to find their tax.... In Mkalama and Singida ... every man was encouraged to seek work on the railway construction.... And to lift the dead weight of the tax ... these men were brought in ... and given tax tickets for their labour on urgently required public works. In this way 500 men were employed ... on the aerodome and new township of Singida—and 500 on the township and roads of Manyoni.

The DC went on to note, that although the Nyaturu would remember that year as the "njaa ya feza" (or "famine of money"), they would also remember how it "saw almost a transformation in the townships and the tribesmen," as the year when windmills, boreholes, dams, watering places and wells were constructed all over the countryside.[18] Hardship provided some of the best opportunities to convert colonial political authority into rural development.

Famine and Famine Relief

Production—like infrastructural development—increased during this "famine of money." From 1930, officials devised "'Grow More Crops' campaigns" which involved new coercive measures—a minimum acreage of cotton to be cultivated or the threat of conscription for those not meeting the tax requirement (Coulson 1982, 48). But the type of agricultural production that officials mandated also increased Singida farmers' vulnerability to food crisis. Farmers began planting maize (a high yielding crop with international demand), rather than the traditional drought-resistant sorghum, and so the risk of famine increased dramatically if the rains were poor. Producing a surplus was increasingly at odds with the project of subsistence. And from 1930 on, small farmers felt themselves increasingly dependent on an erratic world market for their sale of cash crops and on the government for famine relief in drought years (Bryceson 1978, Coulson 1982).

Schneider writes that in 1937, "there was a food shortage noted by a number of informants which was severe enough to be the last time that real bargains could be got in purchase of livestock."[19] In this crisis market of skyrocketing food prices, livestock prices were driven low by people's desperation to trade cattle for food. The 1940s saw a near-decade of drought, with famines in 1943, 1946, and again in 1949. The decade of food crisis culminated in a vast rinderpest and trypanosomiasis epidemic in 1949 that killed "several hundred thousand" cattle in Central, Western and Lake Provinces (Brooke 1967). An elder in one eastern Singida village recalled that in 1949 "I saw with my own eyes how people died of hunger, right here in Unyankhanya." Other villagers remember the hunger of 1949 as the *njaa ya kibaba* or "hunger of the little bowl," in reference to the small amount of aid they received—approximately three *debe* of their own grain stored against emergencies in local silos in the 1940s. Formal records, in contrast to these widely circulated oral reports, state that the colonial state distributed over 16,000 tons of famine-relief food (12,000 of it imported) in the Central Province in 1949 and 1950 (Brooke, 1967).

Throughout these decades of recurrent famine, the British in Tanganyika revised and refined a famine code descended from Britain's first codification of a colonial famine policy in India in 1880. Prior to 1880, Indian famine relief had been carried out on an ad hoc basis, with policies swinging from relying almost exclusively on the private grain trade in the Orissa Famine (1865–66), resulting in 1.3 million deaths, to extreme government intervention in the Bengal and Bihar famine (1873–74), which saved nearly everyone but cost the government upwards of five and a half million pounds (Brennan 1984). Between these two policy poles emerged, according to Brennan (1984), a political climate in the 1870s in which metropolitan ideas about free trade and efficiency were increasingly fused with a sense of government responsibility for providing relief from famine.

The 1930 government circular that first codified the imperial approach to famine relief in Tanganyika reflected the same issues debated in the metropole (cf. Brennan 1984; Singh 1993): (1) Should relief recipients work for aid? (2) How does the government identify those who are truly in need? (3) Whose responsibility should it be to fund and oversee relief efforts? And (4) how can "dependency," (or, what one official called "famine-mindedness") be avoided?[20] Two central premises had emerged from these nineteenth century debates in England: first, that "relief should not be so generous as to encourage dependency among its recipients" and second, that relief should not weaken the economy by intervening in the grain trade (Hall-Matthews 2007, 216–17). This strategy speaks to the broader colonial emphasis on African welfare and development that emerged in this period, specifically through market-oriented efforts.

Like the Indian Famine Codes of the late nineteenth century, the Tanganyikan circular sketched out critical principles of famine relief including standing preparation, observation and test of distress, the declaration of famine, and organization of relief (cf. Singh 1993). In the first place, the circular implored Provincial Commissioners to push Native Authorities to make use of section 9(c) of the Native Authority Ordinance to consistently "compel adequate cultivation" to ensure the food supply, and to develop village or regional grain stores. It also stressed the importance of strong reporting and monitoring systems and mandated that each district officer submit to the PC a food supply report directly after the harvest with estimates of the number of people likely to be affected by famine and the amount of relief food required. To the greatest extent possible, recipients were to pay for (or work for) famine relief and administrators instructed district officers to maintain a list of possible relief works (geographically amenable for the delivery of food, and close enough to allow workers to regularly take food home to their families). Administrators emphasized the role and responsibility of Native Authorities to prevent deaths from famine: a circular titled "Famine Relief" noted that "Failure on [the part of Native Authorities] to report famine conditions or to take measures to relieve them until starvation has set in and deaths take place will be regarded as culpable negligence."[21] But although Native Authorities were to bear the primary responsibility and cost of famine relief, the circular stressed the necessity of European supervision and European monitoring to see that food relief actually reached its intended beneficiaries.

By 1943, the administration was floating more localized recommendations in light of its decade of direct experience with famine in Tanganyika. A flurry of correspondence generated a new mandated grain contribution and communal storage policy and regulated beer brewing more strictly.[22] Additionally, colonial administrators in Tanga and Lake Provinces began lobbying for the cost of famine relief to be transferred more fully to Native Treasuries, as a way of preventing or overcoming "famine-mindedness."[23] Yet at the Provincial Commissioners' conference of 1948, officials from famine-prone provinces objected to this recommendation, noting cases in which "Native Treasuries had been seriously retarded in their development work by the constant drain on their resources necessitated by famine relief. While it was admitted that expenditure on famine relief from Central Government funds equally subtracted from the sum available for development purposes, it was pointed out that in this case the deprivation could be spread throughout the territory without marked effect on any one part of it, while in the case of heavy expenditure by a Native Treasury, the evil effects were concentrated in its particular area."[24] The Conference recommended that surplus balances in any Native Treasury should not be allowed to drop below 25 percent of recurrent revenue, which protected the poorest regions from providing famine relief always at the expense of their own development. In this way, as Tanganyika moved toward independence, famine increasingly became the purview of a centralized and paternalistic government.

A sense of the precarity of subsistence and of the insecurity of well-being pervades the earliest records of life in Singida. Yet while the sense of precarity has remained consistent, its sources proliferated during the colonial period, with shocks produced as much through participation in the market, the extractive orientation of the colonial state, and foreign political events, as from the weather or local political unrest. In the face of this precarity, Singidans imagined anew the concept and practice of governance. Whereas precolonial big men had derived political authority from the provisional and transitory powers of charisma, divination, leadership in battle, and the unpredictable grace of the sun, colonialism brought a bureaucratized, depersonalized, and rather ossified authority always and already implicitly laced with the threat of violence, and mystified by orders and technologies from elsewhere. Colonial authority—embodied both in European officials and the appointed chiefs—readily leaned

on a threat of violence even in the most progressive of its efforts at social, political, and economic change. Jellicoe noted: "During the short time I was in Singida
District, I formed the impression that practically all Government Departments
and local agencies (the Catholic Mission being a possible exception) had uncon-
sciously absorbed the authoritarian viewpoint handed down by the Germans
and perpetuated by the watemi ['chiefs']—namely, that *nothing can be done with
the Wanyaturu except by the use of compulsion* [emphasis added]."[25] Through
taxation and forced participation, a common sense emerged not only among
the government but also among Nyaturu themselves that Nyaturu were *obligated* to their colonial masters—that is, that the government could and would
make material claims upon them with the implicit (or explicit) threat of violence. The audacity of this imposition (especially during years of severe scarcity) was rationalized with a paternalistic colonial discourse laced with tones
of "father knows best," and later, that "father will provide." To be sure, after
several decades of British rule, a very minimalistic sense of entitlement to relief
from famine had also occurred to Nyaturu populations. Thus by independence,
an abstract and incipient notion of membership and belonging to something
beyond Unyaturu—a membership that entailed both obligations and (very minimally) rights—had dawned in Singida, and this concept was integrally related
to the project of subsistence.

Yet these notions of membership and belonging were far from absolute. As
independence approached and leaders increasingly asked Nyaturu to "build the
nation" *kwa moyo wao*, (with efforts of "their own heart"), they were initially
puzzled. Jellicoe, during her community development work' in Singida in the
1950s and 60s, observed that Nyaturu were often bewildered by colonial demands
to think of themselves as "a self-reliant centre of inexhaustible resource and
inspiration." People, she noted, "stood amazed when, about 1960, they were first
exhorted to build roads by 'self-help'—often meaningless and ludicrous when
crudely translated into Swahili" (*kujisaidia*—"to help oneself"—is the Swahili
euphemism for "to go to the bathroom"). She continued: "Many Wahi people
have found difficulty in understanding that they should have a 'sense of responsibility' for Tanzania unless someone comes and explains to them, because otherwise Tanzania is another 'country,' another entity with which they have not yet
fully identified themselves" (1978, 45–46).

This is not to say that the Nyaturu had no concept of voluntarism—an idea
connected to Nyaturu ideas about "the sun's unpredictable 'grace'" (*majighana*)
and complementary beliefs that "the man on whom the sun bestows his gifts
must in his turn willingly take some action before he can enjoy the 'blessing'"
(Jellicoe 1978, 23). But Nyaturu contributions to the building of empire in Singida
were disconnected from this "peace, joy and orderliness of willing cooperation"
and instead carried out under duress in the name of empire (22). It would take

a new leader in a new nation to effectively make a connection between Nyaturu understandings of willing sacrifice to the grace of the sun, and labor and suffering for an authoritarian state.

Building the Nation from the Hinterlands: Socialism and Self-Reliance (1961–1985)

> These days have been agonizing to live through, reminiscent of the dust bowl days in the Midwest. We had nine consecutive months without rain.... The usual greeting this time of year is "the sun is crying intensely," but one lady greeted me the other day saying "The sun is eating us up!"
>
> Missionary Howard Olson, *Footprints*

Late in 1960, the rains failed in much of central and northern Tanganyika, causing a famine not seen since the 1890s (Iliffe 1979). Missionary Howard Olson, resident in Singida at the time, remarked on Singidans' sense that their struggle for subsistence was wrapped up in the politics of colonialism: "Some say that the Europeans have taken all the rain, and that they say without knowing that England has had one of the wettest early winters since 17-. Others say that Nyerere is quarrelling with the British and thus the rains won't come."[26] By 1961, American food aid and 1.3 million pounds in subsidies from the colonial government had helped Tanganyikans survive this famine year (Iliffe 1979, 576). In fact, people in Singida today mark 1961 not only as the year of Tanganyika's independence, but also as the year of "Merika" or "Kenedi," after the yellow maize sent from the United States in large bags labeled "United States of America" (to this day, this type of yellow maize bears the name "Merika" in KiNyaturu). It is not insignificant to note that when Julius Nyerere ushered his country into independence on December 9, 1961, almost half a million of its new independent citizens were receiving famine relief (Iliffe 1979).

To Nyerere, political independence meant little in the context of the poverty in which so many of his countrymen lived. "What freedom has our subsistence farmer?" Nyerere asked. "Only as his poverty is reduced will his existing political freedom become properly meaningful and his right to human dignity become a fact of human dignity" (in Shivji 1989, 40). By 1965 Nyerere was leading his new country along a unique path toward "self-reliance" (*kujitegemea*) and African socialism (ujamaa) that would combat the "hunger, disease, and poverty" faced by so many. He pronounced Tanzania a one-party state and abolished indirect rule. Jellicoe noted that by 1967 Nyerere sat alongside the sun as the key symbol of unity and paternalism in rural Singida:

> Nowadays, the Sun as a symbol of unity is becoming overlaid by other and more human symbols ... the most meaningful symbol is now a national one, the Presidency as manifested in the person of Nyerere ... described in local songs as the herdsman of Tanzania who takes care of all his people as the homestead

> head takes care of the cattle which united the past, present and future.... The
> symbol of Nyerere's delegated authority is his walking stick; this however, has
> in Singida been transformed into the herding stick carried by every homestead
> head—a symbol of protection as well as of rule. (Jellicoe 1978, 30)

Soon after independence, Nyerere was already perceived in Singida as a patriarch who promised protection and peace.

By 1967, Nyerere's key policy tactics were the nationalization of banks and key industries, the rejection of foreign investment for development, and a turn to the production of agricultural surpluses in the rural areas as a national development policy. The first two diverged from colonial policy, while the latter was a continuation of it. The Arusha Declaration of 1967 outlined Nyerere's ideology of Tanzanian socialism (ujamaa) with its core of "self-reliant" rural development—people's use of their own resources for national development and, Nyerere emphasized, a commitment by *all* people to labor for the nation. Ujamaa was intended to revitalize what Nyerere understood to be the "traditional village" through returning to primordial African values of socialism (Ingle 1972, 10). The creation of ujamaa villages—rural communities where production and other political and economic activity could be collectively organized—was to be voluntary. In 1968, Nyerere said of the state's role, "It is our job to explain what an ujamaa village is, and to keep explaining it until the people understand" (Coulson 1982, 243). Socialism asked much of the average Tanzanian. Self-reliance and community development through selfless action were promoted across the strata of Tanzanian society. In many cases civic labor was warmly taken up by Tanzanians of all professions, trades, and classes. "It can be done ... play your part," went one famous independence song. In the name of universal primary education, the government promised each community, "if you build the walls and foundation of the school, the government will bring you a roof." And although many schools were built in this period, the 1980s left a graveyard of partially constructed schools across Tanzania, waiting for roofs that did not materialize.

Between 1967 and 1969 many villages were registered across Tanzania, likely formed by what Raikes referred to as "Ujamaa through Signpainting," or "the registration of preexisting villages with neither significant movements of people nor a significant reorganization of the lives of their inhabitants" (Raikes 1975, 43; Schneider 2014, 88). Between 1970 and 1971 the government began to exert more pressure, and many villages were formed through negotiations between groups of villagers looking for resource commitments (like water contracts and schools) and government officials, who were under pressure to show results of the policy.[27] The TANU Biennial Conference declared in September 1973 that the entire rural population should live in villages by the end of 1976. In November 1973, Nyerere himself was quoted saying that "To live in villages is an order" (Coulson 1982, 249). Middle-level leaders increasingly returned to the colonial tactics of force, taxation, and coercion to extract resources and labor for the nation. "Operations" were organized by many Regional governments (Mwapachu 1979). In Morogoro army trucks transported peasants and their belongings to new sites. In Iringa transport was provided and doors and windows were ripped out and walls and roofs destroyed or set on fire in order to ensure people would not return to their original houses. In Mara the police, army, national service, and local militia were employed to move people. And in Maasailand teams used harassment (including arson) to intimidate people into settlements (Coulson 1982).

In Singida, there was little funding dedicated to implementing or enforcing the villagization policy. By September 1973 only twenty-one percent of the district population had moved.[28] And so on July 15, 1974, party and government officials began to execute "Operation Village" (known as *Operesheni ni Mitaa* in Kinyaturu) among the remaining 80 percent of Singida's population. While in many cases people moved on their own, Singida functionaries ordered villagers' own schoolchildren to use hoes and shovels to knock down the homes of the non-compliant. Such techniques were effective; by 1975 ninety percent of Singida's population lived in officially sanctioned villages.

As was the case with NyaConstantino's family, many of the places Singidans had left behind had offered better opportunities in terms of soil, rainfall, and land availability, but because of their inaccessibility, were not suitable for the planned villages (Oliech 1975, 21). Only a small proportion of the arable land in Singida has the fertile red *nkuhii* soil and these areas were already densely populated. Most Singida farmland is, in contrast, of poor quality: light, sandy, and rocky. For this reason Singida households have long kept their cattle penned in the corral of the fenced family compound from sundown to mid-morning so that the manure can be collected and used to fertilize farmland. With farms now located on the periphery of the village, and no longer contiguous to their homesteads, Singidans could no longer perform the systematic manuring of arable land that had been possible when their cattle lived right on their farms (Dodoma residents faced similar challenges, as documented by Thiele 1982, 1986, in Schneider 2014, 90, 191, fn48). Moreover, they could no longer guard their crops from birds, baboons, wild pigs and other pests. Villagization was therefore devastating to agricultural practice in the area, both for those households relocated away from their farmland, and for those centrally located homesteads who lost their farms to the re-located families. Hence, these "improved" villages did not offer improved lives. Additionally, villagization occurred at a very difficult moment in Singida. 1973 had been a famine year in Tanzania, so there was little food carried over into 1974, which was even worse:

> It will be remembered that 1974 was a year of nationwide famine, which means marginal areas like Singida were badly hit. Hence the movement programme came when the peasants were not in their best spirits ... The famine problem was made worse by the question of water shortage. Hence both animals and

> human beings could not get water for drinking. Furthermore the construc-
> tion of houses could not go on rapidly as water for brick making was not easily
> available. The shortages make it difficult to convince people, who are both
> hungry and thirsty, to move into new areas, whose conditions are unknown to
> the peasants. (Oliech 1975, 26)

The hunger, which carried on into 1975, came to be known as "Vuruga" after the
wheat that was brought in as aid.

Though most Singidans today remain fervent in their respect for President
Nyerere (the "Father of the Nation") they do not look back on villagization today
with nostalgia. Mzee Yusuphu related one village's experience of villagization:

> The life of living together was one of loss, because our farms were far. We were
> given only one acre to build and farm next to our houses. It was difficult to
> get enough food. If our chicken escaped and went into the farm of another
> homestead there would be a disagreement, especially in the rainy season when
> the chicken likes to eat the flowers of bean plants. And we came to dislike each
> other very much.... These altercations disturbed the peace. The farms that
> people had far away were eaten up by wild animals, since we were not there to
> guard them. Later we came to not have enough food. Those who were moved
> were caused great trouble because they had to leave their farms, and those who
> we moved to join were squeezed (*kubanwa*) and were denied their farms and
> so both sides were affected in terms of development. Until today there are still
> cases about that time.

Neither the communal farms (that were intended to raise money for village
development) nor the community stores of grain of that period are remembered
to have benefitted the community: "The ujamaa farm helped only a little. The
leaders sold the harvest but they ate the money themselves instead of bringing development to the village. So the villagers lost hope and stopped working.
The plan was a good one, but it came to be ruined. The thoughtful plan of the
deceased President Nyerere was carried out wrong. It was the lower levels of leaders who didn't understand very well." Accusations of the corruption of local leaders tended to also invoke nostalgia for British colonialism, whose paternalism in
enforcing grain contributions to community stores was perceived to have been
trustworthy. In any event, between 1980 and 1985 many rural Singidans returned
to their original homesteads. Some families who had been able to diversify their
livelihoods while living centrally chose to stay.

No matter the short life of the villagization strategy, it was during this period
that Tanzanian villages, rather than homesteads or empires, became units of
political and economic development. It was also during this period that Swahili
became widely accepted as a national language that united a nation of diverse
ethnic and linguistic groups, and that most of these groups began to identify
with Tanzania not just as *a* nation, but as *their* nation. "Nation-building"—the

political and economic efforts of the first decades of independence to improve livelihoods and conscientize a people—failed to bring many of the promises of development. (In 2005 people in Langilanga laughed when I asked them about the electricity, clinics, and water that they had been promised forty years before and that had still not arrived). Yet this ensemble of initiatives had succeeded in building a nation—a body of people who for the most part considered themselves to share a common history, language, and national vision of development, even as they upheld other histories, languages, and visions from their particular locales. For the people of rural Singida, a concept of nation had developed through the narrative of ujamaa that remains salient in the present day.

Generating "the White Butter of Blessing": Prayer, Politics and Precarity in Post-Socialist Tanzania

By 1980, Tanzania, like most African countries, was caught up in the international economic recession. It also suffered the effects of the state-controlled economy (people refer to this as the time "when you could not buy sugar," that is, when the Singida stores had only empty shelves). A hunger in Singida between 1982 and 1984 ("the hunger of the cassava") once again seemed to herald drastic economic and political change. The Tanzanian government accepted loans under the terms of Structural Adjustment from international financial institutions. In doing so, Tanzanian development entered a new era of international influence on its policies and initiated a remarkable shift away from the rural farmer and the rural village as the locus of national economic development.

The aims and effects of the Structural Adjustments of the 1980s and 1990s are by now widely known (Stiglitz 2003). International monetary institutions sought to create more conducive environments for economic investment and growth in developing countries by reducing inflation, privatizing banks, liberalizing trade and withdrawing subsidies, and reducing the size of the central government and the scope of its work. Through privatization and the implementation of user-fees, the responsibility for services like education, health care, and social development came to be shifted to local governments, families and their communities. It was at this moment that community participation in international development—which had since the 1970s been supported by community advocates seeking to increase the autonomy of local peoples in transnational projects—emerged as a new economically palatable official strategy for international development.

In agriculture, international financial institutions insisted that priority in resource allocation be given to the most productive regions and enterprises so that large farming enterprises came to edge out small farmers in the market (Mbilinyi 1990). These policy shifts reduced credit to smallholder farmers, took away subsidies for seeds and fertilizer, and reduced support for agricultural research related to smallholder farming (Ponte 2001, 2002). Small farmers in Singida continued to labor as usual for their own subsistence and for a small cash crop, but with far fewer resources than their competitors in other regions.

On May 7, 1992, Parliament approved a bill to make Tanzania a multi-party state. In the first multiparty general elections in 1995, Tanzanians elected Benjamin Mkapa union president with 61.8 percent of the popular vote and CCM won 80 percent of parliamentary seats. For the next ten years Mkapa presided over the continued liberalization of the Tanzanian economy, the privatization of state-owned operations, and a Poverty Reduction Strategy Program which sought to elevate Tanzania out of poverty through market-driven economic development. But by the turn of the millennium, faith in liberalization as a tool of poverty reduction was firmly shaken. Primary school enrollment had plum-meted; infant and maternal mortality rates had skyrocketed; the food supply was precarious, and poverty had deepened.

I detail this history of political and economic liberalization more deeply in chapters 5 and 6. For now, I conclude with a few observations about this history and the way in which Nyaturu ideas of the sun's power and grace reveal under-standings of the entanglements of food, farming, faith, hunger, and power. First, this history highlights how natural and political events and disasters (droughts, locusts, famines, tsetse fly, plague, war, economic depression, and economic reces-sion) were occasions through which various colonial and postcolonial regimes could "capture the peasantry" and (though to a lesser extent) through which Singida peasantries could capture state resources. Through mandating labor and personal sacrifice during colonial crises, Singidans were violently pushed into a consciousness of a new level of economic and political order (cf. Klein 2007 on "disaster capitalism" in the United States). But it was these same crises that prompted and permitted Singidans to register moral claims on the government through demands for food aid. The enduring effects of these negotiated bio-politics constitute a significant component of what I call subsistence citizenship.

But there were not only *changes* in the ideas about membership, belonging, and obligation that peasants and politicians (to borrow Schneider's [2014] key groupings) imposed upon each other from the late nineteenth century to the present, for there were continuities as well. Despite the significance of the macro-economic changes and policy shifts that conditioned rural Singidan experiences of precarity over the last 40 years, local narratives about the hardships that lead to hunger still reference the erratic temperaments and whimsical humors of the sun. But these notions of the sun's power and grace have also come to be fused with beliefs in the Christian God and Muslim Allah and historical significance of human sin, alluding to a kind of syncretic trinity that, mediated through elder-ship, controls the heavens and the rains.

Waiting for rain in January 2006 after a year of drought, Langilanga village hummed with nervous explanations, predictions, and accusations. The common

Figure 2.1. A herder leads his cattle to a nearly dry Lake Singidani in Singida Town. Photo by author, 2006.

saayu (the Nyaturu way of extended greeting that often centers on weather conditions and farming activities) bubbled over not only with anxiety about the pending water and food shortage but with a variety of social, political, and religious tensions simmering in Tanzania and the world today. People remarked constantly on the sun's anger, and prayed for its unpredictable grace.

People wondered aloud whether God had abandoned the region. "God has died," (Ny. *Mungu wakue*) mourned one woman. "The end of the world is coming," (Ny. *Kihiriyo kang'i*) predicted some of the elder men. After the 2005 presidential elections were delayed from October to December, people in the village predicted that until the elections (and widespread anxiety about potential violence) had passed, God would prevent the rain from falling.[29] It was up to people to make peace with each other, with their government, and with God.

One thing all these explanations shared was a firm conviction that the overpowering sun, the lack of rain, and the resulting food shortage were the outcome of human vices, political competitions, and misconduct. If, as I argued earlier, regulating the sun's power required praising it during the key occasions for managing gender relations, social reproduction, the building of affinal relations across patrilines, generational change, and the consolidation of new power and wealth, then the increasing frequency of subsistence crises seemed to suggest to Singidans that the whole order had run amok.

Senge, a village youth who had migrated to town, reported on several conversations with elders in Singida Town about the lack of rain. Clad in baggy jeans and with hair braided *kama Snoop* (in the style of musician Snoop Dogg), 26-year-old Senge personified in his appearance many of the complaints about urban youth and "kids these days." He reported on his conversation with one elderly man: "So I went to ask the old people ... I know how to talk in riddles with them. I teased one old man, 'why are you preventing the rain from coming?' And he told me, 'Whoa there my nephew, listen to me. It is the youths who prevent the rain from coming.'" Another conversation with an old woman elaborated on this elder man's complaints:

> Then I met an old woman on the street. I greeted her and after she responded in kind I asked her, "Grandmother, where have you sent the rain?" And she was amazed, "Eeeh, young man, you are asking me where I sent the rain? Don't ask me this. It's not me." And I began to talk with her in Nyaturu instead of Swahili so that she wouldn't think I was just some city person.... So she said, "My child, this world is driving us to a bad place and the rain will not fall as it did in the beginning. This is because you all, my grandchildren, have caused the world to go badly. Why? First, the children do not respect their parents. And you know that your parents are the heart of God, but you sin here and there anyway. The old people get absolutely no respect even though we believe they are the representatives of God, equal to the second God. A man goes out on the street and then he marries a woman and leaves her, because he doesn't have enough money to care for her. Then he marries another and leaves her again. Those whom he leaves suffer much. He throws her out like a dog and she feels much sadness and these tears of hers, God hears. And this is what makes him so angry that he prevents enough rain from falling. And youths do these evil things right out in public. They are not afraid to smoke marijuana all over the place. If you ask him, 'Why do you do this?' he tells you he is just going with the modern times. This is the opposite of the morality of God." And this grandmother she went on to say that the rain is indeed there, but it's necessary that we pray to God for it.

With increasing urgency in early 2006, people again began tending to the relation between forces seen and unseen, times past and present, and matters earthly and otherworldly. Ecological balance (and thus, subsistence) depended on tending divine power: seeing it, feeding it, lifting it up. People saw that it was up to them to make peace with each other and with God. Government leaders implored villagers to keep the peace in the coming elections. The mosque at the crossroads called out to wayward Muslims to pray the five daily prayers. The neighboring Catholic Church called for its congregation to pray for rain with a donation of a thousand shillings (one dollar) during mass: with a big enough voice and a true enough heart, the priests insisted, God will hear.

Groups of elder men and women of all religious persuasions considered that it had been too long since they had paid respects to their ancestors. In the six hamlets of the village (with the exception of the hamlet bordering the village with the Catholic church), elders maintained and protected rock shrines, each of which each bore its own unique history and mandated a specific way of sacrificing a sheep to the ancestors. A group of elder men and women from one hamlet, for example, went to the *ng'ongo a Lissu* (Ny.—"the rock of Lissu"). Mzee Iddi explained:

> At this rock, people are forbidden from cutting firewood there.... There once was a woman who was born in this part of the village. When she died, it was under very strange circumstances. After she died, she went and sat at that boulder there, and the rock began to rumble like rain. Therefore, when it fails to rain, we take a sheep and slaughter it there. And a chosen person will take the contents of the sheep's stomach and paint himself with it. He will enter inside the cracks of this great rock. And we outside will paint ourselves a bit as well. And, I swear to you, after just a day or two the rain will fall.

It was often practicing Muslims or Catholics (only elders) who did this work. Together, Singidans covered all their bases, making sure that God *and* the ancestors had heard their cry for rain.

Finally, in January 2006 many rural Singidans traveled to Lake Singidani to pray for rain together. Senge reported the scene upon his return:

> So I went to Singidani and found many people there that had all come to pray for rain. We arrived early in the morning ... maybe 1,000 of us. There were all kinds of people: men, women, Christians, Muslims, pagans, marijuana-smokers, prostitutes—all saw that they were in a bad state and thought "it's best that I go and pray for rain." From 3 or 4 o'clock in the morning on that day, you were forbidden to give the cows and goats water, so that they would cry as people prayed. By 2 in the afternoon, the cows and goats were making noise, the children were wailing, and people cried because of the burning sun. Those that began praying were the Muslims, and then the Christians followed, then the Anglicans and the Pentecostals, and then those that have no religion prayed in their own way. Each religion was called up by turn and then everyone together in silence with their own language. We sat for four more hours and prayed to Almighty God that he would care for us and bring us rain.

Rain—eventually—it did.

The interconnection of the cosmological, political, moral, natural, and social orders lies at the heart of these narratives of praying for rain and social healing in 2006. The sun and rains are such central referents in people's lives that everything of importance is bound up with them and, in times of crisis, must be tended in relation to them: politics, religion, gender, eldership, marriage, reproduction. In anticipation of hunger, people reaffirm social, political, gerontocratic, gender, and religious hierarchies and cast wide webs of tribute, connection, and obligation. And so it was in Singida. People went to church to pray for rain. They went to the mosques. They gathered at rock shrines to sacrifice sheep to the ancestors. Sometimes they covered their bases and they did all three. And they went to Lake Singidani to pray for rain all together (young and old, men and women, Christians, Muslims, pagans, marijuana-smokers and prostitutes, cows and goats), hoping for the unpredictable grace of God, the sun, or—when all else fails—their government.

Notes

1. These include multiple transcriptions of the Nyaturu ritual "Prayer to the Sun," two scholarly analyses of the prayer, and insights from Nyaturu interlocutors recorded in archival sources and in my own ethnographic fieldnotes.

2. For the translation of Nyaturu proverbs in this book I have been greatly assisted by the Rev. Dr. Howard Olson's (1964) "Rimi Proverbs."

3. I collected several versions of the prayer during my time in Singida. Though each recitation varies, all contain the same basic elements—with some being more elaborate, and later versions reflecting social changes. One version of the prayer recited to me in 2005, for example, included an appeal to the sun for the opportunity for children to go to school.

4. This intermingling is apparent still today. The Nyaturu and their neighbors continue to share many common subsistence, linguistic, and cultural practices. For example, the Bantu-speaking Nyaturu share a tradition of rock-painting, common horticultural vocabulary, and agricultural and gathering practices with their Khoisan-speaking Sandawe neighbors to the south (Newman 1970, in Iliffe 1979, 9; Knisley, Matthew, personal communication with author, 2006).

5. The earliest accounts of Nyaturu custom noted that women and men came of age among the Nyaturu through a set of rituals (Von Sick 1915). The first set of rituals—circumcision for boys, and clitorectomy and menstruation seclusion for girls—served to differentiate young people by gender and fix them in their adult roles. The second set of rituals—known as imaa (Nyaturu for "courage")—occurred only among women. Oral traditions suggest the central purpose of the imaa was to keep this deeply gendered cosmological order in balance through the socialization of young women into their new husbands' villages and through the regulation and moderation of women's reproductive powers (Jellicoe 1978). One of the imaa rituals, *imaa ra ng'imba* ("the lion imaa"), was a purification rite for a woman or a cow who had given birth to twins, which was a sign of great power but required ritual purification so that the whole country might be cleared of the "danger of strife and famine" (Jellicoe 1978, 17). Elsewhere I discuss the decline in the practice of the imaa ritual (Phillips 2009; unpublished manuscript).

6. In 1896 rinderpest caused immense losses in cattle.

7. "Turu Fieldnotes: Summary of Data on Famine," Papers of Harold K. Schneider, Box 13. Vol. 3, National Anthropological Archives, Smithsonian Institution.

8. Ibid.

9. Interview, Unyankhanya Village, Rural Singida District. May 11, 2005.

10. "Turu Fieldnotes," Papers of Harold K. Schneider, Box 13, Vol. 3, National Anthropological Archives, Smithsonian Institution.

11. Liti is a great hero of the Nyaturu, and has been held up by some as evidence of a central Tanzanian resistance to German colonization on par with the more famous 1905 Maji

Maji rebellion in southcentral Tanzania (Jellicoe 1969, 1978). A praise song honoring Liti's valor is still widely sung today at village beer parties and circumcision celebrations.

12. This section title borrows from Sarah Berry's use of the phrase "hegemony on a shoestring" to characterize colonization in Africa (1993).

13. "Provincial Report, Central Province," January 25, 1930, 12–13, TNA.

14. "Singida District Annual Report on 'Native Affairs' and 'Labour,'" December 18, 1934, 3–4, TNA.

15. "Annual Report for Singida Sub-District," DO Annual Reports 1920–31, 1919–20, 2, TNA.

16. "Singida Sub-District Yearly Report for the 9 months ending 31st December 1921," DO Annual Reports, 1920–31, (2–3), TNA.

17. Ibid, (3–4); "The Annual Report on Singida District for the year 1934," January 10, 1935, TNA.

18. "1931 Report," PC Reports Central Province, 1931–1933," January 27, 1932, 3, TNA.

19. "Turu Fieldnotes: Summary of Data on Famine," Papers of Harold K. Schneider, Box 13, Vol. 3, National Anthropological Archives, Smithsonian Institution.

20. "Famine and Famine Relief," Circular No. 33 of 1930 of the Government of Tanganyika, Secretariat in Dar es Salaam, "To All Provincial Commissioners," TNA. "Famine-mindedness" was a central concern of a memo from the Provincial Office, Mwanza: "Famine Relief: Apportionment of cost between Central and Local Government," April 23, 1948, ACC: SECRET: 11500/II, TNA.

21. "Famine Relief," Memorandum from D.J. Jardine to all Provincial Commissioners, April 1930, File 11500, Vol. 1. #58, TNA.

22. "Letter to District Commissioners and District Officers," Provincial Commissioner, Central Province, April 8, 1943, TNA; "Letter to All Provincial Commissioners and District Officers," Chief Secretary to the Government, July 7, 1943, TNA. "Letter to Chief Secretary," Varian, R.W, 1943, ACC SECRET 11500/II, TNA; Provincial Commissioner, Central Province, April 21, 1943, TNA.

23. "Famine Relief: Apportionment of Cost between Central and Local Government," Provincial Office, Mwanza, April 23, 1948, ACC: SECRET: 11500/II, TNA.

24. "Extract from Minutes of Provincial Commissioners' Conference of June 1948," ACC: SECRET 11500/II, TNA.

25. Unpublished paper by Marguerite Jellicoe, in the papers of Howard S. Olson (no date, no title). "This report is based on what I saw and discussed during my stay in Ihanja Chiefdom," ELCA Archives.

26. Personal Letter from Howie, Lou and Children to Rev. & Mrs. Joseph Anderson, Ihanja Mission. July 1, 1960. ELCA Archives.

27. Interview, Ngamu Village, Rural Singida District. September 17, 2005.

28. By September 1973, there were 145 ujamaa villages comprised of a population of 41,687 people (about 21% of the district population). In early 1974, officials regrouped these villages to form 132 larger and more viable ones (Oliech 1975, 20–21).

29. The 2005 elections were postponed from October to December after the untimely death of an opposition party presidential candidate.

PART II: THE POWER OF THE POOR ON THE THRESHOLD OF SUBSISTENCE

3   We Shall Meet at the Pot of Ugali

Sociality, Differentiation, and Diversion in the Distribution of Food

Their staple crops were millet and sorghum, which resisted drought but matured slowly, gave low yields, and required much communal labour. They were the daily bread of most Tanganyikans, enshrined in myth and sanctified in ritual.

John Iliffe, *A Modern History of Tanganyika*

It is very difficult in Unyaturu to make beer and drink it alone.

Anthropologist Harold Schneider, Fieldnotes, Singida 1961

WHEN I FIRST arrived in Singida in 2004, I spent many hours of many days in the district office in Singida town, waiting for letters and signatures and stamps to make my arrival in the region a bureaucratic reality. The office is housed in the old German fort, a part of town known as *bomani* ("at the fort") situated high on the hill overlooking Lakes Singidani and Kindai and facing off against *Ifembe*, the other high rock outcropping around which most of Singida town crowds. On the hike out to *bomani* each day from the hostel in which I was temporarily residing, I passed groups of women trekking into town from the outlying villages to sell their goods in the Singida market. Men flew by on bicycles with large bundles of *mitumbi*, or secondhand clothes, while vendors set up camp right by the lake where government employees passed each morning to get to work. Lines of brightly colored basins held fried donuts and fruit. From a nearby tree hung smart button-down shirts, and knee-length skirts strained across curvy hangers.

One morning, I stopped to purchase a few bananas from a reserved-looking woman sitting among the vendors. As we conducted our transaction, an animated *mukikhuu* (Ny.)—an "old woman" of the old ways—lean and clad in ragged kangas, approached me, engaging me in a rapid-fire exchange of greetings in Nyaturu-laden Swahili. That accomplished, she quickly switched into a caricaturized pantomime often used to express to a foreigner that one is hungry, pressing the tips of her fingers and thumb together and pointing them toward her mouth and batting her eyes soulfully at me. Upon completing the pantomime once, she emerged from it to eye me expectantly, and then repeated it twice more. I asked her in Swahili what she wanted. "*Mapapai mawili*," she answered and motioned toward the last two remaining papaya in the woman's load. I glanced at the vendor, whose face suggested nothing about what I should do. Feeling obliged, and happy at least at the nutritional content of my offering, I consented to pay the 1000 shillings (about one dollar at the time), and I made my way to the district office with my own bundle of fruit.

I spent much of the morning being bounced between offices. When I finally returned to my handler in the district office, I was surprised to find my new papaya-loving friend in the room (amid what was clearly a familiar comradery) dealing, what else, but papayas. We eyed each other anew and I laughed sheepishly, feeling simultaneously a bit embarrassed, impressed by her entrepreneurial innovation, and, I'll confess now, just a smidge of indignation. She left quickly.

The incident—that turned on an almost sit-com-ical interaction about what this *mukikhuu* wanted, what I thought she should want, what she thought I thought she should want, and what she thought she could get—stuck with me throughout my fieldwork. It highlighted to me how—in this social world riven with inequalities—individuals with vastly different stores of social, symbolic, political, and economic capital congregate regularly, and sometimes theatrically, over questions about the distribution of resources. My discomfort, born of the unspoken moral assumption on my part that this elder woman owed me honesty while I owed her nothing but could bestow at will, spoke directly to these "nervous conditions" of neoliberal and postcolonial life.[1]

But the incident also encapsulates many themes that emerge from a close study of the social and political life of food in Singida. It reveals the creative social work required to divert the papaya from the commodity phase of its career into a different type of thing altogether, and then back again. It is about the mukikhuu effectively communicating to me that her circumstances are dire, that help for her is within my means and within my grasp, and situating her request publicly, so that an audience will ultimately bear witness to the choice I make. To call this interaction politics is not to question or judge the authenticity of her need and her claims. As Tania Li has argued, "those who demand that their rights be acknowledged must fill the places of recognition that others provide, using dominant languages and demanding a voice in ... power-saturated encounters, even as they seek to stretch, reshape, or even invert the meanings implied" (Li 2001, 653). Regardless of the desperation of her situation, a redistribution of resources in this moment required of this elder woman to set a scene, engage a narrative, construct stakes, and invite an audience. Such claims-making and resource-staking, I go on to describe, is a highly elaborated political practice in rural Singida.

Describing the life cycle of the subsistence grains used to make the staple Nyaturu food ugali—bulrush millet, sorghum, and maize—illuminates how grains travel and transform between four non-linear phases of their social life in Singida—social entitlement, commodity, gift, and aid. Such projects of transition and transformation are wholly grounded in and animated by the value of food in Singida and beyond and the social ideas, relationships and acts in which food is implicated. This biography serves as a foundation for a later analysis in chapters 4, 5, and 6 of the politics of subsistence and redistribution currently at play in Tanzania through three salient discourses of distribution: those of the market, rights, and patronage. Following this highly condensed social fact through its social life sheds light on food's many meanings and the social and material roots of its value in subsistence agriculture contexts.[2]

Theorizing Food and its Distribution

Theorists have long recognized that different rules and norms govern the distribution of food in different times and different spaces. Such a point is essential to conceiving of the way that the papayas circulated in the opening story to this chapter—sometimes in reference to perceived supply and demand (as a purchase), sometimes in reference to a moral system (as a gift). But there has been little consensus on how such differential rules and norms are organized or constituted. To position my own approach to this question, I briefly review two well-known theories used to explain the circulation or distribution of food, and outline the major challenges that critics have put to them.

In the 1980s Nobel Prize-winning economist Amartya Sen proposed greater attention to the mechanisms of food *distribution* in a conversation that had previously been dominated by one of food *supply*. His work helped to temper faith in the market's ability to humanely regulate the distribution of food and the commonly held view that famine is *caused by* natural disaster. As a discourse of distribution, Sen argued, the market is fairly inflexible and not easily swayed by social work. To get food, you either have something to trade or you do not. Sen's idea of entitlements distinguished between what people own in theory (their endowments), with what they actually have access to in practice (their entitlements). For example, a household may own a cow, but it is not everyone in the household who has access to its utilities (its manure, its milk, its meat, and its social status). Starvation, Sen argued, results when the sum of one's entitlement to commodity bundles like food (food one grows, buys, works for, or is given by others) does not suffice for subsistence.

Sen proposed that two different sets of conventions frame people's entitlements to food: a legal sphere framing a household's ability to command food in the market, and a moral sphere framing an individual's ability to command food within the household. While such a theory acknowledges the way different norms seem to govern the circulation of food between kin and the circulation of food between strangers, many theorists have found it wanting. First, Sen's separation of the legal and moral spheres of entitlement map all too easily onto the public/private dichotomies that have been so thoroughly critiqued by feminist theories (Pateman 1983). These separations threaten to devalue women's labor, obscure commodity exchange relations within households, as well as between them, and to miss the moralization of markets that takes place in everyday village life. Indeed, as we see in the case of the two papayas, *multiple* overlapping discursive frames govern the distribution of the papayas on a single Singida street. Second (and by Sen's own admission) the theory relies on essentially "fuzzy" concepts of the "individual" and of "property" that often turn out to be *most* fuzzy in rural subsistence economies, the very economies with which theories of famine are most concerned (Devereux 2001). Finally, critics have called Sen's understanding of distribution as a function of fixed moral and legal codes both ahistorical and de-politicized, noting that it ignores how norms are contested and negotiated in the everyday and how they change over time in relation to local events and broader historical shifts.[3] Remedying these analytical limitations to explain food distribution—that is, why people have the food they have, and how they come to get it—requires closer attention to the divergent regimes of value in which food is embedded for those living on the threshold of subsistence and a more detailed analysis of the way it travels through them.

Anthropologist Arjun Appadurai offers another way of understanding how varied normative frames govern the distribution of food in different times and contexts. He famously theorized "the social life of things," arguing that a commodity was not a *kind* of thing, but rather a particular *phase* in the life of a thing, in which a thing's exchangeability became its dominant feature (13, emphasis added). He maintained that one needs to recognize "the commodity potential of *all* things rather than searching fruitlessly for the magic distinction between commodities and other sorts of things" (13). Things, Appadurai went on to note, move in and out of the commodity phase in ways that can be "slow or fast, reversible or terminal, normative or deviant" (13). He theorized "commodity contexts" as the social arenas that "help link the commodity candidacy of a thing to the commodity phase of its career" (15). An auction or a market, for example, could establish a commodity phase, and cue people to its activation.[4]

One of Appadurai's key contributions to later work in anthropology was to point to the way that an opposition between these two "types" of things (commodity and gift) ignores that the same object may take the form of *both* commodity and gift at different times, even between the same social agents (cf. Weiss 1996). Distinctions between legal/moral and commodity/gift become far more useful when understood to be, not essential properties of a thing, a social system, or (per Sen) conventions of a fixed code or particular sphere of action, but rather discursive choices (at times made under severely strained conditions) employed strategically by social subjects. Returning to the story of the two papayas illustrates this point.

A woman sits by the roadside with piles of fruit on a blanket, among other women who have similarly arranged themselves. From the way they have arranged themselves, I know they are not giving away fruits and vegetables, but selling them. When I ask the cost (exchange value) of the papaya, and pay cash for them, they are squarely in the commodity state. But the old woman standing next to me has quickly established a social relationship—we are both human, she is hungry—and makes a claim on my resources. I acquiesce to this claim and she receives the papayas from me irrespective of their equivalent market value. A short time later, she walks between district offices with two papayas. Her appearance (ragged kangas that contrast with the smart clothes of the district employees) and the rhythm of her words ma-pa-pai, ma-pa-pai (papaya! papaya!) mark her as a vendor as she weaves through the offices, reinstituting the papayas' commodity status, and claiming cash in exchange for them. A while later, we might presume, a district employee will take them home to her spouse, children, and dependents that live with her. These will consume the papaya the next morning, without necessarily giving her anything in return. In this short period, the papaya has circulated from hand to hand, constituting a commodity, and then something else, and then a commodity again, and then something else altogether. Throughout these encounters, it is peoples' (including my own) complex and divergent ideas and understandings of the economic, social, political, and moral values of food that animate these transactions.

While attending to "things-in-motion" in this way does a lot to illuminate this social context, Appadurai's frame also has its limits for grasping this scenario and others like it. First, Appadurai argues value is produced through economic exchange; that is, it is derived from others' relative desire for the object. Graeber has argued that this stance reduces exchange to people's self-interested maximization of their relation to things, and erases the way things (some more than others) circulate with particular regard to relations between people (2001). Second, Appadurai's framework privileges the commodity phase in the life of things, naturalizing it almost as a resting point in the life of an object. (He writes, the "diversion of commodities from specified paths is always a sign of creativity or crisis, whether aesthetic or economic" [26]). For him, what begs explanation in the contemporary economy is how and why market goods sometimes circulate (or are "diverted") away from their prescribed market "paths," an approach that seems to naturalize the market. Missing is an analysis of how, why, and through which diverse interpretive frames goods circulate without regard for the market, and in turn how they come to be subjugated by or incorporated into it. Food is not just sometimes a non-commodity; it can be several *different* things that situate it outside the commodity paradigm. And people use these divergent frames of meaning of both food and their social relationships to drive food's circulation. So if—as this story of two papayas illustrates—food is not always a commodity, then what else is it? When does it transform? And how does it get there?

Remedying these analytical limitations requires not only closer attention to the legal, market, and moral conventions of food circulation (as Sen would have it) or the regimes of value produced through exchange (as Appadurai proposes), but to the divergent *frames of social and moral meaning* in which food and people are embedded when they are situated on the threshold of subsistence. In this chapter, I examine the life cycle of grain in Singida, which often seems to shape-shift as it flows through the region, transcending easy analytical distinctions between the legal and the moral, the commodity and the gift, the economic and the social. In its focus on subsistence and food insecurity, my analysis centers on people for whom the material value of food for physical survival is never taken for granted. At the same time, it highlights how the circulation of food that is needed for subsistence is driven by a diversity of interests, impulses, inclinations, and ideas about food that reflect its much more robust social and moral value in rural Singida. This type of attention to the meaning of food highlights how "apparently similar forms of action" around food "can have vastly different meanings and consequences" (Weiss 1996, 77–78). I argue here that food's capacity to hold many contiguous meanings— and people's ability to make use of these to pursue life, livelihood, and human connection—allows food to transcend the fixed codes of distribution that Sen theorizes and to follow unpredicted paths. Following this highly condensed social fact through its social life sheds light not only on food's many meanings but also on the significance of food's periodic scarcity in subsistence agriculture contexts.

Food and Sociality in Singida

Food is the material means to avoid, satiate, and heal hunger. But it is also so much more. In rural Singida, food organizes, mediates, and constitutes sociality (as it does for so many other people), providing the means through which human connection, productivity, hierarchy, and authority are practiced, instantiated, and communicated. As Brad Weiss has noted, "food is a central symbolic vehicle *in*, as well as an objectification *of*, constitutive collective practices. Food is a locally privileged means of organizing and experiencing the material and immaterial features of a lived world" (1996, 28). Comprehending these complex patterns and multiple meanings of food is therefore central to grasping the significance of its uneven distribution, its meaning as it travels from hand to hand, its ability to be contested and diverted in unanticipated ways, and the experience of its dearth at certain times and for certain people.

What does it mean to say that food organizes, mediates, and constitutes sociality? *If* one eats, *how* one eats, *what* one eats, *where* one eats, *with whom* one eats,

Figure 3.1. Cooking ugali.
Photo by author, 2005.

when one eats, all mean something to people in Singida. Food *signifies*: it binds and excludes; it marks power, hierarchy, and difference; it sanctions belonging and membership; it mediates membership and legitimacy. As people produce, eat, gift, exchange, and ritually engage with food, they affirm, negotiate, reconstitute, and contest their place in the world and the social categories that mark them and others. Such engagements, no doubt, bear consequences for present and future actions.

Let us start with the question of *what* people eat in Singida. Despite the long pastoralist tradition of the Nyaturu, and their reliance on a variety of crops, it is predominantly grain that structures peoples' diets, livelihoods, and labor. Indeed, though people in Singida rely on a variety of foods to sustain them through their day as well as to mark and celebrate important occasions, *chakula* ("food") for Singidans—including the family of NyaConstantino—refers almost exclusively to the grain used to make the staple food ugali. Ugali is a stiff porridge of water and maize, millet, or sorghum flour that is stirred and roasted into a thick paste in a locally fired clay pot over a hot indoor cooking fire built between three large stones (see fig. 3.1) or sometimes a charcoal stove.

People's ugali preferences in Singida reflect both the embodied experience and the performance of class. As a matter of taste, middle classes and urban Singidans tend to prefer a soft white ugali made from the flour of hulled maize kernels (hulled maize has its outermost fibrous layer removed). This is the white Wonderbread of ugali varieties and is most commonly served in urban areas. But NyaLukas, Petro, and the majority of those who farm for a living still prefer the brown sorghum ugali, light green bulrush millet ugali, or unhulled maize ugali because it is coarser and dense and "sticks with them" the whole day, whereas with hulled maize ugali they complain of being too quickly hungry again.

Ugali is invariably prepared without salt, oil, or other spices. Flavor, in a meal, comes from the *mboga* ("side dish") that ugali is served with—well-salted meat, dried fish, beans, or greens that are usually prepared with oil and often onions (a regional specialty in Singida). For many families like that of Nyalukas, meat and dried fish are a rare treat, though she may slaughter a rooster if an important guest visits, or if the rooster itself is nearing death. *Mlenda* is the most common mboga in Singida and is one of several concoctions of wild leafy greens (fresh or dried) boiled with tomato, okra, salt, milk, or ground peanuts to make a slimy bright green sauce. Mlenda is the signature food of the Nyaturu, teasingly referred to by Nyaturu urbanites as an example of the backwardness and poverty of their rural kin. Mlenda provides next to no caloric value, but is the source of important vitamins and a modest amount of flavor in most Singida diets. The wild leaves used to make it are available to be picked year-round and it requires no cooking oil so it can be made by even the poorest to accompany their ugali. When available, a bowl of sour milk is passed around as well. I encountered a pervasive self-consciousness about the hierarchy of identities that food choices (made of preference or necessity) expressed. In Langilanga village, people often apologized or laughed when they served me mlenda. Sometimes a similar nervousness accompanied their serving of ugali made of sorghum or millet.

Among most households, ugali is eaten communally, and when possible twice a day (mid- to late morning and evening). Different groups eat in stages—men and older boys first in an inner sitting room, women and small children later in the kitchen—with the pot placed on the floor at the center of those who are eating. The server (usually a mother or child) washes with hot water and sometimes soap the hands of those who will eat. Those who eat sit on stools, with the size of the stool usually reflecting age and status. Each person grasps a small hunk of dough with their right hand, kneads it into a ball, forms a small depression with the thumb, and then uses this small "bowl" to scoop some of the shared mboga. It is considered impolite to only eat ugali from the center of the pot (this is the softest ugali) and people are obliged (some more than others) to eat the crustier ugali from the sides of the hot pot (the *chungu* pictured in fig. 3.2). Though hosts will urge guests to keep eating, it is never polite to finish the pot. Even after all groups

Figure 3.2. Eating ugali, cabbage, and *maya* (fermented milk).
Photo by author, 2017.

Figure 3.3. Eating mlenda, greens, and ugali.
Photo by author, 2014.

have subsequently eaten in the household, it is expected that there will be *ikokho* (Ny. "leftovers") to serve an unanticipated guest or to reheat for the children to eat as a morning meal.

In households that are part of the professional class (teachers, government officials, clergy, etc.) with more cosmopolitan experiences and tastes, separate bowls or storage containers may be used to create individual portions of ugali and the mboga (seen in fig. 3.3), especially for men or guests. Spoons are now and then offered to visiting guests if rice or makande is served. But throughout Tanzania, even in urban restaurants with professional patrons who would normally use utensils with other food, ugali is always eaten by hand. The social and material act of eating ugali is in part a tactile one as well.

It is significant that it is really only the grain used to make ugali, *uji* (a thin porridge of finger millet, sugar, and fruit or groundnuts), and *makande* (a typical Swahili dish of boiled whole maize kernels, beans, oil, and salt) that many rural Singidans consistently perceive to be food. Even the boiled peanuts, greens, beans, pumpkins, wild and domesticated fruits, sweet potatoes, cassava and (on very special occasions) rice that supplement the rural Singida diet at various times of the year fall outside what Nyaturu perceive to truly satisfy their appetites, and to nourish them for the grueling labor of rural life. The phrase *"hamna chakula"* ("there is no food") refers specifically to the lack of grain in the household.

Ugali, in particular, is recognized for its social symbolism, as the glue that holds the family together. In times of conflict between household members, or if a child has run off from his parents, the Nyaturu saying is invoked: *Guutanania unyungu a nkhomba* (Ny. "we will meet at the pot of ugali"). This saying is meant to remind a deviant that one cannot escape one's intimate connections with others, or the effects of one's mistakes or trespasses, because we are all bound to come together again around the pot of ugali. Being able to prepare and provide food are also important markers in gendered constructions of personhood and the achievement of adulthood. As I describe in the following section, in Singida, new wives come to achieve both adulthood and belonging in their husbands' households not by relocation, but by feeding, and feeding well. Preparing ugali is the most difficult and most important test for gauging cooking ability.

Yet food may also mark the boundaries of belonging and identity or of hierarchy and difference. At a beer party or other gathering, not everyone may be invited to eat the ugali that the hostess may cook. At many rural weddings men and women eat separately, and depending on their status and proximity to the family, may eat different foods and in successive order. During my fieldwork, pilau (a seasoned rice dish with meat) was considered the most festive meal for such occasions and was reserved for the high-status or most proximate relations. (Because rice is not grown in Singida, its price is much higher than other grains). These groups will be invited inside the house to eat in an inner room, removed from the rest of the attendees and often served soda or beer. Other attendees will eat (without drinking) from large shared plates of makande (whole maize or sorghum and beans boiled together and then sautéed with oil and salt) that will be distributed strategically on the ground where people are seated. For some attendees, food will be simply, and literally, out of reach. As I go on to describe, these concentric circles of people that form around plates at such gatherings are illustrative of the gradations of identity, proximity, and affiliation that drive the distribution of food in conditions of scarcity.

Distribution and Diversion: The Social Life of Grain

The harvest time in Singida is one of jubilation. Prior to missionization of the area the Nyaturu celebrated the harvest with the *ilanda* festival, where men and women gathered to dance, drink, cavort, and celebrate a new food year. Today, the successful harvest of a greater variety of crops extends and disperses enjoyment, but the relief and joy with which the harvest is met is the same. Farming work is hard work (as I described in chapter 1), but it is social work, and the time leading up to and following the harvest—threshing millet, shelling beans, tying maize cobs to drying structures (fig. 3.4)—is one of intense labor, cooperation, and interaction between men and women and the young and old. Harvested grains are thus the

Figure 3.4. Maize cobs hang and dry following the harvest.
Photo by author, 2007.

outcome of social relationships, obligations and collective (even if divided) labor (cf. Strathern 1988). And although harvesting and storing grains is the culmination of the food production cycle, grain is merely in the infancy of its social life.

Grain, I show below, moves betwixt and between four non-linear states of being: social entitlement, commodity, gift, and aid. That is, grain circulates in a variety of contexts and with a diverse set of norms and purposes. Amartya Sen wrote that a "person's ability to command food has two distinct elements, namely, his 'pull' and the supplier's 'response'" (Sen 1990, 43). I suggest here that in addition to "pulls" and "responses," there are also "push" factors—socially significant impulses for circulating grain *out* of one's hands, not just into them. People "push" food from their own hands into others' to fulfill social obligations, to exchange, to respond to moral or political claims, and to forge or reinforce relationships. And they "pull" grain with a range of discourses of redistribution. Thus, entitlements, gifts, and aid—like commodities—are neither certain kinds of things, nor are they progressive phases occurring always in the same sequence. Rather they are *non-linear phases* in the biography of staple foods (millet, maize, and sorghum). Below I trace this social life of food in Singida, beginning with the entitlement phase.

The Entitlement Phase

Subsistence grains that are harvested by members of a household are used throughout the year for household consumption and sorghum is also used to brew beer (both to consume and to generate income). Once dried and threshed or plucked, grains are stored out of sight in adult women's sleeping quarters. Women are charged with budgeting grain consumption throughout the year for household subsistence, to discharge social obligations through feeding and brewing (fig. 3.5), and to keep seed grain for the following year. Upon harvest, subsistence grains that are born for the most part of household members' own labor are often in the social entitlement phase, when grain's meaning and value is derived in the context of social norms and obligations. Some or all of this grain may quickly be diverted *into* other phases or may be added to grain diverted *from* other phases where a purchase, a gift, or aid renders it household property.

Grain is the property of a house (*nyumba*) within a household (*kaya*). So in a household with several houses (either inter-generationally constituted or polygamous), each able wife/mother farms and keeps her own grain supply. An outsider could not walk into a house and take grain without being charged with stealing. But that outsider *could* invoke a social relationship or entitlement context in order to make claims (which may or may not be honored). In the social entitlement phase, consumption of grain is premised on *relationships*, relationships that are themselves produced, reinforced, or undermined through such interactions. One is entitled by nature of social belonging: "we have a social relationship, therefore I may eat." This is not to argue that there is never a material return on the fulfillment of social entitlements, but rather that, on the push side, fulfilling social and moral obligations within and between households is primary to the exchange function of food.

Entitlement arrangements help coordinate the use of household goods. In Singida, food entitlements are generally centered on female subsistence grain producers and organized by radiating circles of identity and affiliation: the house, the household, kin, clan, village, tribe, humanity. As Parker Shipton has noted, "feelings about entrustment and obligation are inextricable from feelings about social proximity and distance" (2007, 118). The closer an individual's relationship lies to the center, the stronger the food claim. Claims on food are governed by social norms: obligation/responsibility (*wajibu*); respect (*heshima*); generosity/hospitality (*ukarimu*); compassion/sympathy (*huruma*); and cooperation (*ushirika*). When the food supply allows and relationships are acknowledged, social entitlements are reliable claims. But one's claims on food are subject to fluctuation over time in relation to the food supply that is available. Hinged to this cyclical variability in food supply is variation in the understanding of exactly how proximate one is to the person who governs the food supply. For example, in flush

Figure 3.5. Neighbors gather around two women brewing beer.
Photo by author, 2006.

times, one may call an elder neighbor "mother." In food-poor times, one might refer to her as the widow of one's father-in-law's brother. Yet this female elder may consciously invoke closer kinship discourses to shift and influence her social membership and the claims her status makes possible. The social work of establishing entitlements turns on both establishing the relation as well as pressing the obligation.

Ideas about wajibu, or responsibility and obligation, govern the entitlement relations within houses and households, specifically in relation to gender and age. In this virilocal system a woman is charged with the daily feeding of her children, her husband, and her husband's parents if they reside in the same household. Other kin and guests of her husband (brothers, cousins, etc.) can expect to be fed as guests now and then, but must rely on their own wives and/or mothers to feed them on a regular basis, for as a Swahili proverb goes, "he who depends on his relative dies of poverty" (Ny. *Mtegemea cha nduguye hufa umaskini*). Elder kin outside the household may be able to expect additional assistance with food and/ or labor for cooking and often invoke the value of respect, generosity, and hospitality to make claims on food. I often had elders arriving at my doorstep asserting

"Nene mughenyi ako! Ughai kufei?!" (Ny. "I am your guest! Where is the ugali?"), greetings that are also a half-joking command to a host to cook for the guest. Men are most often the beneficiaries of hospitality, and women the laborers for it, for it is mainly men who travel and who do not cook for themselves or others.[5] While hospitality may be directly reciprocated between families, it is often not. Rather, most people seemed to engage in practices of hospitality as a way of both paying respect to particular social relationships, as well as of honoring the norm of respect for social relationships that is seen to be so central to rural life.

People in Singida have long placed a high cultural premium on women's role in food distribution and preparation. These notions of a woman's work and her role in the respectful, generous, and hospitable distribution of resources were highly emphasized in the "house imaa" rituals carried out from at least the late nineteenth century through the 1970s in Singida. Imaa rituals took place only among women and focused on establishing unity and order among them—a challenge in this context of virilocality, where women married into other clans (descent-based groups of men arranged spatially) to live among strangers. The imaa socialized new brides and brides-to-be into their roles as wives and mothers and into the ways of their husband's village (Jellicoe 1978; Phillips 2009; Schneider 1970; Von Sick 1915). The *imaa ra unyumba* (Ny. "house imaa") was the first of two imaa (usually held in the dry months) that occurred around the time of birth of a young woman's first child.[6]

The house imaa evaluated and celebrated a cohort of girls' internalization of the social order in both their old and new kin networks. That is, a girl's elders rewarded her *utii* ("subservience, discipline, tractability") and punished her *dharau* ("contempt"). The primary adult women in her life—her mother, her mother-in-law, and her husband's sister (if herself already initiated)[7]—would praise the girl for good deeds like cooking well, following the advice of her mother- and sisters-in-law in the kitchen, and being generous with her neighbors. At the imaa she would be rewarded with kind words, good songs (like the one described below), and the gift of the *mwimo* (the "secret ritual object" understood to be central to the imaa). Alternately, they would shame her with "bad songs" for a failure to be generous, or not cooking her ugali thoroughly, or not listening to her mother-in-law. In this way, new wives came to achieve belonging in their husbands' households not by relocation, but by feeding, and feeding well.

There is an imaa song that is still sung today by women in Singida that praises subservient girls and indexes these two poles in behavior and the way people assess them in relation to food. In the song, neighbors would reward a "good girl" for her generosity and assistance by bringing to her the salt, mlenda, and flour that the girl has lent her in the previous year, during which she was "tested" for her generosity. These she would lay at the girl's feet and, as NyaSafina told me, "her birth mother will feel pride because she knows she has a generous daughter who helps her neighbor when she is in difficulty." The neighbor would then tell the girl, "continue to live with a heart to help other people," and then lead a Nyaturu song of thanks to the girl that praises her generosity of spirit:

Mughenyi waja	A guest comes.
Kamufa itumbi ra ighuu	I gave him a footstool.
Wafuma kure ino nyanda	He came from very far away.
Ho haya hwee haa egu hekua.	*Ho haya hwee haa egu hekua*
Ni waja nimufe itumbi.	If he comes I give him a stool.
Ni waja nimufe ikhokho.	If he comes I give him the leftovers...
[Whoops and catcalls, and then repeats].	[Whoops and catcalls, and then repeats].[8]

NyaJuli, an elder woman with seven grown children explained to me, "If she has done well by her elders she will be sung good songs and dances. They will be songs of praise and she will return home happy. She will return home having learned many things and knowing that she should continue to do well by her elders and by those younger than her." If the young girl has failed to be generous, she would be humiliated with a song of contempt that protests her behavior. Rural Singida women still sing these songs today at beer parties and boys' circumcision celebrations where new wives may be present, and through these songs women continue to send and receive social messages about the rules governing the circulation of food.

Within households, of course, it is in the family's interest that a woman should be frugal with food-sharing and that she should attend to preserving the grain supply, as well as the social standing of her family. One woman recalled being a young girl of twelve or thirteen and sitting by as she watched her mother be too generous with the household grain for cooking, brewing, and assistance to neighbors. So she dug a hole inside her room, and little by little took grain each day and created a secret store. As prices skyrocketed and the family began to worry about food and to strategize about how they could purchase it, the young girl revealed her secret store to the joy of the family. "Were they angry that you were taking food from them?" I asked the woman. "Not at all!" she replied. "They were surprised and happy I had been so 'clever' [*mjanja*] and were very grateful. Now we could eat, and not have to sell a goat!"

In general, however, the history of hunger in Singida drives a social system that emphasizes cooperation and reciprocity. One can expect reciprocity from some more than others. Someone you can turn to for help is often referred to as "someone you can take fire from." This is a neighbor with whom you are on good enough terms to take burning embers from for your cooking fire when your own have gone cold in the night—a reciprocity that also extends to food. (Most people bury hot embers in a pot of ashes after cooking, thus eliminating the need for fuel or tinder to start the next fire). In the case of men, one you can seek help from is called an *mbuya* (Ny.). Anthropologist Harold Schneider wrote about the *mbuya* relationship between men in Singida in the late 1950s. His informants told him that a man likes to have an mbuya in each direction: north, south, east and west. Mbuya is a man who you can ask for food, beer, or a place to sleep. A man with whom you have no such relationship is called *watiti* (the Nyaturu word for a pot of ugali), for he is one whom you will sooner or later "meet at the pot."[9] It is significant that even the most anonymous of relations is understood to be someone with whom you will eventually share food.

There are individuals in each community (widows, the ill, the disabled) who one knows might never return the favor. It is compassion and sympathy (*huruma*) as well as Christian and Muslim practices of alms-giving that will feed them no matter how much the food supply has shrunk, for as the Nyaturu say, "a locust in famine is divided" and "he who cries for food shall not be rebuked." Both compassion and alms-giving call for quiet giving, and little ceremony or eye contact. For those suffering, it is reliable, but often comes at a cost: of losing voice in the village, or political or sexual autonomy. For those in great need, it is the use of crisis and kinship narratives, the presentation of signs of famine, and threats not to subsist that pull the transfer of food.

There are of course those who reject the obligation to fulfill social entitlements to the extent that others believe they should. Such a person is subject to accusations of being not just a selfish person (Ny. *moraku*), but also a thief (Ny. *mwivi*), a murderer (Ny. *mweoragi*), a witch (Ny. *mworoki*), or a "snob"— one who "looks at others as though they are not people."[10] Also during times of food scarcity, there are ways to both dodge obligations and to press others' hospitality with one's claims-making. A guest may strategically arrive at the door at the time of the mid-morning meal. His host, likewise, may delay cooking or serving the ugali. But the guest, if very hungry, may remain until he has been fed. And it is said that still today in hungry times people do not cook their ugali all the way through, since ugali that is thoroughly cooked gives off the savory aroma of roasted corn. It is better not to let one's neighbors know when one is eating.

Finally, social and material circumstances (such as individual poverty, a communal food shortage, weak entitlement relations, social deviation, or simply the opportunity to fill a hungry stomach) do lead to cases where people steal food from farms, kids scrounge, or daughters sneak food while cooking. One middle-aged woman shared with me how during the food shortages she experienced as a girl, she loved to cook because she was able to sneak more than her share while cooking, and then be praised for her selflessness by her parents during their one meal of the day for letting her younger siblings eat first. Such tactics point to the creative ways in which people angle to meet their material needs as well as to fulfill their social commitments and roles. People regularly engage with food both as a means of individual physical persistence as well as a means of affirming, negotiating, reconstituting, or contesting their place in the world and the social categories that mark them and others.

The Commodity Phase

To paint a picture that suggests that people in Singida *have* nothing but food or *want* nothing but food would contradict the social and material realities of rural Singida as they are indexed both in the historical record and in the ethnographic present. Certainly between 2004 and 2014 rural Singidans' desires diversified, as did their paths to achieving them. And it was not just production, but *exchange* (as it is for most people in the world) that provided the key means of obtaining goods and services and of achieving economic improvement at the household level. Through both subsistence and cash crop agriculture, subsistence grains were both an object and a currency for achieving basic needs, adulthood, and development (*maendeleo*).

Between 2004 and 2014, Singidans generally agreed upon what constituted basic needs in rural Singida, though costs doubled or tripled in this decade through inflation. For a family without livestock (but a few chickens), cash for "basic needs"—cooking oil, lamp and cooking fuel, soap, salt, matches, mill fees, basic agricultural implements, and clothing—was eked from subsistence agriculture through brewing sorghum beer (fig. 3.5), selling eggs, or engaging in day labor. From these basic necessities, cash was sometimes diverted (and in some families more than others) to purchase beer, meat, rice, sugar, or soda.

Cash for "development" on the other hand—corrugated aluminum to replace thatched roofs, school fees and uniforms, second-hand clothing and shoes, cell phones, phone vouchers, store-bought food and drinks, start-up costs for a small business and solar panels—could only be accomplished through the cultivation of cash crops like sunflower and finger millet, migration to urban areas, remittances from emigrant kin, or the sale of livestock. Likewise, young men in rural Singida who wanted to be able to "grow up" (*kuwa mtu mzima*) early in the new millennium relied on these latter strategies to build a house and to be able to court a young woman with gifts of kanga cloths, flip flops, and body oil.

In any event, it is certain that *subsistence* in Singida (that requires both food and non-food goods) cannot be achieved without the commoditization of food. Appadurai defined the commodity phase as one in which a thing's "exchangeability (past, present, or future) for some other thing is its socially relevant feature" (1986, 13). Brad Weiss, alternatively, argues that commoditization is characterized less by exchange than by the process of establishing equivalence or the commensurability of objects, even when this universal equivalence is not always applied (15). Both ideas of the commodity situate it in a system of value in which the meaning an object takes on is *in relation to other goods* (both objects and services).

Appadurai speaks of the social work—born of creativity or crisis—that diverts objects *from* commodity status. But in rural subsistence contexts, there is equal if not more social work required to divert food *to* the commodity phase from the social entitlement phase. The context of the village—where food distribution norms prevail along non-market lines and where social relations are thick and multi-dimensional—diverting food from a phase of social entitlement to its commodity phase is no easy feat. People use a wide range of strategies to "help link the commodity candidacy of a thing to the commodity phase of its career" (1986, 15); that is, they employ social codes to convince people they need to *buy* a particular thing, not be given it straightaway. Diverting food to a commodity phase is much more difficult for women than for men, is harder in the home than in the cattle market, and is a much greater challenge deep in the rural footpaths than on the roadside, where the volume of human traffic and the mix of people from many clans create more of the social distance required for selling.

On the roadside, people use a variety of strategies to link goods with their commodity context. They create a physical and formalized separation between buyer and seller (by organizing selling space with a counter or shop window—as in the case of many village shops). Women who sell beer on the roadside, often construct a separate mud brick house called a *kilabu* (derived from the English "club") in which customers gather to drink. Away from the roadside, women brewers in remote hamlets may rely on a male relation (spouse or brother-in-law) to ensure payment, keep the peace among drinkers, and effectively serve as a bouncer when drunk relations try to register entitlement claims. Other social cues for selling include the aesthetics of presentation (produce like peppers or onions or tomatoes are usually grouped into piles that have a particular price) and displaying a multiplicity of goods—for people know that one never makes one's food assets conspicuous unless they are squarely in a commodity context. (In my early days in residence in Langilanga, I once hung up a flat basket normally used for winnowing rice and filled it with produce in an attempt to make my cement-walled room in the village office less austere. I was very quickly advised by friends to hide the produce, for if people can see it they can make claims on it). Finally, the commodity context is characterized by the simultaneity of exchange—for the commodity context in Singida is known to be undone by any kind of credit.

In comparison to food's other phases, laying claim on food in its commodity phase is as reliable as the market and one's own capacity to participate in it. The economic relationship within which a commodity circulates is socially thin and fleeting, mediated through money. While a social relationship may exist between those exchanging, it is often denied or not considered primary in the commodity context, where relations between people are masked as those between things. Commodity exchanges, it is true, represent "an effort to exchange things without the constraints of sociality" (Appadurai 1986, 10). And yet at the cattle market taking place each week at the crossroads of four villages, people will prefer to purchase tomatoes, beer, doughnuts or spinach from the same woman week after week. A woman interested in starting a small trading business in used clothing or small livestock requires a "friend" to take her money and bring her inventory. This person must be close enough to be known and trusted, but distant enough to not use a blood relation to manipulate business transactions with kinship discourses.[11] In rural and urban Singida, like in many places in the world, the market is never fully divested of moral and social interests.

The Affiliative (Gift) Phase

While grains spend the majority of their life cycle either in the social entitlement phase or commodity phase, two other non-linear phases characterize its biography in Singida: the affiliative phase and the aid phase. The affiliative phase (or gift phase) is the phase in which food's dominant and primary feature and value is its capacity to forge, strengthen, or shape relationships: you eat my food, so therefore we have a relationship. While these relationships may ultimately be productive of social entitlements, they cannot be reduced to mere exchange. Unlike the entitlement phase—in which the relationship drives the circulation of food—in the affiliative phase, the circulation of food drives the forging, strengthening, or shaping of relationships. The exchange of food either constructs new kinships, or it cements old ones. It is a signature feature of this phase that the circulation of food occurs often without reference to material need, and sometimes even in inverse relation to it.

The affiliative phase is characteristic of two types of food circulation: ritual and patron-client. Engagement and marriage are one context for the ritual circulation of food—when decorated dahwa gourds filled with flour and beer are sent between families. Deaths are another, in which presents of food (Ny. *rambirambi*—which translates to "lick lick") are sent to mourning families to express condolences, fund funerals, and heal wounds. Likewise, in the construction of the extramarital sweetheart relationships between men and women common in the 1960s and 70s (Jellicoe 1978; Schneider 1970), gifts of flour between a man's lover and his wife disclosed the relationship and helped to legitimize it. As one elder couple described to me in 2005 of their past:

> If you want to build a relationship with another man outside of your marriage … it should only be one. And you should have a good relationship with his wife. You are required to take her presents. You send her a dahwa [gourd] of flour so that she knows you are building a relationship there. And she will come visit you. And you will help each other, for example with the weddings of your children. You will help each other with presents of food or with cooking on the wedding day. If there is a funeral, she will accompany you.

Like these attempts to newly configure an extramarital love affair as a socially legitimate link, gifts of grain between households can send messages packed with highly complex (even fraught!) social meanings.

Patron-client relations, what Pitt-Rivers once referred to as "lopsided friend-ship" (1954, 140, in Wolf 2001, 179), are the other main category of relations in which food is a key transmitter of social messages and builder of relations. Patron-client relations in Singida are formed when basic financial protections (wages, assistance in times of need) are provided in return for the expectation of labor or political support. But with respect to any food that circulates between the rich and the poor in such relationships, people understand that it is the *relationship* (and arguably society itself) that needs to be "fed"—often in highly conspicuous and symbolic ways. Diverting food aid into gifts, as we will see in chapter 4, is one way in which politicians cultivate political relationships. Harvest gifts of cowpeas and sweet potatoes from the poor to the rich are another.

While many different kinds of impulses and inclinations lead people to form new relationships (that include, but are in no way limited to rational, logical choices intended to maximize one's own self-interest), for the purposes of this book it is helpful to consider and compare the material outcomes of gifts, com-modity exchanges, and entitlement transfers. These might be most easily illus-trated with the metaphor of a tree. Watering someone else's tree in the hopes that it may—sooner or later—bear fruit (affiliative act), is quite different than picking the fruit of a tree one has planted (claiming entitlements) or directly exchanging water for fruit (commodity exchange). It is fundamentally a very different act. There is extraneous value, inherent risk, and necessary sacrifice in watering a tree (or "feeding a relationship") rather than directly exchanging the water for fruit (or grain for cowpeas). The tree provides shade, even shelter; it might provide comfort, a ritual space, connection, purpose, or meaning. Yet it may also die or deceive; it may be infertile and never bear fruit; or someone else may take all its fruit. A commodity exchange is certainly quicker and neater than a patron-client relationship. There is less risk, less messiness, and less opportunity for loss or deception (though even these qualities too, may be debated). But, concomitantly, there are also fewer possibilities and less meaningful interactions. There is less risk that one's investment will not be returned, but less safety when one has noth-ing to trade. What a person both gains and sacrifices when relying on patron-client relations for subsistence will be explored further in chapter 6.

The Aid Phase

Finally, a last phase through which food passes in Singida is the aid phase. I use the term "food aid" for the provision of food to combat hunger in emergency situations as well as that provided to help with longer term food insecurity issues.

The distribution of aid is widely understood to be determined by a fixed legal or moral code, but, as we will see in chapter 4, is always negotiated through relationships. Communities in Singida are the recipients of *relief food* (food aid distributed widely by the state or NGOs in emergency situations, either free or for a fraction of market value); *targeted food aid* (food aid that is narrowly distributed by organizations like UNICEF to support particularly vulnerable populations like children, the elderly, or the disenfranchised); as well as *project food aid* (food provided over longer periods through specific programs like the school food program, see fig. 3.6). Internationally-, regionally- and locally-sourced food is diverted from commodity status to the aid phase when state and international actors agree that systems of social entitlements and commodity markets are failing to meet the basic needs of much (but not necessarily all) of a population. Regardless of its intended beneficiaries or program category, all three types of aid arrive in similar form, mostly as grain delivered in synthetic gunnysacks on the back of trucks to government-owned buildings (like schools or the village office).

As aid, food takes on its value in relation to perceived *membership* in a polity (Tanzania), a species (humanity), or a religious community (God's family). In Singida food aid is distributed by international organizations (UNICEF, the United Nations World Food Programme); by the Tanzanian government (often purchased through concessional arrangements with governments in the global north); by religious organizations (Roman Catholic charities or Islamic organizations, for example) and by invested individuals (wealthy migrants from the region, for example) who give food as Christian tithe, Muslim *zakat*, and/or perhaps with political ambitions in mind. Since food aid tends to be procured overseas, or at the regional or national level, the supply relationship in which aid is embedded is often socially thin, fleeting, de-personalized, and devoid of social content for those who receive it. Yet, unless ready-to-eat food aid is dropped from the air for direct consumption by its beneficiaries (which does not occur in Tanzania), food aid is always diverted into other types of relationships as it moves closer to its distribution points (from nation or sponsor to district to division to ward, to village, to hamlet to household). That is, it becomes re-embedded in social entitlement relationships, commodity exchanges, or affiliative practices. Food, like some other "inalienable" objects, has the capacity to retain a history (cf. Weiner 1985; 1992). Food's capacity to retain a history (that is, to be understood as the product of one's own labor, a gift born of patronage, or aid in the name of civic or human rights) inflects its circulation and consumption (by producers, politicians, or those with the purchasing power to buy it) with different kinds of social and political meaning. These meanings, we will see, are significant for the practice of subsistence citizenship.

Grain is diverted *from* the aid phase into social entitlements, gifts, and commodities, in both legitimate and illegitimate ways. First, it is diverted from the aid phase into social entitlements once food reaches claimants (usually the heads

Figure 3.6. A school cook prepares the daily fortified porridge (donated by an international organization) for primary school students.
Photo by author, 2005.

of households, or adults in the household). Legitimate diversions occur when other members of the household (often children) make claims on the food. But illegitimate diversions also occur when intermediary distributors (for example the heads of hamlets or ten-house cells at the tail end of the political distribution chain, or school officials who may oversee the storage of food aid until it is distributed) divert food from its intended recipients for their own consumption. Second, food aid can be diverted from the aid phase into commodities when aid is distributed through sale. This occurs with social and political legitimacy when distributors make decisions to distribute the food not for free but for a price far below market value (this becomes sort of a commodity/aid hybrid; often the poorest households still receive aid for free). This is a common strategy by both church missions and the government in Singida to stretch aid in ways perceived to be most beneficial for the community. But illegitimate diversions also occur when intermediary distributors divert food to sell for their own profit, which is often alleged when government appointees in a village (like village executive officer or a head teacher) suddenly become grain traders, which was not uncommon in the 2006 food crisis. In this way, when food aid is delayed, there is much speculation about it having been "eaten" by local government officials. And indeed these accusations (or the fear of them) often work to the advantage of hungry communities to put pressure on the government.

Food aid is understood by rural Singidans to be a benefit of political membership in the nation of Tanzania that they have earned through their participation in "building the nation" or contributing labor and resources to local rural development projects in education, health care, and agriculture (see chapter 5). Food is diverted *to* the aid phase from the commodity phase when food is purchased on markets for free distribution by governments, organizations, or individuals. Those suffering from hunger (and their government leaders) can help to trigger this phase when they communicate crisis narratives, bear witness to the signs of famine, and threaten not to subsist—that is, communicate warnings that they may die of hunger. Because of the social and geographic distance between those suffering and those providing, the aid phase depends on a political, legal, and media apparatus to communicate crisis and involves a negotiation of signs and symbols between potential donors and beneficiaries to come to a consensus on suffering. As Alex de Waal has noted, "Who defines an event as famine is a question of power relations in and between societies" (1989, 6).

Food aid, as many have argued, is rarely ever perceived to be a reliable source of food. Peter Little, in his study of dependency discourses in the context of Ethiopian food security, notes that "few farmers are foolhardy enough to depend on food aid in rural Ethiopia since its delivery is nontransparent, uncertain, and poorly timed, and the amounts are insufficient" (2013,140). De Waal, likewise, in his 1989 tour de force *Famine That Kills* notes that food relief "is generally merely a footnote to the story of how people survive famine" (1). Indeed, the amount of food aid distributed to rural communities is often negligible, given the duration of food shortages. However even a small amount of aid has a longer-lasting effect on the price of grain in the market, and, as the Langilanga village chairman noted in 2012, this is what makes the greatest difference to poor households.

The Power of the Poor and the Politics of Subsistence

People exercise agency in their daily give and take of food. A person who needs additional resources can remind someone of a relationship to access social entitlements; he can build a fruitful friendship; or he can access aid by convincing officials of his suffering. But it is significant to note that it is not just pulling and pushing *within* these four non-linear phases (entitlement, commodity, affiliative, and aid) that moves food from hand to hand. Rather, people also manipulate food's multiple and contiguous meanings to *divert* food from one category to another in order to make new kinds of claims possible.

Within a day, a papaya might travel from commodity to aid and back again, and then finally be consumed as an entitlement. Village women pull subsistence grains from social entitlement to commodity when they brew beer from sorghum (that they would otherwise consume for food) in order to obtain cash. A brother-in-law might pull it back to entitlement by making a kin-based claim on the beer. A village might pull food from commodity to aid when they endanger officials' political legitimacy by threatening not to subsist (claiming that some people in the village are close to dying from starvation). But government officials might pull the same food from aid back into commodity when they sell or "eat" aid for their own consumption or profit. Or they may pull it from aid to gift when they use government food subsidies to build patron-client relations.

In this light, Sen's idea of an inflexible market, unswayed by social work, is untenable. This highly apolitical understanding of both the market and of hunger goes a long way in letting "the market" off the hook for the consequences of the system of distribution that it organizes. As we have seen, it is social work ultimately that constitutes the market; that is, it is *people* who ultimately sometimes give precedence to the notion that a certain amount of one thing is equivalent to a certain amount of another without regard for the relations or well-being of the people that exchange them. And it is social work—E. P. Thompson's moral economy of the English crowd, as it were—that also conditions and constrains the market; for food is never fully commodified. As we will see in chapter 4, when the cost of food threatens to cost a life, people (both "haves" and "have-nots") reject the market frame of distribution and invoke instead the frames of patronage or rights to organize the distribution of food.

So what makes food distinctive from other things of value? Food, as we have seen, has the capacity to retain a history (though this history may at times be erased or misrepresented). This history implicates the people whose actions it chronicles, marking them as legitimate or illegitimate in their authority, as effectual or ineffectual in their social or political role, as morally sound or ethically bankrupt, as having achieved adulthood or social standing or being divested of it.

Food in Singida is marked by the seasonality and temporality of its value. Food means different things at different times to different people—and sometimes different things at different times to the same people. As we have seen food can be used towards ends that are social, biological, political, or economic. It can mean nourishment, labor, or the achievement of adulthood; it can communicate friendship, generosity, or the promise of allegiance; it can send messages of obligation, identity, alliance, or adultery. It can be conceived as money, belonging, or development. And these meanings shift from season to season, moment to moment, person to person.

Finally, food is understood to be more of a *moral* issue than, say, flip flops, or cash, or clay pots, or cell phones. When the elder woman introduced earlier in this chapter registered a claim with me for two *papayas* (as opposed to two cell phone vouchers or two kanga cloths that she could go on to sell for the cash she needed), she moved our interaction into a moral realm. This discursive move changed the stakes of our conversation not only for herself, but also for me, as I was forced to consider our relationship and my own relative wealth in moral rather than in disinterested terms. In this way, food presents more fertile discursive opportunities to divert resources than many other goods. Local norms, ideas, and practices support this notion, and international human rights discourses reinforce it. This is not to make a judgement on whether or not this elder woman's situation was indeed desperate or not, but rather to acknowledge that in this situation, centering our interaction on *food* allowed her to engage a moral narrative and to construct moral stakes that effectively provoked a redistribution of resources.

This analysis shows that the social labor—productive, symbolic, political— that produces access to food, can never be taken for granted. It highlights not just the fuzziness of concepts of the individual and of property (Devereux 2001), but points to the fuzziness of belonging itself; that is, the way in which understandings of social membership and notions of "the household" (and as we shall see in chapter 4, "the community" and "the nation") change over time, often directly in relation to shifts in the availability of resources. Attention to this social life of food underscores how the dualisms of moral/legal, household/market, gift/commodity are not distinctive domains governed by separate rules for different groups of people. Rather they are discursive choices selectively engaged by the same individuals and groups at different moments and in diverse contexts to negotiate materiality and meaning. To understand how Singidans map these practices, tactics, idioms, expectations, and obligations onto their government, let us explore the *politics* of this social and moral value of food and its inscription on *citizenship* in Tanzania.

Notes

1. "Nervous conditions" is a phrase that was used first by Jean-Paul Sartre in his introduction to Franz Fanon's *Wretched of the Earth*. Zimbabwean novelist Tsitsi Dangarembga then took the phrase as the title of her 1988 novel.

2. I bound this discussion rather tightly, focusing on aspects of food's meaning and value that relate to the *distribution* of food, rather than comprehensively laying out its entire semantic landscape.

3. In reaction to this critique, later work on the "extended entitlements approach" (Gore 1993; Leach et al 1997) developed Sen's work to see entitlements as the outcome of negotiations among people that involve power relationships and contested meanings.

4. Following Appadurai's influential volume and its constituent analyses of material culture many have taken up the call to trace what Appadurai coined the "social life of things." Such a framework has been particularly generative in studies of material culture (Meskell 2005); media (Morley 2003; Silverstone 1994); consumption (Corrigan 1997), and things (Latour 2005). A few studies have also analyzed the social life of food. Brad Weiss, for example, studied consumption and commoditization among the Haya of northwestern Tanzania, tracing how food items move back and forth between gifts and commodities, always embedded in social relations (1996). Rebecca Galemba brings politics into the picture in her study of the moral economy of corn as it traveled back and forth between commodity and contraband on the Mexico-Guatemala border (2012).

5. However, in our wanderings through remote parts of the village, my middle-aged female research assistant—a resident of the village—and I were ourselves often the beneficiaries of such generosity.

6. The exact timing varied from girl to girl, depending mostly on when a ritual was to be held in given village.

7. The prominent role of the husband's sister in imaa and other ritual occasions references the strong ties that women maintain to their natal households, even after marriage.

8. Nyaturu song recording, Feb. 2, 2005, Rural Singida District. Groups of elder women who gather to drink *ntui* (Ny. sorghum beer) several times a week still sing these songs. In addition, boys' circumcision ceremonies and wedding engagements offer more ceremonial occasions during which women convene in ritual fashion.

9. "Turu Fieldnotes." Papers of Harold K. Schneider. Box 13. Vol. 2. National Anthropological Archives, Smithsonian Institution, 1959, 297.

10. "Turu Fieldnotes." Papers of Harold K. Schneider. Box 13. Vol. 1. National Anthropological Archives, Smithsonian Institution, 1959, 137.

11. As NyaWilliam noted, "You can't trust your blood relation and be helped by him like by a good friend. Even if you were born in the same womb. Better that you are helped by a good trustworthy friend. Or a distant cousin."

Plate 1. Failed maize crop in the valley hamlet.
Photo by author, 2017.

Plate 2. Nyaturu homestead in rural Singida. A Tanzanian flag flies near the roadside.
Photo by author, 2007.

Plate 3. At the cattle market.
Photo by author, 2005.

Plate 4. The valley hamlet.
Photo by author, 2017.

Plate 5. Finger millet field in the rainy season.
Photo by author, 2005.

Plate 6. The same finger millet field (as shown in Plate 5) in the dry season.
Photo by author, 2004.

Plate 7. Heading home.
Photo by author, 2014.

Plate 8. The author with friends.
Photo by author, 2007.

4 Crying, Denying, and Surviving Rural Hunger

> Famines are not a naturally constituted object, subject to a scientific definition.
>
> Alex de Waal, "Democratic Political Process and the Fight against Famine"

In late 2005 and early 2006, drought and hunger spread across East Africa. In the Singida region of central Tanzania, food prices skyrocketed, stores of grain dwindled, day labor opportunities vanished, and the state continued to delay on its promises for relief food—what the Nyaturu refer to as *ufoni* (Ny.), or the "healing" of their hunger. As conditions intensified, villagers struggled to lay claim to assistance from their neighbors and aid from state resources.

As we have seen, diverting subsistence grains from one phase in their social life to another requires creative social work. That is, social work can transform one person's entitlement to another's, or an entitlement into a commodity, or a commodity into a gift or aid, (and sometimes back again). Just like the claim registered by the woman who coaxed two papayas from me in the previous chapter, and regardless of a claimant's desperation, a redistribution of resources requires people to set a scene, engage a narrative, construct stakes, and invite an audience. Should one narrative fail, a new one must be invoked. Indeed, as Dorothy Hodgson (2011) has shown—people rely on broad repertoires of discursive strategies to provoke redistributive efforts.

Here I extend this analysis to describe how Singida villagers first tried to access food aid in 2005 and 2006 by registering claims through narratives of crisis and paternal obligation. As we shall see, when food aid failed to materialize from the state, the tone of villagers' protest against their condition changed. Hungry villagers who were not eligible for aid countered the government's seeming paternal neglect and abandonment with claims to their "rights" to food, accusations of corruption, and a threat to no longer participate in (i.e., to labor for) development projects. This filial rebellion and shift to rights rhetoric as the discourse of claims-making endangered not only the material achievement of district government development goals (and consequently the livelihood of village and district officials who would be evaluated on those outcomes), but—through a withdrawal of filial loyalty—also threatened to unravel the narrative of the political family on which the government so substantially relies. And yet following the wider distribution of food aid that resulted, villagers dropped their use of rights language and willingly reinstated the paternal narrative through ceasing their accusations and thanking leaders for their "gifts." Rights, I argue, are risky, and are most viable and effective as a form of claims-making in contemporary rural Singida at the threshold of subsistence, as a "last-gasp" when there is virtually nothing left to lose (Scott 1976). Patronage claims, while often equally unreliable, do not threaten relationships; rather they preserve more enduring moral connections to those in power. Such subsistence politics are integral to the practice of citizenship in rural central Tanzania.

Hunger: Definitions, Scale and Impact

When Singidans declare a year to be one of hunger (*njaa*), what exactly do they mean? Famine, Alex de Waal argues in the Darfur context of his forceful 1989 treatise *Famine that Kills*, that famine has three constituent concepts: hunger, which you just put up with; destitution, which you do your utmost to prevent; and death, which is beyond your power to influence. A fourth concept, he notes, also looms near famine—that of relief, which you do not rely upon. I focus here mainly on hunger, which includes subjective feelings of severe and prolonged deprivation, a socially defined sense of a lack of acceptable food, and a measurable fact of undernutrition (de Waal 2000). But I also attend to the anxieties about destitution and death that constitute key aspects of the experience of hunger in Singida. As de Waal notes: people's key goal during food crises is to "preserve the basis of an acceptable future way of life, which involves not only material wellbeing but also social cohesion" (1989, 227). During such hungry times in Singida, poor people are often pressed to walk the thin line between eluding death and avoiding destitution, between eating one's daily bread and keeping one's livelihood, and between sharing what one has and surviving till the morrow. A "famine that kills"—what Singidans today refer to as *njaa kabisa* ("total hunger")—is when such choices cease to exist for large parts of the population. Famines that kill, then, are always anticipated, predicted, and desperately avoided, but have not often actualized in postcolonial Singida on a widespread basis. As the chairman of Langilanga village noted of the 2011–12 hunger, "No one died; there are ways of turning assets into cash."

While Singida is one of the more food insecure regions in Tanzania, it is by no means exceptional in the pervasiveness of hunger nor in the degree of its seriousness, which ranges from mild deprivation and discomfort to physical debilitation and financial devastation. Approximately 20 to 25 of the 169 districts in Tanzania experience such food shortages on an annual basis. In rural areas, food shortages are deeply shaped by the rainy and dry seasons, which determine the lean and harvest seasons.[1] Twenty-nine percent of Tanzanian households are characterized as *highly food energy deficient*—with a daily deficit of more than 300 calories. Some of the most serious consequences are born by children, whose growth and development is permanently affected by diet deficiencies in the form of stunting and wasting.[2] Food insecurity also shapes everyday life for young and old, taking emotional, psychological, and physical tolls (Hadley & Patil 2006). When surveyed in 2010–11, 36 percent of mainland Tanzanians had worried about not having enough food in the last seven days. Thirty-four percent had experienced negative changes in their diet—by having to rely on less preferred food or limiting the range of food in their diet. And 32 percent reduced their food intake (either by limiting their portion size at meals, reducing the number of meals they ate in a day, or restricting their own consumption so that children could eat), borrowed or were given food, had no food of any kind, or went an entire day and night without eating anything (United Republic of Tanzania, 2012).

Hunger in Singida certainly leaves its mark on the individual and social body. A 2013 USAID-funded study in Dodoma, Singida, Njombe, and Iringa found in its sample that 30 percent of primary school students in Singida were categorized as "thin" according to their BMI (as opposed to "normal" or "overweight") and that 17 percent of women were underweight (Tanzania Food and Nutrition Centre & TAHEA Iringa 2013). The *2010 Demographic and Health Survey* estimates stunting in Singida at 39 percent and wasting at 9 percent (compared with national rates in 2010–11 of 42 percent stunting and 5 percent wasting). 44 percent of children and 29 percent of women in Singida suffer from anemia (National Bureau of Statistics and ICF Macro 2011). As a Nyaturu proverb notes, "Pain doesn't kill you, but it does weaken you."

An ethnographic focus on this more banal experience of rural hunger and impoverishment in which death looms and threatens but does not often strike is theoretically productive. The workings and implications of such food crises are not only largely invisible in media reports and the general public consciousness (which tend to highlight famines with high mortality crises), but also in the literature on the politics of hunger and famine. As de Waal has noted, the famines that have been theorized the most often and with the most sophistication have have been "class-based, rapid-onset, and high visibility" as opposed to the less spectacular but all too common agrarian and pastoralist famines that are "paradigmatic" in many African contexts (2000, 8,10). Moreover, he argues, most theorizations of anti-famine political contracts center on urban areas, where "since colonial days, governments have felt keenly obliged to provide cheap food to townspeople—because this is where their power can be threatened" (24). De Waal goes on to note that even in the most severe agrarian famines, coping is more important than relief (9). And yet little is understood of the sociopolitical practices that allow people to survive episodic hunger and/or to protect themselves against it in rural African contexts.[3] If indeed, food relief is "generally merely a footnote to the story of how people survive famine" (de Waal 1997, 1), then how exactly do rural people experience and cope with hunger? What are the politics of rural subsistence?

De Waal's own proposal for a political contract against famine focuses on the development of what he calls *secondary mobilization* institutions (human rights or democracy institutions acting on behalf of others suffering from hunger) (2000). He calls for the development of political triggers; technical expertise in famine-relevant fields like economics, nutrition, health, agriculture, migration, among others; public education on the need for famine prevention; laws that ensure a right to be free of famine; and electoral, democratic, legal and professional accountability systems. Such recommendations are surely key to effective famine response by states and international entities. But a better understanding of what de Waal calls *primary mobilization* (activism by people affected by famine in pursuit of their own interests) in these "invisible" rural famines offers important insights into indigenous and more agentive forms of rural famine response.

Citizenship and the Politics of (Not) Eating in Singida

Novelist Kamala Markandaya once depicted the suffering of hunger as that of a gnawing pain that evolves into a vast emptiness.

> For hunger is a curious thing; at first it is with you all the time, waking and sleeping and in your dreams, and your belly cries out insistently, and there is a gnawing and a pain as if your very vitals were being devoured, and you must stop it at any cost and you buy a moment's respite even while you know and fear the sequel. Then the pain is no longer sharp but dull, and this too is with you always, so that you think of food many times a day and each time a terrible sickness assails you, and because you know this you try to avoid the thought, but you cannot, it is with you. Then that too is gone, all pain, all desire, only a great emptiness is left, like the sky, like a well in drought. (1954, 91)

In the rural Tanzanian context, this emptiness that Markandaya so evocatively describes characterizes both the physical and social discomfort of hunger. If food constitutes sociality in Singida, then hunger is experienced not only as a lack of food, a shrinking body, or a painful gnawing feeling in the stomach, but also as a marker that one lies outside the social relations that produce and distribute food. For those suffering, hunger is shameful, to be suffered quietly. If feeding and feeding well is the means to achieving personhood and adulthood for men and women in their separate roles, then not being able to feed one's family undermines not only one's position in the household, but also one's sense of self. It is no wonder that during times of widespread hunger, many younger men vanish to the cities leaving villages (and hunger itself) a function of the feminine, the very old, and the very young.

Tanzanians extend these larger frames of social, moral, and political meaning that adhere to both food and hunger into the political realm. Making sense of the hunger that struck Singidans in 2006 requires attention to this interplay between the material, social, and political discursive realms and, specifically, to Singidan ideas about the connection between political legitimacy, the appetites of the state, and material well-being. This includes understanding food, hunger, and feeding as idioms through which Tanzanians negotiate the rights and obligations of citizenship.

Early in the new millennium, idioms of food, feeding, and political providership saturated Tanzanian political discourse and bore potent meanings in this context of widespread vulnerability to hunger amid mounting disparities between the rich and the poor. These idioms for articulating and negotiating politics and citizenship in Tanzania have of course deep roots in Tanzanian postcolonial history (Phillips 2009; 2011; 2015; Schatzberg 2001) as well as in longer-term regional political discourses (Bayart 1993; de Waal 1997; Schatzberg 2001; Watts 1983). Nyerere, unlike many of his post-independence presidential contemporaries in Africa, was praised by Tanzanians for his "thinness"—his prudent lack of personal feasting on what Bayart has termed, "the national cake" (1993).

I discuss the specifics of kinship and food idioms in politics in more detail in chapter 6 and elsewhere (Phillips 2009; 2011; 2015). For the present purposes, it is sufficient to note that in the first decade of the new millennium, and particularly during presidential election years, politicians widely invoked metaphors of food, fatherhood, and the provider role of political leaders to garner political authority. For example, during Jakaya Mrisho Kikwete's visit to Singida as the CCM candidate for the 2005 presidential election, his speech was peppered with such allusions. After Kikwete's speech at Namfua Stadium one young Singidan glossed it in the following way:

> The opposition candidates come with a hunger and they are not suitable for your votes. A person with hunger, if you give him your vote, he won't implement a thing. He will just go to feed his family. And a youth of thirteen years old, would you give him a wife to take care of? And people agreed you can't trust a thirteen-year-old with a wife and children. And CUF (the main opposition party in Tanzania in 2005) is only thirteen years old since it was born, so you can't give it your vote because it's still too young. The vote must go to our father Nyerere's party, the father of the nation.

In this and other speeches in 2005 Kikwete laid claim to the presidency through tracing his lineage to Nyerere and establishing himself as the "family" provider, arguing that only CCM possesses the qualities, resources, accumulated wisdom, and descent from Nyerere to be the political father. He argued that opposition parties were still "too young" and "hungry," drawing on gendered and generational stereotypes to cast Civic United Front (CUF) candidates as teenage troublemakers: out-of-work, discontented, with illicit appetites, and bearing all the strength of youth, but using it toward violent, self-serving, or exploitative ends. Such images make the case that a political father must himself be so well nourished and able to provide for others that he would have no reason to use his position for material gain. A "hungry" politician in this view is one who lies outside the wealth, access to state resources and patronage networks of the dominant party, and one who will be more focused on eking a subsistence from the system than doing the state job of development. In these political terms, to be hungry means to be forced to focus on one's own immediate needs, unable to think beyond the short term and necessarily unconcerned with the general welfare.[4]

Yet political metaphors are most powerful in the way they can be adopted and co-opted toward a variety of ends. Media commentators as well as individuals I spoke with also invoked themes of food, family, and political providership as an idiom of critique of the conspicuous consumption of the Tanzanian elite and the increasingly visible suffering of the rural and urban poor. To many Tanzanians, political leaders (generally speaking) appeared more concerned with brokering aid money and translating their political service into money-making endeavors than with representing constituent interest in national politics. Charges of "over-eating" their share and of "starving" the populace permeated the political sphere in response to the increasing economic disparities of liberalization and unevenly distributed benefits of the booming aid industry. The headline of a Tanzanian *Guardian* article (September 3, 2005) charged, "Ikulu [the Tanzanian presidential palace] only good for a big stomach, heavy pockets." A 2005 editorial cartoon (see fig. 4.1) showed a pot-bellied man in a smart business suit holding out a bowl labeled "food aid." With his other hand he is dragging an emaciated half-naked villager by the hand saying, "Come! You'll make the perfect impression on the donors. Don't forget to yawn after every 5 minutes." (In Tanzania, yawning is associated with hunger and is often used to signify hunger in cartoons). A bubble above his head shows that the politician is daydreaming of a pile of money. Here the sign of hunger invokes a moral commentary on politics in Tanzania that taps into local ideas about disproportionate inequality, social injustice, and the exploitation of the vulnerable for elite gain.

"They ate the money" was a frequent charge laid at government officials when questions emerged as to the whereabouts of development funds. People often accused leaders of overeating their share. During the hunger in January 2006 a newspaper political cartoon by Anwary depicted a member of the Tanzanian parliament seated at a table, getting ready to dig in to a whole roasted chicken while he demands a larger salary. A small citizen sits at his feet, holding an enormous burden of "sickness," "poverty," and "hunger." A sideline observer asks the

Figure 4.1. Cartoon by David Chikoko. *Guardian*, February 21, 2006. Reprinted with permission of David Chikoko.

parliamentarian in Swahili: "Have you seen the condition of those who put you up there?"

Singidans, like their Tanzanian compatriots, map local meanings about food, morality, and sociality onto their concepts of political legitimacy. In this context, political careers can be both made and unmade during famines. As Michael Schatzberg has noted, in the predominant paternal discourse of many "middle African" contexts, "if the father nourishes and nurtures, he has the right to rule ... and the right to 'eat' as long as his political children are well nurtured" (2001, 150). Feeding—and feeding well—in Singida produces not only person-hood and adulthood, but also successful political careers. People often articulate their support of a particular politician in terms of how people "ate" during the leader's tenure. Political leaders, too, gain many points for supplying food in times of need, and even if the timing of aid is awkward or suspect, this is usually overlooked in retrospect as long as food does arrive.

On the flipside, one's perceived ability to administrate or govern can be seriously undermined by a failure to avoid famine. This link between food security and political legitimacy is crucial leverage for food insecure populations. As de Waal has argued more generally: "The basic reason why a government prevents famine is because its interests—the power of its leaders—depends on it. There is a political *incentive* to prevent famine. Elected politicians fear the retribution of their constituents in the polling booths, and hope for the electoral reward of successfully delivering famine prevention. Civil servants fear disgrace or demotion if their failure to prevent famine is exposed, while hoping that they can use the opportunities of a famine emergency to prove their capabilities and win promotion" (2000, 13, original emphasis). Yet with this in mind, one might conclude that there is a perverse incentive to let communities slide to the brink of famine, but not actually into it. In any event, with political legitimacy understood to be so inextricably tied to a well-nourished and well-nurtured populace, it is no wonder that when hunger predominates in Singida (as we will see below), political fathers—as well as biological ones—flee or steer clear of the villages.

This link between political authority and food security means that the representation of Tanzanians' well-being becomes a site of intense struggle during hungry times. When the newly inaugurated Tanzanian president Jakaya Kikwete spoke again at Namfua Stadium in Singida in January 2006, the *Sunday News* reported that he warned regional and district officials that they must report on hunger in a timely manner.[5] Acknowledging that some leaders prefer to paint a rosy picture of their jurisdictions in order to further their own careers, he demanded that they provide accurate and timely reports. He ended this stern warning with the oddly worded statement: "I will not tolerate press pictures of lean and bony people who we are later told are victims of famine." This warning speaks to the temptation for local government officials to overestimate or misrepresent their populations' well-being. It also speaks to the social and political shame that death from hunger produces up to the highest levels of government.

The above examples allude to a set of widely accepted ideas about the connection between political legitimacy, the appetites of the state, and the material well-being of citizens in Tanzania. Grasping the significance of subsistence citizenship and the workings of rural mobilization around hunger requires recognizing this interplay between the material, social, and political discursive realms. A study of food politics in Tanzania must consider food simultaneously as (1) the object of the struggle for scarce resources; (2) a sign of political legitimacy, sociality, and human universalism; and (3) a site of confrontation over larger political and economic issues. Food and hunger are material outcomes of citizenship, markers of citizenship, and idioms for contesting and negotiating citizenship.

Crying, Denying, and Surviving Hunger in Singida

Let us now turn to the circumstances of the hunger in 2006. During the previous year, the rains had been insufficient and ill-timed, and the harvest had produced a mere one-third of the village's food requirements. Villagers had immediately sold much of their meager harvest to pay off debts and make mandatory contributions to the school and to village development projects. With dwindling household stocks, they soon began to purchase back imported grain sold at the local market at increasingly astronomical prices. The price of sorghum and maize increased nearly threefold, while the value of the livestock that they traded for food dropped to a third of its normal value. Villagers lamented, "You can't get even one bucket of grain in exchange for a goat!" "Mlenda leaves have no price if you try to sell them!" "You can't even *work* for food!" Livestock owners and salaried government employees who had bought grain low and could resell high made a significant profit, but most cash-poor villagers suffered a great loss. Late rains in 2006 then exacerbated the situation. And when the internationally-sponsored school food program active in Langilanga ceased its delivery of two meals per day to rural Singida schoolchildren between October 2005 and February 2006 (the hungriest months of the annual cycle) without explanation, the situation became grim. The families I knew, even the village chairman's family, had reduced their food intake to one meal per day.

From November 2005 on, people were anticipating the food aid politicians had promised them during the electoral season. In the early months, when the more well-off villagers were still hopeful that the rains would fall early, they hired day labor to help with rigorous plowing and cultivating. Women still brewed beer to make a small profit with which they could buy other necessities. And life seemed to be going on as usual in the months of scarcity. But by February, when the rains had still not come, and women woke at three in the morning to draw water from the sometimes-trickling well, distress was palpable. The lack of wage labor opportunities was due not only to wealthier villagers tightening their purse strings and not hiring, but also because the lack of rain meant there was so little agricultural work to be done. A widowed mother struggling through these months explained: "If it is raining, then at least there is wage labor to do. And if it is raining, people are willing to give help and to hire people. But when the rain refuses, there is no help and no employment. Everyone is hoarding what they have."

Having traveled out of the country in November and December 2005, I arrived back in Singida in January 2006 to a village already in crisis. Across the board—rich and poor, young and old, men and women, city-person and villager, landed and landless, cattle-owner and she-who-does-not-even-own-a-chicken—everyone was feeling and lamenting the hunger. Not everyone however was experiencing this crisis in similar ways. Senge commented on the conditions of hunger in Singida town, where increasingly more of the village population was migrating or sending their young people to seek work:

> Everyone is hiding money right now. No one will give help. There's no money to be earned or spent, even by those who can afford it. Normally it is the villagers who come to town to spend money here. They come in to buy their basic needs. But the villagers are the ones who are starving. Now here in town, if people know someone has money, they will attack him. There's no begging now, because there's no one giving out money to strangers. People are being mugged lately around the lake [where I often walked for exercise while in town]. It's not a good time to take walks out there. The youths are hiding money so they can leave town if they need to.

But he went on to compare townspeople's opportunities to eat in comparison with those in in the village: "A town person can't die of hunger. He has friends. He will be welcomed. He can go from meal to meal in a day being invited to eat. He has resources. And he's clever [*mjanja*]. In town there is wealth. There is more to be redistributed when things get bad. Only the villager can starve."

For some in the village, the escalation in food prices involved the mild deprivation of preferred foods or inconvenience. With the increase in maize prices, the head teacher's family (with whom I had lived for three months in the previous year) had stopped eating meat and ceased to hull their maize, leaving the fibrous external coating on in order to further stretch their food supply until the price of grain dropped once more. Yet they still ate breakfast plus two full meals a day with assurance. Although the larger food crisis was felt by all, and arguably palpably so, for some the *promise* of food never dimmed. Thus, it is important to note that some people who *lived in* the hunger and experienced some of its effects, never actually *knew* it. The Nyaturu have a proverb that captures the insurmountable existential distance that privilege affords, despite physical proximity and shared experiences: "He who lives in the shade cannot know the burning heat of the sun."

There were unfortunately those who never knew this proverbial shade. NyaMariamu, a widow in her early forties, was known as a villager who "doesn't even own a chicken." By February word had spread that she and her three children were in trouble and NyaRosalia—who at the time was the chairwoman of the Committee for the Children from the Most Vulnerable Environments (MVC)—and I set out to visit her.[6] Finding her not at home, we checked in with two neighbors. "She is truly in a bad state," said a woman from NyaMariamu's deceased husband's clan. "Unless she goes to pick wild greens to sell now, she doesn't eat." NyaRosalia, herself a widow who had been spurned by her in-laws after her husband's death, later lamented, "If her neighbor says she is that bad, she must be *really* bad. We get envious of each other and don't like it when others get help and we don't. If her sisters-in-law are saying she is in a bad state, she is truly in trouble."

When NyaRosalia and I finally found NyaMariamu at home she looked exhausted and had shrunk dangerously. The small dirt yard outside her mud-roofed house was littered with pits of the small watery *zambarau* fruit. "For a while, when it was raining, greens had no value," NyaMariamu said, "but now that it has stopped, they have a little. I get 50 shillings [approximately 5 cents] for one bowl. So I have to sell 8 bowls to get 1 liter of grain a day."[7] The day before she had walked the twelve kilometers to town to sell her greens, and had kept walking further in the other direction to find a buyer. She had left her small child at home and returned at eight o'clock in the evening, having walked 30 kilometers in the round trip to finally sell her greens at a very poor price. She continued: "My children leave school at noon and pick fruit in the valley and then we try to have one meal at night. We get a little flour from the neighbors [her mother-in-law's family] if I promise to pay them back after the cattle market." I was acquainted with NyaMariamu's older son, Hassani, a tall 17-year old in seventh grade whose buttons strained on his too-small school uniform. According to NyaMariamu, Hassani was studying for the all-important seventh-grade exam—the narrow gateway to higher education—on barely a meal each day.

A European sister at a local mission noted that the 2006 hunger seemed much worse than that of 2003. She lamented, "At least then kids were getting food in school through the school food program and looked healthy. Mothers were even sending kids too young for school there to get fed, and the head teacher was just feeding them because—as he said—'What else can I do?' We [the mission] have planted beans *four times* so far this year, and none have survived without the rains. We are giving people about 1000 shillings [approximately one dollar] when they come for help."

An excerpt from my fieldnotes recorded a visit from Nyaamani in late February 2006. She was a widowed mother of two that I had come to know when I interviewed her in 2005.

> Nyaamani just came by. So thin. So tired. She came and just cried. Her Standard 4 son is truant. He refuses to go to school. She thinks he's sick but she's not sure. He lies all the time. She's off trying to work every day to try to get food. She is hoeing for people, now that there is rain. Her hair has become like peach fuzz. So thin. So tired. She says all she can do is cry, worry and cry. She gets one bowl of grain per day for her work. Her Standard 7 son continues to go to school. He is doing well. The younger one just doesn't understand.

The bowl of grain Nyaamani was able to earn for a day's work was enough for one meal for one or two people. This she shared with her two sons. While Nyaamani and her elder son both grasped that "hunger is something you live with," her younger son (owing perhaps to his age or temperament) struggled and suffered more.

Neighbors and kin played a vital role in these months in the survival of the poorest community members. But as January turned into February and everyone's stores dwindled, help became harder and harder to come by. Rumors of people starting to swell and eating grass inspired new efforts at assistance, sometimes arriving from relatives in Dar es Salaam or concerned local leaders. Crisis narratives were key to prompting this aid. In February, a story from the 1998 hunger circulated widely in Langilanga. I never verified its truth, but it certainly functioned as a "rural legend" that served to remind people of the shame involved when someone, receiving no assistance, died of hunger. As NyaRosalia narrated:

> In 1998 a woman from—I think it was [a neighboring village]—had run out of food. That year, there were many wild fruits. She saw that she had no food left and she went to go look for day labor. She searched for work until dark to

no avail. So, she went to pick fruit to take home to her children. The children ate it, even though fruit is not the food that takes care of hunger. They cried with hunger, but in the end, they bore the discomfort until the next day. In the morning, she left again to look for work in another village. But she wandered again until evening without any luck. She wanted to find sweet potatoes, because in that year, that was all there was to eat after the grasshoppers ruined all the food. On her way home, she asked herself, "Again I have failed to get food. What will I do for my children?" So she put stones in her bag so that when her children came to greet her, she could tell them, "I brought you all potatoes. Go on and play outside while I cook your dinner." So they stayed outside and played with joy because today there would be no lacking food. They would eat! Their mother, on going inside, took a clay pot and put the stones and water inside it. She lit a fire and covered the pot. And then she went into the bedroom. The children, when they investigated the first time, asked, "Mother, aren't the potatoes ready?" They heard only silence, but saw that the pot was beginning to boil. So they went outside again. The second time they came in to the kitchen and saw again that their mother was not there. They started to cry from hunger, so they opened the pot to see if the potatoes were ready. When they opened it, they saw only rocks and cried. On looking into the inner room they saw that their mother had hung herself. They began to "cry the cry for help" [-*piga yowe*] and people came to see this horrible sight.

The circulation of the story reminded villagers of their most vulnerable households—those who are female-headed, living among hostile or unhelpful neighbors. Although in the story it is the mother's shame that drives her to suicide, the story functioned to shame everyone else involved—in particular those better off who refused her plea for work or assistance.

In another tragic example from 2006, word spread across Langilanga that a young girl from a neighboring village had died at the hands of a witch. According to her family and village leaders, she had been cursed and poisoned, dying of illness with black spots on her body. A local medical missionary had a different interpretation of the reported skin condition, more shameful to her village and family: that the young hungry girl had begun to fill her stomach with whatever grew nearby and had accidentally poisoned herself. Regardless of whether witchcraft was at play, these accusations helped to diffuse blame for the girl's death to the periphery of the family. Widespread sensitivity to the shame of hunger enhances villagers' power in claims for assistance when they begin to assert to government leaders that "people have started to eat grass" and "they have started to swell."[8] Such words signal growing desperation, and people use them not only literally but also strategically, to precipitate government action.

Some argued that such crisis narratives may not be indicative of actual crisis. One teacher in a remote rural Singida village noted that, "Here people say *njaa njaa* ['hunger, hunger'], if they begin to hear other people talking about hunger. It is necessary to say it too, or everyone will say that they are rich. So they begin to say '*mimi pia nina njaa*' ['I too am hungry']." This teacher's observation points to the ways in which "crying hunger" can be more than the report of a condition or the declaration of suffering that prompts redistribution from the "haves" to the "have-nots." It is also a discursive act that positions those afflicted by hunger in relation to *each other*. By "crying hunger," people can socially situate themselves as clients, not patrons.

Surveillance, Invisibility, and the Social Erasure of Rural Hunger

> How is violence like this taken for granted in state institutions such that it disappears from view and cannot be thematized as violence at all?
>
> Akhil Gupta, *Red Tape*

The suffering had not come as a surprise to the local government in Singida; they had anticipated it since the previous year. In June 2005, once the growing season had finished, leaders submitted their annual report of the estimated shortfall of food (*matarajio la mavuno*). Then in January 2006 they sent in their annual report estimating the number of people in three categories: those who had no ability to buy food, those who were able to work to buy food, and those who could buy food at subsidized prices. As the food crisis dragged on, village officials continued to survey households. Such monitoring and reporting was tedious, particularly for those suffering most. The head of the household of one of the poorest families reportedly waved the village chairman out of the tree-lined *kraal* adjacent to his *tembe* compound, cursing him: "All you people do is show up and write reports on us. Help never arrives! Don't come back until you bring me assistance. I don't want to answer your questions in vain anymore. Perhaps it is you who have 'eaten my right!'" The scene echoed a political cartoon published around the same time by the civil society organization Hakielimu, in which villagers reject poverty researchers from the city: "We are fed up with your endless studies." "Give us some money first!"

Rumors began to fly that people in the valley were dying of hunger, that even in Langilanga people were "starting to swell." It was impossible for local officials to remain unaware of the suffering. The two salaried government officials in the four-village ward received a constant stream of guests whom they were obliged to feed. One lamented his own dwindling grain supply: "They will come all the way to your home to ask for help, to the ward councilor, to the head of the district, even to the head of the region. Since the weekend they have been at another local leader's house, saying they have not eaten in three days. Then they move on to my house. Before you even drink your tea in the morning, you have guests. Hunger is the worst. It's even worse than war. War you can run from. But hunger ... where will you go?" Still officials did have a way out. When their guests became too many, the leaders simply left the village.

Political leaders are aware that hungry times are volatile times. In both rural and urban areas, young men have been known to participate in group violence and vigilantism. While such violence is rarely directed toward anyone with political power (for fear of legal retribution), the potential for violence during periods of hunger cannot be ignored; as one ward leader told me upon passing through, "people have become very angry!" Many district and national leaders, in fact, do not show their face (or more significantly, their bellies!) in rural areas until the hunger has passed. As one village leader noted, "Our leaders will not come to visit us now. People have become too angry. They are demanding the promises made last year during the elections."

In 2006, President Kikwete's motorcade passed by the periphery of Langilanga village along the inter-regional road en route to Singida Town. Anticipating his passing, villagers waited many hours on the road to see him. He was late—no doubt other villages had had the same plan. One woman reported: "People had to force him to stop. He talked a little bit, but people were disappointed with all the preparations they had made to sing and dance. People said, if he's going to pass without saying hi to us, he's going to sleep on the road. So, we sat on the road until he stopped. Some people were given t-shirts and head scarves as presents. But there was no *ngoma* [singing and dancing]. People were very bitter." After the greetings, the motorcade proceeded as quickly as possible. As many people remind themselves in the hungry months, there is a fine line between a rally and a riot.

Reflecting in 2011 on his interactions with constituents during periods of food crisis, Singida East's MP Tundu Lissu (of the opposition Chadema party and from whom we will hear more in chapter 6) departed briefly from his usual radical populism to make note of his increasing sympathy for leaders and officials who begin to avoid their home constituencies: "Resources—it's the perennial problem. We don't have the money. The life of a Tanzanian MP. I've learned a few things ... that I could never understand before. That is: why the CCM MPs were running away from their constituents. I now know. If you are a Member of Parliament, you are an uncle to every child who has been ejected from school because they don't have school fees. You are a brother to everyone who is going hungry." Without the resources dedicated to alleviating suffering, it is not difficult to see why those who are not suffering stay away from rural areas during hunger. Yet this avoidance also places further social and political distance between those who suffer hunger and those who proverbially "do not know the burning heat of the sun." Such aversion to interaction only further "reinforces the 'otherness' of famine, and its isolation from ordinary life" (de Waal 1989, 31).

An excerpt from my field notes on February 15, 2006, reveals the kinds of interactions I had with district and regional officials around the issue of hunger when I traveled to Singida town.

Hunger … when I brought it up this week at the regional office or district office, it seemed that some just laughed it off. I told N- today in the regional office about the village man who kicked out the village leaders because all they were doing was counting [doing surveys] and he laughed and said, "*Ni utani tu*" ("That's just joking"). I stopped by the district office today to talk to my connection there and told him my concerns. He was serious, and said that they expected food at the end of this month, or the beginning of next. They are basically waiting on the region, who are waiting on the nation. He was very nice. But another district official I spoke with blamed it on the villages for a lack of reporting. "It's the villages who haven't sent in their reports yet. The District can't know that people are starving if it's not reported. The villages are in the process of sending in reports." This I know to not be true [because I had seen copies of the reports that had already been submitted]. When I followed up in another office with A-, he told me that the school food is set to arrive next week, and that government food aid had already been taken to the village. He said he had passed by Langilanga and "there had been good rain; the crops looked healthy; so what is the problem?"

At the time, I was furious that the state of hunger in rural villages could be so easily dismissed; that food aid had not yet, in actuality, arrived in the village; and that the current state of the (still fledgling) crops could be bandied about as an acceptable assessment of people's current food situation. In retrospect, the one official who took my questions seriously was very gracious. The defensiveness I encountered among other local government officials was likely in part a reaction to me as someone from a wealthy country with the presumption to tell local officials (whom I otherwise knew to be hard-working and committed) their business on such a highly politically loaded and sensitive matter. (And indeed a European medical missionary who also pressed them on the issue of food aid reported that she was told quite pointedly that this was not her business). Also, several of these officials seemed to bear a genuine sense of helplessness and dependence on the creaking of bureaucratic wheels outside of Singida. They were in the difficult position of explaining the delay of food, and not actually being able to do much about it.

But it is also important to note that these officials were not necessarily in a position to "know" or to "see" hunger. With "reporting" one of the few modes of communication between villagers and district officials during hungry months, it is easy to see why state bureaucracies have been called machines for "the social production of indifference" (Herzfeld 1993). While nutritional reporting renders hunger bureaucratically visible, it also obfuscates hunger's human effects and buffers the sharp edges of other people's suffering. No wonder it has been said that nutritional surveillance creates a "citadel of expertise" in which famine becomes "a technical malfunction, not a human experience" (Hewitt 1983, 5; de Waal 1989, 31). The technocratization of reporting and monitoring, a *general* lack of funds and time to regularly visit the rural areas, and a *specific* disinclination to visit them during the hungry months all contribute to the social erasure of rural hunger.

A Shift to Rights

In February, as the government continued to delay on food aid and school food still failed to be delivered, suffering and anxiety mounted. People articulated a sense that the moral economy of patronage appeared to be broken and began to openly politicize the food situation, framing their claims to aid in the political terms of rights. Concerned about the delay of village development projects and the loss of government funding, village leaders threatened young men at a village assembly in February 2006: "If you don't do the work of building the nation, you won't get any food aid." The young men offered a counterthreat: "If we don't get any food aid, we're not building the nation!" Such disputes laid bare the political contract, in which rural citizenship obligated Tanzanians to labor for state development and entitled them to be free from famine.

Since the political advancement of government functionaries in Singida hinges on the success of development projects, Singidan labor is critical. In Langilanga and other villages, labor strikes against village development projects were an effective means of accessing food aid in the first decade of the new millennium. Such strikes appeared not to be limited to Singida. According to a 2006 newspaper article in the *Guardian*, village authorities in Same district, Kilimanjaro region, complained that: "'All development programmes are doomed to failure, as many are not willing to work unless they are given food.' School building, road maintenance, trench digging and others are some of the activities that people boycott. The Village Executive Officer . . . told the paper that the majority of business people refuse to participate in development activities claiming that they have been marginalized on the food aid issue." According to the article, village authorities noted that "People will tell you . . . let those who have got food, since they are energetic, go to work."[9] From both sides of this political contract—the state and the villagers—we see efforts to entice into an obligation *and* to evade reciprocal demands.

In response to the continued delay of aid, accusations also flew that district, village, or school leaders were "eating the rights" of their constituents by selling it off for their own profit—pushing the debate from a purely moral realm to a moral-legal one. "They're selling it!" complained Abdallah, a notoriously querulous father of four in his fifties. "Thieves, all of them! Worse than lions, they are hyenas! They don't just eat that which fills them. They eat everything and its remains!" The news that some regional and district leaders had been involved in selling grain at elevated prices raised suspicion about the real whereabouts of food aid. Hunger in Singida invited charges that leaders were "eating the rights" of villagers, consuming or profiting from the sale of food-stuffs intended for hungry communities. My neighbor in Langilanga came over to grumble one day: "They cry and they cry that food is coming, next week, next week, and next week. Every week it's next week. So where's the food? Who is eating it? Is it the village government? The ward councilors? Meanwhile, we die of hunger."

The uncharacteristic absence of school food during the hungry months exacerbated speculation and suspicion about the involvement of local leaders in the sale of food aid.[10] Such suspicions are reflected in a March 2006 *Majira* political cartoon by Nathan Mpangala that showed sacks of food aid with grain spilling out of large holes. A large fat rat labeled "*Watendaji*" ("Village Executive Officers"—village government appointees charged with overseeing the distribution of grain, among other responsibilities) sits on the high walls "guarding" the food aid, but is presumably responsible for the "leakage" of grain. There may be some truth to these accusations (which may help explain the peculiar timing of food aid, which often arrives *after* prices have already fallen or food has once again become available). Yet one can read accusations of corruption not only as the censure of individuals' behavior but also as a critique of the overall regime that organizes access to political power and economic resources. As Daniel Jordan Smith has noted, "In many ways, corruption has become the dominant discourse of complaint in the postcolonial world, symbolizing people's disappointments with democracy and development, and their frustrations with continuing social inequality" (2007, 9). Accusations of corruption (which is illegal) also allowed Singidans to push their claims on food into (or at least closer to) a national and supra-national legal realm that otherwise offers people few means to adjudicate their human right to food.

During the worst of the hunger, prior to government aid, I realized that my own private gifts of food to friends and neighbors who asked for help were not necessarily reaching the people who needed it most. The village chairman, the chair of the Committee of the Children from the Most Vulnerable Environments, and I made it our task to come up with a list of villagers likely to fall through the cracks of social and aid networks (the list was composed almost entirely of *vikon-gwe*, elders whose age made them unable to work and who lacked the children that would qualify them for most aid efforts). I purchased several gunnysacks of grain to be distributed to these households but asked to remain anonymous, as I had long since learned how acts of assistance complicated my research. I anticipated that there might be some complaint about the fact that we had distributed this aid to specific households, instead of spreading it around more equally, but our concern for one elderly woman in particular, who had allegedly "started to swell," overrode this concern.

Yet as it turned out, most people agreed with the tactic, as it was these very destitute households that were draining the resources of their neighboring kin. People were relieved that the village was taking some responsibility. What concerned them was the notion that the donor wished to remain unnamed. At the next village government meeting, several men insisted, "Tell us to whom we are indebted. We must know whom to thank." As Marcel Mauss has noted, "The gift is therefore at one and the same time what should be done, what should be received, and yet what is dangerous to take. This is because the thing that is given itself forges a bilateral, irrevocable bond, above all when it consists of food" (1990; 1954, 59). Food, as previously noted, has the capacity to retain a history (though this history may at times be erased or misrepresented) and define a relationship. And people were unwilling to not know the conditions of the relationship to which they were submitting, nor to remain in the dark about to whom they were bound and beholden.

In response to this query about my identity (at which I was not present), two members of the village government who had been party to my purchase of the grain seized the opportunity and took credit for the gift. Yet they quickly leaked the truth about my role after they were overwhelmed with demands for assistance that their newfound but short-lived status mandated. Unlike the state officials who took personal credit for state and international food aid, these local leaders did not have the permanence of the state's wealth and authority to back them or the ability to disappear when claims overwhelmed them. My own wealth and status were understood to have their limits. As Singidans pragmatically say about their *wazungu* ("white") guests, "The guest is a river": it brings good things but does not stay, so you take what you can from it before it passes.[11]

Singidans know that "there are no free gifts," either to give or to receive; for "gift cycles engage persons in permanent commitments that articulate the dominant institutions" (Douglas 1999; 1954, ix). Because food aid tends to come from overseas, or to be purchased at the regional or national level from faceless farmers in other places, the supply relationship in which aid is embedded is socially thin, transitory, de-personalized, and devoid of social content for those who receive it. Yet, as I describe below, as it moves closer to its distribution points (from nation or sponsor to district, to division, to ward, to village) this same food aid becomes re-embedded in social entitlement relationships, commodity exchanges, or affiliative practices. There are no anonymous gifts, no state entitlements that are not marked by the hands that pass them on, regardless of their original source. Every gift has a face that gives it, and a face that receives it. These transactions put both of these faces in relationship with each other and make them different from each other. It is here that distinctions between clients and patrons, and between citizens and the state, come into sharper relief.

Resolution after Rights: Food Aid and Social Healing

"*Ufoni uaja!*" (Ny. "The healing has arrived!") In March 2006, word traveled quickly from homestead to homestead, along cattle paths lined with tall young sorghum, across Langilanga village's 40 square kilometers. Within hours, hundreds of villagers were milling around the village office and its surrounds. Groups of men rolled tobacco into old newspaper and exchanged news of the newly arrived government food aid. The young men who had been playing *bao* at the roadside when the grain arrived recounted the number of sacks they had hauled from the truck into the village office, where two elders now sat in constant vigilance of the padlocked door. Women, too, congregated, with ragged empty sacks bearing the faded blue emblem of the World Food Programme (WFP). They soberly exchanged guesses about the amount of food the leaders would distribute to each household. In a side room representatives of the village government—a council of elected men and women of various ages—gathered to "do the math." Days would pass before they issued any rations.

The mood was less celebratory than I had anticipated. The word on the path was that the food aid would not suffice for all those suffering in the village. As we sat in my room at the village office, NyaJuli, a mother of four in her forties, predicted that with the limited amount of aid, leaders would target only the hungriest of the hungry. "But hunger has now settled with every person!" she lamented. "We are all sick with hunger. That is why we say: 'Old age is miserable. Famine is better.' At least for famine there's a cure." This seemingly indigenous medical model for understanding hunger, in which state therapy cures rural pathology, struck me as a rather odd euphemism for the situation.

Thirty sacks of grain (each approximately 100 kilograms) had arrived. The village government relayed district orders that food be distributed only to the poorest households. Langilanga erupted in protest as people demanded "their right." Several men refused to do the heavy work of building the rock wall for the village cattle watering place unless they too were given food. The rest of the villagers not designated for food aid soon followed suit. With no alternative, the village representatives returned to several days of calculations to decide how the grain would be distributed. In the meantime, two elders stood guard outside the village office each night. I wondered at this, for the office had often stored more economically valuable items like construction tools for development projects and no such precautions had been taken. The chairman explained, "Yes, but this is food. The tools are not so desirable. But right now a person can be killed for just one bucket of grain. In Nyaturu we say, 'The year of the lions does not loan doors.' You cannot trust anyone with food when it is the time of hunger." According to a January 2006 article in *Nipashe*, thieves as well as guardians had best be wary: it reported that neighbors had caught and beaten to death one resident of Shinyanga region who had broken into a private home and stolen three buckets of grain worth a total of 10,000 TSH (US$9).[12]

In the end, village leaders in Langilanga made their allocations according to the village government's three-tiered grouping of households: at the top level, those who could buy grain received no aid; at the lower level, a few of the poorest households were given a small amount of grain (12 kilos) at no charge. Everyone else was allowed to buy 12 kilos of grain at 50 shillings (less than 5 cents) per kilo. While this policy spread the aid more widely to include the middle households, it meant that those in the most dire situations received very little relief from their more desperate hunger or from the weariness of eking subsistence from such a barren economic landscape.

The rain did return in March and April 2006. The prospect of a decent (though late) harvest lifted people's spirits and with a few ears of fresh maize, the few kilos of grain distributed as aid, and the lowering of grain prices, hunger dissipated. But so did the outspoken critique against the political and economic circumstances of rural Singidans. "*Tule, tupone!*" ("Let's eat, so that we may heal!") people called to each other from doorways. Presents of pumpkins and peanuts flowed from those who had borrowed and begged to those who had helped. Resolution was in the air, not revolution.

District and elected leaders became much more obliging with visits to rural Singida. In speeches they often took personal credit for feeding hungry communities, reminding constituents that they had been remembered, and framed state food aid as a "gift" from the party or as a donation of personal wealth from leader to citizen, or (invoking the local political metaphor) from a father to his children.[13] One leader implored Singidans to help him continue building the nation, but he steered clear of the language of rights. Instead he took credit on behalf of himself and his party and asked his constituents to remember both in their votes.

Singida villagers had awaited this aid with a very different narrative. Under the duress of hunger, vocal Langilangans (the vast majority of whom are men) stripped the veneer of paternalism embedded in the narratives of charity and gifts that politicians invoked. While they too couched their claims in the rich language and metaphors of ujamaa (Nyerere's policy of Tanzanian socialism and self-reliance), they adopted a rhetoric that emphasized rights and equality. If they were to do the work of building the nation, they reminded their leaders, they were all equal and the food in their hands was the food of the nation to which they were entitled. However while such language leveraged the rhetorical power of rights to remind a leader that "you are not above us," this democratic discourse of *asocial equality* (to twist a phrase from James Ferguson) also obscured the fundamental *inequality* that existed at the village level. By arguing that every villager should receive the same amount, This rhetorical flattening of very real socioeconomic differences rendered invisible the many households—often female-headed and/or without access to farmland—who had sunk to more desperate levels of poverty. It also revealed the attributes of the citizen who can make democratic claims on the state—the laboring male head of household. The village chairman, though aware of the risks of spreading food aid too widely, sighed resignedly when I asked him about it: "they demanded their right, what can we do?" In this instance, we see that the moral economy of the poor may be articulated at odds with the interests of those who suffer most.

So how can we understand these contests over resources, existing as they do in this slippery field of overlapping and contradictory narratives and histories? When politicians refuse to speak in terms of rights or entitlements, what exactly are they eliding? And when villagers shun the idea of the gift, what do they gain? Today Tanzanians and their leaders are negotiating a rapidly transforming system of distributing wealth and resources. If we think about the exchange going on around food aid, it helps if we understand that it is not only an exchange of nourishment for power, but also a debate about the terms under which wealth and poverty are produced. It is not only a conversation about food, but a conversation about postcolonial and postsocialist politics.

When politicians refuse to frame food aid as an entitlement, they affirm their own right to private property, and to become rich and powerful individuals. They deny claims of the masses to the resources at their disposal, even when it is not their own property. When villagers refuse to speak in terms of gifts, they capitalize on the language of ujamaa that has long been used to nationalize resources. They not only assert their claims to food and their right to receive aid, but they also protest politicians' power to give it. But it is important to remember, as E. P. Thompson once wrote, that "even 'liberality' and 'charity' may be seen as *calculated acts of class appeasement* in times of dearth and calculated extortions (under threat of riot) by the crowd: what is (from above) an 'act of giving' is (from below) an 'act of getting'" (*emphasis added*; 1978, 150). Food aid in Singida is therefore as much (if not more) an outcome of rural political mobilization and action (however transitory) as it is a marker of postcolonial dependency. And elite preoccupation with food security in Singida references not only a paternalistic concern for the hunger and suffering of others, but also a wary concern for the security of property and person of those who are far more comfortable. Food security is vital to well-being, to be sure; but it is a question worth asking, in appeasing the hungry masses, *whose* well-being is *most* secured?

I sat in my room in the village office on the morning when those being given food at no cost were called to pick it up. These poorest of the poor families trudged in silently and left with little comment. Yet I was also present in the afternoon when food was distributed to those middle-level households (still poor by all standards) who had fought to access some of the aid marked for their poorest neighbors. I noticed that there was something in their posture besides relief at being handed the food. They straightened their spines, stiffened their lips, and ceased their accusations. They resumed a respectful stance toward government leaders. At the time, I understood this shift as an appreciation for being recognized by the government; of having the state of one's life and hardships honored and recognized as deserving of assistance. These were the people who had fought for their right to assistance and who, in receiving it, felt vindicated.

But I have also come to understand that villagers were healing the ruptures and disruptions that rights rhetoric had generated and were reinstating their filial connection to the government. Rights are grounded on a notion of membership (to a nation, a state, and/or a species), a membership that self-consciously renders *social* relationships irrelevant, even problematic. Rights thus imply, as I noted above, *asocial equalities*. So while rights have their time and place in subsistence agriculture contexts—that is, at the threshold of subsistence—they are somewhat counter-intuitive in a political space in which distribution is governed on a daily basis by relationships and their social work. As I go on to show, it is the political code-switching between and code-mixing across these two forms that allows rural Singidans to capture as much of the state as they do. *Relationships* saw Singidans through the everyday, while *rights* were a last gasp that kept them hanging on at the threshold of subsistence, when they could no longer wait on the unpredictable grace of the government. In the remaining two chapters, I explore how this subsistence citizenship shapes the practice of politics and development.

Notes

1. The pattern is much the same in urban areas, though it is less pronounced and there is less variability during the year. This variation is likely to reflect less reliance by urban residents on agriculture for food and more access to food through other means (United Republic of Tanzania 2012).

2. Stunting is defined as short height for age. Wasting is low weight for length/height. Both are important public health indicators.

3. A notable exception is Lisa Cliggett's ethnographically rich monograph *Grains from Grass* (2005) that highlights the highly gendered strategies elder men and women in rural Zambia deploy to evade and survive hunger.

4. It must be noted that CCM's dominance of the electoral realm has been supported not only by such symbolic work but has also been structurally produced through the constitution as well as the ruling party's dominance of the media and state resources (Makulilo 2015; Phillips 2011, 2015).

5. Abby Nkungu, "JK Warns Districts on Food Reports," *Sunday News*, January 15, 2006.

6. In February 2006, I helped members of the village's Committee for Children from the Most Vulnerable Environments to carry out a survey on the food situation of the village's poorest households.

7. If NyaMariamu and her two children living at home were to eat two meals a day, they would need 3 liters of grain.

8. See, for example, A. Lugungulo, "Starving Villagers Now Eating Grass," *Guardian*, February 25, 2006.

9. P. Kisembo, "Food Aid Must Go with the Will to Work," *Guardian*, March 16, 2006.

10. A district official explained to me that the school food could not arrive because the government had monopolized lorries and trains for its own food aid. Finally, in late February, the school food program resumed. It is notable that during the absence of school food (which was assumed to be temporary) attendance did not drop significantly at the school.

11. Due to rural Singida's remote location and lack of exploitable resources, virtually all people of European descent living in the district between 2004 and 2014 were either volunteers, missionaries, or representatives of development organizations. Nearly all came bearing resources to support their particular agendas. There was neither tourism nor Western business operating in Singida during the time of my fieldwork.

12. L. Mamushu, "Apora debe tatu za mahindi na kuuawa," *Nipashe*, January 15, 2006.

13. In addition to hearing this rhetoric in these 2006 visits, I had also attended numerous election campaign visits by parliamentary and ward councilor candidates and officials from the ruling party in 2005 that were filled with this kind of rhetoric about the food aid they had given during the 1998 and 2003 famines.

PART III: SUBSISTENCE CITIZENSHIP

5 Subsistence versus Development

> The peasant family's problem, put starkly, was to produce enough rice to feed the household, buy a few necessities such as salt and cloth, and meet the irreducible claims of outsiders.
>
> James Scott, *The Moral Economy of the Peasant*

BETWEEN 2005 AND 2010, demands on villagers to contribute labor and resources to development projects (what Tanzanians call *michango*, or "contributions") snowballed amid normal seasonal food insecurity and years of irregular rainfall and more intense food crisis. As Singidans were repeatedly pushed to the threshold of subsistence during this period, the terms of the political contract between rural Singidans and their government (in which their labor for the nation guaranteed them a minimal set of rights) were set askew. State officials justified the increase in michango (that came in the form of extractive, unregulated, and sometimes even violent taxation) with the contemporary political narrative of "participation." With such narratives, officials suggested that rural Singidans are poor because they have not yet contributed to national development. But the more untenable such demands became, the more Singidans switched political codes, from an idiom of helping their political fathers to build the nation, to their labor as a market commodity that entitled them to wages, to a political critique of the differentiated terrain of citizenship in Tanzania that distributes the rights, obligations, and protections of citizenship in vastly uneven ways. To start, let us sketch out two scenes from Singida that are suggestive of the sociopolitical and rhetorical backdrop of these events.

Each year, the *Mwenge wa Uhuru*, (or "Torch of Freedom"), is "raced" across Tanzania to highlight accomplishments in national development.[1] On its journey, it passes through each region in the Republic to symbolize freedom and light, bringing "hope where there is despair, love where there is enmity and respect where there is hatred" (Consulate of the United Republic of Tanzania, 2015). In 2005, blustering October winds greeted the caravan of sports-utility vehicles when Mwenge finally arrived in rural Singida, snaking its way southward from Iramba district. Singida region held the 2005 honor of being the last region to receive Mwenge after its three-month race around the nation to honor and motivate development.

Figure 5.1. Two Singida men collect sand to make bricks for a primary school construction project.
Photo by author, 2005.

The 2005 Mwenge tour of Singida promised to be a festive one, culminating in the arrival of President Mkapa himself to extinguish it in Singida Town. On the Singida-Iramba border, district officials, schoolchildren, a bugling brass band, and female dancers wrapped in brightly covered cloth received the torch's six beret-capped bearers, who quickly donned gas masks to protect themselves from the fumes and huddled around the torch to protect it from the dusty gusts. From the border, the festive caravan made its way through Singida district, stopping in several villages along the way to preach the 2005 Mwenge message of development and to commemorate the successful completion of school buildings, clinics, and other development projects.

In Langilanga village, the leaders had prepared well. A new monument to "Participation" stood erect by the roadside. And the head of the Participatory Rural Appraisal (PRA) committee detailed the history of Langilanga's accomplishments to the assembled crowd: through the much-lauded participatory approach the village had constructed a primary school, a pre-school, and teacher housing and they were preparing to dig a deep-water well. They foresaw a health clinic, a dam in the wetlands, and even electricity in their future. In spite of their hardships, the "light"—the elder recounted—had come early to the village of Langilanga.

A few villagers then performed a skit for the visitors, who now sat ceremoniously protected from the wind in a temporary shelter erected for the special guests. With a hand hoe, the village chairman traced a wavy line in the sandy courtyard of the village office, and pretended he was farming next to a river. In the skit, three people came upon the farmer and announced they needed to cross the river to go vote in their village election. But the river was overflowing with water so they asked the farmer: "Say, farmer, how can we cross this river?" The farmer responded, "I will help you." He carried the first person across the river on his shoulders. The second person was carried, but he fell into the river. The third person refused to be carried and asked that he be shown how to cross the river himself. And so the third traveler followed in the footsteps of the farmer until they crossed the river. The farmer wished them well with voting and continued with his work.[2]

A village official then asked the Mwenge audience: "What does this skit teach us?" One man responded. "In the years past we were used to being helped, just like the first person who was carried over the river. But now we need to learn from our specialists so that we citizens may rely on ourselves. We should no longer rely on the district, the region, or foreign sponsors to carry us." The Mwenge guests murmured their approval and the leader of the Mwenge caravan stood to deliver to Langilanga the message he had taken across Tanzania that year: of hope for peace in the upcoming presidential elections, the election of good leadership, and a call for unity and non-discrimination in the war against HIV/AIDS. Though his dress was militant, and his urban coastal Swahili rapid-fire, his tone was fatherly—typical of mainstream Tanzanian political rhetoric: scolding, teasing, tender, persuasive. He congratulated the people of Langilanga on their impressive monument and their enthusiastic participation in development. "If only all Tanzanians could participate so well." "But," he reminded them, "*usishirikishwe, ujishirikishe*." Taking advantage of Swahili's conjugational forms, the leader urged the villagers not to wait for someone else to participate *them* but rather to *make themselves* participate—a distinction, I will go on to elaborate, deeply relevant to the contemporary ideology of development in rural Tanzania.

This local celebration of Mwenge serves as what Murray Edelman has called a "political spectacle" in which the production of stories and histories of the Tanzanian state comes to light (1998; cf. Haugerud 1995). It is a ritual of solidarity, in which all Tanzanians stand together behind the project of development through their commitment to "participation." Yet the occasion serves also as a rite of differentiation, one that delineates historical distinctions between groups of people and their rights, responsibilities, and roles in development. Participants are divided into those who perform their mastery of state ideology, and those who appraise the performance; those who are paid for "performing the nation" and those who pay for it[3] (see Askew 2002). The event showcases the production of the "up-there state" and the "social and imaginative processes through which state verticality is made effective and authoritative" (Ferguson & Gupta 2002, 983).

A teleology also emerges in this performance of participation and self-reliance: one that implies that those individuals who already have schools and hospitals have already helped themselves and that those who do not, are those who have not yet made their contribution to the nation. The script of the skit quietly alludes to the "free-loading" of villagers, at the expense of the labor of the state, embodied as an industrial rural farmer who carries the villagers toward progress. In the process of re-writing history, the skit suggests to Singida villagers—"enough taking without giving—it's your turn now."

The story embedded in this ritual, replicates much of the international rhetoric of participation and development (namely, that top-down policies have disempowered people, producing dependency rather than self-reliant citizens). However, it belies both the histories of rural extraction and coercion that I detailed in chapter 2, and rural Singidans' experience of citizenship in the present day. To consider this contemporary experience of citizenship, let us turn to another slice of life from contemporary Singida.

One night in 2005 a regular shipment of internationally-funded school food arrived in Langilanga village. Because of the late hour, none of the older students who normally unloaded the trucks were present at the school. So, the head teacher called on eight village men to help unload the sacks of maize and beans. With their task complete, the men demanded a total of ten dollars for their labor. The head teacher refused, but the men continued to insist, so the head teacher agreed to at least consult the rest of the school committee on the issue.

The school committee met a few days later for its monthly meeting. The head teacher explained the situation to a chorus of tongue clicks of disapproval from the other members. "But this food is going to feed *their* children!" argued a primary school teacher. "Why can't they volunteer simply for the good of their children?" "It took only a short time, and it's for the good of the community," argued the village executive director. "How can they demand money on top of that?" "We will give them 'tea,' or, a 'tip,' but not a 'wage.' It must be only a 'little something.' If the villagers start demanding a wage now for everything, will they ever 'participate' again?" In the end, the committee agreed to offer the men 50 cents, "as tea only, not as a wage."

"Community participation" is a cornerstone of contemporary development policy. In return for the aforementioned supply of school food, for example, communities are required to give cash and in-kind contributions to support school cooks, supply fuel and water, and construct a school kitchen. To most on-lookers, these contributions seem a fair exchange for two well-balanced meals served to primary school students each day. Yet the episode above raises the question of why and how those who are paid for labor that serves their children, their community, and their nation (the schoolteacher and the village executive director, for example) may determine that others shall not be remunerated. In this scenario, different kinds of rights and responsibilities are apportioned to different categories of citizen (McGovern 2011, 204). The social projects of participation and development re-group and re-order people to grant them uneven rights to their own labor, property, and means of subsistence. It also highlights a key mechanism of subsistence citizenship; that is, the way people pull labor (similar to the way they pull food) in and out of different discourses of distribution. In different times and different spaces and to different people, labor may be a market commodity, a duty of a client to a patron, part of a political contract that guarantees certain rights, or a donation born of good will to a social entity beyond oneself.

Rural communities in Singida participated in state and international development initiatives during a period of severe food insecurity between 2005 and 2007. This participation consisted mainly of the snowballing of mandated contributions (cash, labor, and in-kind) to village development initiatives during a famine year. The differentiated citizenship at play in these politics of participation "uses social differences that are *not* the basis of national membership ... to distribute different treatment to different categories of citizens" (Holston 2008, 7). These categories included their spatial relation to existing development infrastructures, the market value of people's labor, and the fulfillment of responsibilities in return for rights. This "unsettling" of citizenship is exemplary of larger trends identified across the globe and it has been one way that the state and its subjects have dealt with scarcity of labor and resources amid soaring expectations of economic development (James 2013; Kymlikca & Norman 1994; Li 2007). These political shifts have high stakes, for onerous development demands pushed many rural Singidans to the threshold of subsistence between 2005 and 2010. Singidans' political backlash in the 2010 elections against these excessive demands by the state will be the subject of chapter 6.

The New Participation: Development Policy in Tanzania since the 1980s

The contributions of labor and resources so central to development projects in Singida in the first decade of the new millennium were not necessarily anything new, even if their logics, intents, and discourses had shifted. As I detailed in chapter 2—and as Jellicoe and Jennings have written of the colonial and early socialist periods in Tanzania, respectively—community labor and taxation was essential to the emergence of regional infrastructures and the rural state from the late nineteenth to throughout the twentieth century. (Jellicoe 1978; Jennings 2003). I pick up on this history now in the 1980s to describe the new constellation of policy, ideology and practice attached to "participation" in the new millennium.

The terms of structural adjustment (accepted in return for loans from international finance institutions) included the privatization of state services. Through the implementation of user-fees, Tanzania's debt-laden government shifted the responsibility for services like education, health care, and social development to local governments, families and their communities, which devastated the social sector (International Monetary Fund 1999; for further discussion see Vavrus 2005). Similar to many other African contexts, this "outsourcing" of government and market-oriented vision of citizenship emphasized individual responsibility for well-being and livelihood. As Deborah James has noted in the South African context: "A generalized social and cultural 'pressure' was emerging, with the aid of but not solely determined by the government, in which only those who fulfil their responsibilities would be entitled to the rights of the citizen, and in which such rights would not necessarily be guaranteed by the state" (James 2013, 27).[4] Of course, this was not exactly a new turn of events, given earlier practices of withholding famine relief from those not doing their part to build the nation (by moving into ujamaa villages, for example; see Schneider 2014). But this shift in governance clearly contracted the scope of entitlements promised by national citizenship and employed the emerging commonsense of the development industry—"community participation"—to legitimate this.

By 2000, the intensification of poverty and the new impetus provided by the Millennium Development Goals led the Tanzanian government to implement new measures to reduce poverty and expand access to educational, health, agricultural, and water resources. At this time, the same policies that had called for the privatization of social services also created a fertile environment for "community participation" to emerge as an economically palatable national strategy for development. Such approaches to development had been supported since the 1970s by left-leaning advocates seeking to increase the autonomy of local peoples in transnational projects. Yet these strategies also complemented international organization agendas to shrink state responsibilities and state expenditures and to increase "local buy-in" (and hence—the logic went—sustainability) in development projects.

This decentralization trend in Tanzania's national development policy also converged with the mainstreaming of grassroots participatory development techniques like Participatory Rural Appraisal (PRA; see Chambers 1983; 1995; 2002; 2008). Despite its reputation for obstinacy in the face of development initiatives, Singida emerged as a frontrunner among Tanzania's 26 regions in employing PRA to implement development projects. PRA owed much of its early success to the leadership of former Singida Regional Commissioner Anatoli Albibi Tarimo as well as to two nongovernmental organizations—HAPA and Caritas—and to their Singida offices' charismatic leaders.[5] After two relatively successful pilot phases by the NGOs in a total of seven Singida villages, Singida became the first region in Tanzania to adopt a "participatory approach" as a regional government strategy for village development. Subsequently, other regions adopted a variety of pre-packaged participatory programs. In line with international pressure to democratize and decentralize, "participation" was soon incorporated into nearly every Tanzanian policy, from primary school reform to the development of water infrastructure. Again, this language was not necessarily new but participation was now part of a different constellation of ideas and practices that included the abdication of the state and its obligation to care (Jellicoe 1978; Jennings 2003; see Schneider 2014).

Underlying these Tanzanian policy shifts are deeply embedded international and local institutional beliefs in how participation works as a sustainable development strategy. A seminal World Bank study by Deepa Narayan is oft-cited as evidence that participation has a more positive effect on sustainability than projects with no or minimal participation (1995). Other studies identify upfront cash contributions and the provision of labor and other materials by community members as essential features of rural development projects (Sara & Katz 1998; Kleemeier 2000). According to these studies, citizens develop a sense of community "ownership," "value," and "stakeholding," which encourages the maintenance of development goods because they have purchased them (932).[6] As one American NGO director in Singida stated flatly in 2007: "if they don't contribute, they don't value the project. It doesn't matter how small the contribution is, as long as they give something" (see also the critique by Palotti 2008).

Three other national policy reforms roughly coincided with the adoption of explicitly participatory strategies in Tanzania. First, beginning in 2001, the Tanzanian government abolished primary school fees. Second, a 2003 tax law abolished the local development levy (a flat rate development tax on each individual) (World Bank 2006). As an alternative, any "self-help" project voted on by the village council legitimated the collection of a cash or in-kind contribution. This reform intended to abolish flat-rate local taxes in favor of restructured property and business taxes on the more well-off and to improve morale at the local level by providing greater transparency for the use of development taxes.

The third major change in the development policy context took place through the Local Government Reform Programme (LGRP) beginning in 2002. This involved the decentralization of fiscal management and an attempt to train and structurally empower village councils to produce and implement their own development agendas. In addition to bringing governance closer to the people, the reform sought more coordination among ministries carrying out contemporaneous development projects in the same place. Yet the LGRP and the abolishment of the development levy tended to work as opposing forces, with the LGRP increasing the authority and responsibilities of village, district, and regional councils and the abolishment of the development levy essentially taking away a good part of their operating funds (for further discussion, see REPOA 2006).

In any case, it was through PRA that Singida villages produced ambitious development agendas at the turn of the millennium in a context of ever-increasing uncertainty about who would fund them. With school fees and the development levy abolished, schools and village councils became more dependent on funding from the central government. Though the government was promised "basket funding" from foreign donors for these reforms, the transfer of funds was often exceedingly delayed and there was speculation that it had been "eaten" by upper level officials (Phillips 2009). Reform, on the other hand, was at the forefront of expectations, both among rural populations and policymakers at home and abroad. With pressure from "above" and "below" to realize the promise of development, village governments (like Langilanga, as I describe below) began increasingly to draw on old techniques—false promises, the seizure of property, coercion, even criminalization—wrapped in shiny new paper, (the language of "participation") to secure the resources necessary to move their technical development agendas forward.

During this time, the implementation of PRA in Singida had fundamentally changed from its early implementation as a small-scale strategy for a kind of Freirian conscientization and empowerment of rural communities to make use of their own resources, to its appropriation as a mass mobilization of labor and capital in the pursuit of a state and international agenda driven by "accountability" and "results." In its earliest incarnations in Singida, HAPA and Caritas had used PRA not only to come to consensus about technical problems and solutions they would seek, but also to talk about relationships within and beyond the village. The latter objective quickly fell to the wayside in the face of the mass production of "participation" and state and donor deadlines for tangible results.

In any event, the PRA process in Singida was quickly reduced to the production of a laundry list of projects for which the government might provide pre-packaged technical solutions. A 2006 REPOA report found in its study of six districts in Tanzania that "bottom-up planning was in practice an *ad hoc* exercise, with the actual planning carried out by the council management team" (1). This certainly seemed the case in the PRA planning exercise I observed in 2004 in one rural Singida village. In contrast to the detailed reflection I had discovered in the written records of Langilanga PRA exercises (that had taken place during the pilot phases of PRA), the 2004 exercise was constrained by the short timeframe for discussion as well as expectations from the community and the district government that certain kinds of solutions should quickly emerge (recommendations to build schools, clinics, wells, etc.). As a regional leader of Caritas (a Nyaturu man himself) reflected in the case of Langilanga: "We wanted to address the issue of livelihood. But people always see development as the development of infrastructure only. They don't look at decision-making.... Community participation requires time to discuss issues, conflicts, and find new ways of dealing with them. PRA became something different though: 'look how many schools, how many buildings we've constructed.' And politicians want physical trophies. They don't look at the development of people." PRA had become an exercise in defining community problems in direct relation to pre-packaged technical solutions rather than exploring community problems as rooted in social, political, economic relationships—as well as technical deficiencies.

Michango in Singida

Langilanga village, as I have already described, is a village not unlike others in rural Singida. In 2005–2007 (the period in which these events took place) it had a population of approximately 2600 people. In 2006 the majority of households in rural Singida earned an annual income between 150,000 TSH (US$120) and 300,000 TSH (US$240) (Chastre & Kindness 2006). It was regularly difficult to make ends meet, even without paying mandated contributions.

Early in the new millennium Langilanga had shown itself to be a village worthy of development investment. It participated in the regional pilot program for Participatory Rural Appraisal and was one of the first Singida villages in the new millennial development wave to construct its own primary school with cash and labor contributions from community members and government funding for cement and roofing material. Though a few villagers complained that some of the financial contributions were coerced (with goats and chickens forcibly seized from those unwilling to contribute) there was a strong sense of accomplishment when I began my fieldwork toward the end of 2004.

A few months into my fieldwork in early 2005, I was approached by village leaders for a loan of US$500. A major international finance institution had arranged with district authorities to dig a deep-water well in Langilanga, but, in line with the participatory zeitgeist of the day, the project mandated a commitment of 10 percent of the total cost from the district and 5 percent from the village. The institution was now demanding its first installment as evidence of "commitment" from the village and as a requirement for work to begin. Langilanga leaders, thrilled to be chosen for a project that would guarantee the village access to water year-round, scrambled to collect 6500 TSH (approximately US$6 at the time) from each villager by the deadline. But after an initial round of contributions from villagers to the project, collections had stalled. The main reason for the shortfall, apparently, was that villagers had refused to divide up the debt in any way but at a flat rate. Whether cattle-owner or landless widow, all were required to pay the same amount. The village government was not without compassion, however, and its officials forgave or halved the debts of some of the village's oldest and poorest members. But the result was that even if everyone else contributed fully, the total would fall short. I agreed to contribute the money to the project, not as a loan, but as an initial installment of supplemental rent to the village for my residence in Langilanga (like the teachers and agricultural expert who also rented rooms in the village office where I lived, I regularly paid rent equivalent to one dollar per month).

Within a year's time, work on the well began, but the village remained indebted to the international finance institution. The village government subsequently announced a second wave of water contributions (to meet the shortfall) in what was to be by far the most intensive year of "contributions" that people in Langilanga had experienced yet. Many households resisted this second contribution, charging the village Water Committee with "eating the money" they had so far collected for the project. Consequently, the Water Committee, in an effort to defend its honor, went on the offensive against all who had not contributed. They seized chickens, goats, cattle, until they unknowingly seized the goat of the Ward Executive Director, whose elderly mother had not paid the contribution. He called property seizure to a halt and requested that the Committee instead provide the Ward Office with the names of non-contributors, so they could be dealt with appropriately. It was a slippery slope from defining rural populations as "underserved" to defining them as "underserving," and criminally so.

Meanwhile, as the harvest season approached (the time of year most contributions are mandated), the government announced one contribution after the next: for improvements to the division secondary school; for gas for the Mwenge parade; for the salaries of cooks and guards for the school; for construction of desks and chairs; for celebrations for International Women's Day and seventh grade graduation; for the Committee for the Children from the Most Vulnerable Environments, and for the CCM campaign. And these mandated contributions came on top of parents' additional contributions to the school for lunches, books, exam fees, and school uniforms as well as everyone's routine voluntary contributions to needy kin, to life events (weddings and funerals), and to their religious organizations. (With the exception of aid to needy kin, all of these financial transactions are also referred to as michango).

Community labor was also required for all funded development projects such as the digging of school latrines, the construction of classroom buildings and teacher housing, and the construction of a cattle watering place in the wetlands. Women were asked to carry water and sand and men would use these to make bricks and also carry heavy stones. All this came in the midst of a severe drought in 2005 (and subsequent food shortage in 2006) that drained cash reserves, lowered the value of labor and limited opportunities to be paid for it, and heightened anxiety throughout the region.

What pushed many villagers from complaining compliance into outright refusal was a 2006 order that came from Tanzanian Prime Minister Lowassa himself, that a secondary school be built in each ward before the start of the new term. Though the reform guaranteed funding in return for community "in-kind" contributions, ward officials had received no funds to implement the directive.

Figures 5.2 & 5.3. Rural Singidans make and bake bricks in the sun for a primary school classroom construction project.
Photos by author, 2005.

Figure 5.4. A man who has been asked by village government authorities for the use of his ox and cart (for the reconstruction of school latrines) demands to be paid.
Photo by author, 2005.

The ward therefore mandated a new "contribution" of TSH 24,000 (US$22) per head (four times the contribution that had been mandated for the water project). Still waiting for any government funding, the ward eked out a Form 1 building by the deadline with community labor, contributions, and some assistance (the "gift" of sheet iron for the roof) from its parliamentary representative. (Other wards were not so successful, to the point that, on the outskirts of Dar es Salaam, secondary students were shocked to find themselves allocated to "ghost schools.")[7] In other gross distortions of the policy, ward officials—in desperation to meet the deadlines—began converting primary school buildings into secondary schools and creating virtually overnight certification programs to turn primary teachers into secondary teachers. A 2006 cartoon by David Chikoko from the *Tanzanian Guardian* caricatured a very westernized "witch" casting a spell to turn "*Usinigeuze*" ("Don't Convert Me") Primary School into a secondary school.

The reaction of Singida communities to the exorbitant secondary school contribution was, in general, one of dismay. Although the rains had eventually arrived in 2006, people were still recovering from the food shortage, and the

2007 rains did not promise abundance. One resident of Suna village declared the policy absurd:

> Yesterday we said, "let's build a secondary school for our ward." They said each person should pay 24,000 shillings. So, I stood up and said, *jamaani*, right now we have the construction of a teacher house … and then there's contributions to the desks, the water project, and Mwenge, and now today you say a secondary school contribution. We won't refuse, but let's look and see. If we think this secondary is so important, then let's leave these other contributions for a while, because even rich people don't plan like that. They plan and say this year, let's accomplish this and next year, we'll accomplish that.

In early 2007, one of Langilanga's leaders confided in me: "The food shortage this year … it will be worse than last time. What is killing us is this contribution to the secondary school. They tell us we will receive 5 million shillings from the central government and 2 million shillings from the district, but we have seen nothing yet." "What happened to PRA?" I asked him. "What of prioritizing village projects and finding manageable ways to realize them?" "No," the chairman replied, "This is not like under Mkapa. 'Cooperation' is very far away now." The "will to improve" the conditions of rural life in Tanzania had taken on a life of its own. And in placing the responsibility for development squarely on the shoulders of "incarcerated" rural communities, "participation" had begun to look very much like a targeted tax on the poorest of the rural poor (Li, 2007).

Between 2005 and 2012 I interviewed people about the practice of michango. All Singidans I spoke with agreed upon one thing. Despite the consistency in *rhetoric* used to elicit michango (often in terms of self-reliance and nation-building), the *practice* of michango was quantitatively and qualitatively different than it was 30 years before. The amount of contributions mandated had skyrocketed; the rate of requests had snowballed; and the tactics used to elicit and collect michango had become far more coercive.

People described this difference in tactic in terms of two Nyaturu concepts: *majighana* (Ny. "voluntary action") and *witegheyi* (Ny. "listening to each other"). For example, one elder noted: "During colonialism, there was no listening to each other. There was no witegheyi. It was just a command. 'A school will be built someplace,' the Chief would say. And it was done. They were given a command, an order that comes from afar, even if you don't know the benefit of the school. There was no voluntary action. They would take your chicken, your goat, or cow. There is no meeting. Only the Chief knows. You are given work without agreeing to it. It's someone else's decision." He went on to describe Nyerere's michango, which he related in idealized terms: "During Nyerere's time, leaders would say, 'Let's have a meeting so that people understand the importance of school and the problems of the school.' And we'd say, 'yes, the children have to walk very far. There's no school here.' And so we would decide, let's make bricks, like this, like this, and like this. And people would say, *ndiyo!* (yes!)." He noted that the present is a mix of these two histories: "These days—sometimes it's like Nyerere's times. But other times, like with the ward schools, it's just a command. So sometimes it's like Nyerere, and sometimes it's like colonialism." This characterization of Nyerere's michango certainly whitewashes the history of coercion in development during the socialist period. Yet it also suggests that people perceived the overall constellation and intentions of michango under Nyerere to be far more politically legitimate.[8]

A middle-aged village woman in Singida also drew on this same distinction to explain the shifts in michango. "Majighana," she explained, "means to do something voluntarily, by your own decision, for your own happiness. It means to not be forced." Witegheyi she described as "listening to each other and sitting together." According to her, both criteria for peaceful michango were possible in the present, but not always practiced.

My neighbor in Langilanga village, Mzee Omari, noted that nowadays, the problem was that there was no *siasa* (politics) involved in michango. I prodded Mzee Omari for additional clarification here, given that siasa often carries a negative connotation in rural Tanzania, implying conflict and disagreement in a political context that has prioritized consensus. He responded, "Siasa is good!" and went on to explain it as the need for political persuasion regarding community contributions and the time required to listen to each other debate the pros and cons of a particular project or plan.

In any case, there was general agreement that contributing to development efforts through cash and labor was nothing new—such initiatives had been common throughout people's lifetime. Yet people complained now about the complete lack of legislation or coordination of michango, now that school fees and the development tax had been abolished. Now that the development of rural infrastructure had been so decentralized and privatized, village governments had to be self-enterprising entities and were therefore reluctant to turn down any prospects for infrastructural investment, which bound the village into contributions. They also felt that the cancellation of school fees, far from releasing them from the costs of educating their children, allowed teachers and school committees to place unlimited demands on parents for educational costs, for which, they suspected, government money was supposed to be there. As one parent complained:

> People were surprised that school fees were abolished. They thought, "I am poor and now I have the right to send my child to school." But later they discovered that the primary school reform policy had some problems. The government was very clever, it abolished school fees so that they could benefit. With school fees the contribution for one student was 2500 shillings. Every once in a while, you would contribute for desks or other materials. But now people say better to pay

fees than to continue paying these michango to the school, which now exceed 6000 shillings. They say the fees have been abolished but now we contribute much more than in the past. And there are many things they try to cover up. They are given money for books but most of it is paid by the parents with michango.

Another parent noted: "They should stop saying education is free. Education is not free now."

When I interviewed a Tanzanian development official employed by the World Bank, she acknowledged that michango had emerged as a serious problem in the implementation of poverty reduction policies. She noted a study carried out in Kilimanjaro where, despite the abolition of school fees, parents were required to contribute an average of 58,000 shillings (about US$53 in 2006) per year, far more than the official school fees had been prior to their abolition. She observed that requirements to pay michango were not actually legal and that as far as donors were concerned, education should be free. An official of a European embassy that was funding and helping to plan the secondary school reform emphasized to me in a 2006 interview that school construction was fully funded and expressed dismay at my reports of mandated contributions. According to official plans, villagers were not to be contributing any money, though small contributions of time and labor were expected.

People acknowledged that these excessive michango were primarily a rural phenomenon. Senge, a 26-year-old man from urban Singida explained: "To pass from house to house asking for michango? It is very hard here in the city. People are too clever. But villagers are bothered a lot. Every time a person is told by a leader that there will be michango, he has to be afraid. If he doesn't have the money he goes to borrow it from someone else or he sells something that could have helped him later so that he can pay these michango." In a 2006 interview, an upper-level official at the Ministry of Education and Culture (later re-named the Ministry of Education and Vocational Training) agreed with this perception, noting that, "Urban people are too clever (*wajanja*). Rural people contribute a lot of money; urban people won't."

Local leaders spoke to the issue of coercion in the collection of michango. I asked one village leader why it was that Langilangans were so much better at participation than their neighbors in Suna village (with whom they were often compared), was it their *moyo* ("heart" or, colloquially, "conviction") or their leaders? He replied, "These villagers are better participators because they have been taught. It's like with a student. If you hit him with a stick without teaching him the lesson, it won't help. If you hit him with a stick and you also teach him, it will be good. He will understand." But he also lamented the waning enthusiasm of villagers to "participate." "People don't want to volunteer. Everyone wants to be paid. It's necessary to push them with force more than before."

I also inquired among village leaders about the ethics of mandating labor and cash contributions to development in a hunger year. One explained the frustration of villagers' position and their choice to "work by pushing themselves" in the face of hunger:

> A person might have eaten in the evening, but in the morning he hasn't even eaten his breakfast, and it's required that he go to the community development projects. And we can't delay the projects because we have been sponsored, for example as in the case of the cattle watering place. If you finish digging the cattle watering place you can't wait, it's time for people to carry the rocks and lay them. Now, if rocks are the responsibility of the people to bring, it's necessary that we just continue so that we don't lose our sponsorship so that we can get ourselves some development. If we let up, we have to return the money.

Villagers sometimes used this immediate demand for labor by the village government to negotiate for food aid. As I described in chapter 4, in the hungry months of 2006, people went on strike, refusing to participate in development projects until food relief was brought and distributed to all those in the village.

The year 2005 was one of elections, and though michango was not a primary campaign topic, one opposition candidate from the Civic United Front told me it was a major concern for some of his constituents. In any event, CCM dominated the 2005 elections in Singida, and the politics of michango continued as usual. The political side of this story will continue in chapter 6.

Dividing the Labor of Development: The Duties of Subsistence Citizenship

To be sure, many participatory development initiatives have very different intents than the effects I have described here. Many well-meaning people and institutions intend participatory approaches to give villagers' voice in decisions about development initiatives. Yet when taken to scale participatory development projects and policies are never carried out without an official eye toward pressurized accountability frameworks and sluggish, inadequate and leaking funding chains. Nor can they be easily disentangled from local histories of colony- and nation-building, in which contemporary policies find firm footholds. But what emerges clearly from the situation presented here is that entitlements from and obligations to the state in Tanzania are born unevenly by Tanzanians. What remains to articulate is the way in which they are born, by whom, and to what effects.

Several distinctions among citizens become very apparent in the situation presented here. There is a distinction between those who already have access to basic infrastructure and services (schools, clinics, water, etc.), and those who do not who are expected to labor for it. Onto this distinction is mapped a narrative of labor for the nation—that those who have already have schools and clinics within a reasonable distance have already made their contribution to the nation, while those who do not have those services, have not yet gotten on board with development. What this narrative of "good citizens" and "bad citizens" muddles however, is the spatial dimension of infrastructural development, in which planning and implementation occurs using the bureaucratic gradations of the Tanzanian government. In Tanzania, the government initially committed to building a secondary school in every region, and then in every division of that region, and then in every ward of each division. Those people living in the ward where the original regional secondary school was built contributed cash and labor one time for the construction of a secondary school. Those who lived in the ward where the division secondary school was built contributed two times. Those living in outlying wards contributed three times. The story does not end here, for it is planned that Langilanga itself will soon split into four villages, becoming a ward unto itself that needs its own secondary school and villagers will pay a fourth time. The same phenomenon occurs with the digging of wells, and the construction of clinics and primary schools, and so on. In the process, the labor of "building the nation" radiates out from political centers, disproportionately burdening the most rural populations.

Another distinction of note here is the division between those who decide how and when development happens (the state at the national and local level) and those who bear the costs and labor of development (rural citizens—some more than others). Those in formal employ or who possess specialized skills (masons or carpenters or local businesspeople, for example) are not generally asked to contribute labor for free, for their labor has value on the market. But just because some labor is virtually valueless, does not mean that its supply is limitless; those whose labor is assumed to be inexhaustible are those most struggling to eke their basic needs out of a relatively unaccommodating environment. Moreover, this group who has the least access to a means of subsistence is asked to contribute *most* to community development projects and yet they have the *least say* in how and when it happens.

This is not to say that those who make decisions do not face their own set of constraints, tensions and concerns. In these intercalary, or interhierarchical roles, state agents perform the political work needed "to align the interests and strategies of high-level state actors and those of local actors, down to the level of farmers in villages" (McGovern 2011).[9] It is the village leadership who grapples to reconcile communities' ambitious development agendas in a context of ever-increasing uncertainty about who will fund them. Leading villagers in the effort to "work by pushing themselves"—even in the face of hunger—in order to capture state resources is neither an easy nor an enviable task.

And yet in spite of all these distinctions, there also exists *a failure to distinguish*—between the ways different individuals and groups are positioned to financially contribute to these initiatives—by instituting a flat-rate contribution, instead of one which considers people's ability to pay. Such a strategy reflects both a local and a national rhetoric that insists, "we are all poor here" and must come together to build the nation. Yet it belies existing disparities in wealth, both at the national and local level. In the decision to implement a flat-rate mandated contribution, there was insufficient consideration of the relative cost of such an amount to different households. For some households the opportunity cost of such a contribution might be the sale of a goat and the loss of that money for business investment. For others, it might mean the loss of two days' worth of food.

The local legitimacy of such projects could be said to be measured by the extent to which mandated contributions push a household to the threshold of subsistence—which varies across households. The divisions drawn by these differing experiences no doubt underlay the tensions between groups of villagers who are said to "like development" (and are held in favor by the local government) and those who "don't like development" (and are held in contempt by it). Ultimately, those who cannot contribute are released from the debt if they truly cannot pay. But this debt forgiveness only reinforces their dubious standing in the community. And the variation in political voice produced in this kind of extractive participation both generates and deepens the gradations of membership so characteristic of subsistence citizenship.

What then, were the mixed effects of such initiatives? The secondary school was up and running by the end of 2007, though it was understaffed and under-resourced. Many Singidans complained that the kind of education their children received in these hastily constructed schools and their emergency-certified staff would not significantly alter their or their children's economic situation. One college-educated Singidan living in Dar stated flatly: "These secondary schools that Lowassa is building are *shule za siasa* ('schools born out of politics'). They are schools for poor kids. But they're failing. The rich kids can afford English-medium schools or international schools." Likewise, a Lutheran minister noted: "These schools that we construct so rapidly for MMES [the Primary Education Development Plan], we call them '*yebo yebo* schools' with *yebo yebo* teachers ... [*Yebo yebo* are plastic or old rubber flip flops]. These secondhand schools cannot change our poverty." Another local religious leader lamented to me:

> What is education for? How do we achieve it? It is not these school buildings we desperately race to erect all over the country. If we do not watch we are creating even bigger problems: The gap between rich and poor widens, families impoverish themselves for education, and yet kids still fail because there are no teachers or materials. Meanwhile rich kids go to schools with science laboratories. We just make fools, not educated people.... In this time to come, I fear for the young people. The ones in the cities will get by. But the ones in the rural areas will be lost.

And in Suna village, one outspoken critic of the ruling party was moved to a tirade: "The children of the government people ... go to private schools where one child is told to pay $400 a year. *Je*, someone like me, if my child is intelligent and wants to study ..., am I really going to educate him? I'll educate him according to my poverty."

By 2013, civil society leader Rakesh Rajani noted that even the government had acknowledged the poor quality of learning going on in schools:

> When I was working at Hakielimu [an NGO dedicated to improving access to education and quality learning opportunities for all Tanzanian children], we used to say, "The Emperor has no clothes! Kids are not learning." And yet the Government would argue that there is quality as well. But right now, no one in the government will tell you that. There is complete consensus that quality in education is poor. Just yesterday I was talking to [a top education official] and he said, "We all agree that quality is poor. What we disagree on is what it will take to change it."

Cartoonist Nathan Mpangala poignantly captured these disparities in educational quality in one of his cartoons. It depicts a little girl (representing the *watoto wa walalahoi*—the "children of the destitute") trying to peer up onto a desk, labeled "higher education." On the desk sits a little boy (representing the *watoto wa vigogo*—"the children of the 'dead wood' government"). The little girl exclaims: "Now I understand why they call it 'higher' education!" The cartoon points to people's frustration with their lack of access to higher education and the likelihood that [to paraphrase Paul Willis], governing class kids will get governing class jobs. And what seems to frustrate people most in rural Singida, is the extent to which their labor to construct educational opportunities for their children simply legitimates an educational system that has little to offer them in terms of social mobility.

Yet by my most recent visit in 2014, villagers were also commenting on the benefits of the ward secondary school. Though it was ill-equipped to teach, the school at least offered the opportunity for educational credentialing necessary to pursue other types of opportunities (like trade schools or technology training). Though most students ultimately failed the Form Four examination, some noted that for young people to sit in a classroom without a teacher, was preferable to having them sit at home. This "secondhand" secondary school was a step ahead for rural populations, and *pole pole ndio mwendo* ("slowly is the way") to development. From this perspective, these participatory politics had generated success, even if achieved through suffering. Some villagers had succeeded in capturing state and international organizational resources through showing support for national development agendas and contributing their labor and scarce resources.

In any event, if (as James Scott argued in 1976) exploitation is marked by the tipping point at which clients experience demands by patrons as threats to subsistence, then—given the number of people pushed to this threshold between 2005 and 2010—it is perhaps no surprise that the "safety-first" principle of politics broke down. In December 2010, Langilanga's voting district—Singida East—overturned five decades of loyalty to the ruling party, Chama cha Mapinduzi, to vote in Tundu Lissu, a charismatic candidate from the opposition party Chadema who promised, above all, "no more contributions." The smoke was clearing. A new politics of protest was at play in Singida. Let us turn to these politics in the next chapter.

Notes

1. The Mwenge torch has been raced each year since the eve of independence in 1961 when Peoples' Defence Forces army officer Lieutenant Alex Nyirenda planted both a Tanganyikan flag and a torch of freedom on Mount Kilimanjaro.

2. I came across the rough script for this skit in the office of the Singida Rural District Cultural Officer. It seemed to be an excerpt (written in English) of a larger program (that I did not locate) of community education on "participation."

3. The expenses of Mwenge (the most significant one being gasoline) are paid for by local contributions.

4. See also Chipkin 2003.

5. HAPA, the Health Action Promotion Association, was formerly a British NGO but is now a Tanzania-based organization. Caritas Tanzania is part of the Tanzania Episcopal Conference (TEC) and has coordinated charitable as well as social development activities in Tanzania since 1971.

6. This belief in the power of purchase, even when it is nominal, is articulated by Georg Simmel in his 1978 book, *The Philosophy of Money*. Simmel elaborated: "We desire objects only if they are not immediately given to us for our use and enjoyment; that is, to the extent that they resist our desire. The content of our desire becomes an object as soon as it is opposed to us, not only in the sense of being impervious to us, but also in terms of its distance as something not-yet-enjoyed, the subjective aspect of this condition being desire ... value does not originate from the unbroken unity of the moment of enjoyment, but from the separation between the subject and the content of enjoyment as an object that stands opposed to the subject as something desired and only to be attained by the conquest of distance, obstacles and difficulties" (Simmel 1978, 63–64).

7. Bilham Kimati, "Students Are Allocated to 'Ghost' School," *Guardian*, April 15, 2006.

8. I thank Leander Schneider for helping me to formulate this point.

9. In the present context, in which international donors and international organizations weigh in heavily during the production of national policy, national state actors as well as village leaders can be understood to occupy interhierarchical roles. I have discussed this extensively elsewhere (Phillips 2011).

6 Patronage, Rights, and the Idioms of Rural Citizenship

The outspoken lawyer and activist, Mr. Tundu Lissu (Chadema) was on Wednesday declared the new Member of Parliament for Singida East.... This is the first time in history since the multiparty politics was introduced in the country that an opposition party wins a parliamentary seat in the region.

Tanzania Daily News, November 3, 2010

IN 2010 THE gusty dry season winds brought political change to rural Singida. The Singida East parliamentary constituency overturned five decades of loyalty to Tanzania's ruling party (Chama cha Mapinduzi, or CCM) to vote in Tundu Lissu—a charismatic candidate from the opposition party Chadema (*Chama cha Demokrasia na Maendeleo*, or the "Party of Democracy and Development"). In this fourth-ever multiparty general election in Tanzania, rural Singidans declined for the first time CCM's claims to political seniority and continuity and opted instead for a candidate with a radically new platform: no more *michango*— the practice of mandating (sometimes forcefully) cash and in-kind contributions to state development projects.

That Lissu won the vote despite CCM's increasingly desperate measures to defeat him (including the re-drawing of constituency borders and a mass influx of funds for campaigning and ultimately contesting the elections) is testament to the political nerve he had tapped into with his michango platform. But Lissu's candidacy and subsequent victory provoked not only debates about how to achieve development and who should pay for it; but also about how Singidans are situated in relation to their government and how they practice politics. It raised important questions: What shifts (and possibly even continuities) had effected such a seeming transformation in rural Singidans' political preferences? How and why did Singida East constituents, whose political discourse in 2005 had been saturated with idioms of patronage and paternalism, endorse one of the most critical and radical opposition candidates in Tanzania to represent them? And to what effect?

The post-election reports I had out of Singida by phone and text were ones of jubilation. He had won! No more michango! On a national scale Lissu quickly became one of the most outspoken, critical, (and—by some—despised) figures in Tanzania's Parliament—a role that soon earned him the rank of Chief Opposition Whip. True to his word, the incessant—and at times violent—claims by local government officials on rural households in Singida slowed. Yet the high expectations generated during the three years of Lissu's campaign were dampened by Singidans' ongoing challenges to subsistence (2012 was another hunger year) and by their continued frustrations in accessing the development pledged to them in national policies. Lissu's leadership of an effective resistance against state predation had, some charged, resulted in the immobilization of development agendas meant to provide access to basic needs and services. What theoretical frame could make sense of this all? Had anything really changed?

The answer to these questions, I argue in this chapter, rests in the idea of subsistence citizenship. It lies in the way that Singidans have analyzed, understood, and come to navigate the conditions of rural life—driven as they are by cycles of scarcity and plenty, unpredictability, anxiety, invisibility, and unbearably high stakes—amid tremendous and increasing inequality. The escalation of michango—in a context of rising government mandates for development and yet the apparent evaporation of funding for them—was the tipping point at which Singidans experienced government demands as persistent threats to subsistence. Electoral rebellion occurred when a new political choice appeared on the scene and the "safety-first" principle that had long privileged CCM broke down. For a constituency that had long opted for political patronage (however sporadic and unreliable) over democratic representation, electing Lissu was a last resort in the face of rapidly disintegrating livelihoods.

These events and their aftermath also point to another key feature of subsistence citizenship: the oscillation between rights-based forms of political claims-making and patronage-based claims—a discussion begun in chapter 4. The ethnographic data presented in this chapter highlight patronage and rights as two forms of political practice that rural Tanzanians engage in contemporaneously but unevenly, as sometimes distinct discourses but with always overlapping practices, values, and assumptions. I first consider the predominance of patronage politics in Singida, its roots in the paternalism of the socialist period, and its symbolic, practical, and structural terms during the 2005 presidential and parliamentary elections. I go on to discuss the shifts that Lissu's michango politics introduced in rural Singida prior to the 2010 elections and Singidans' post-2010 efforts to re-embed Lissu's rights talk into a relationship-based politics. With perspectives collected between 2011 and 2014, I identify core values, uses, and constraints of rights- and patronage-based idioms of claims-making from the perspective of rural Singidans. The key tactics that constitute this political subjectivity are political code-switching (or oscillation) between rights- and patronage-based idioms of claims-making as well as code-mixing (a selective and partial synthesis that borrows from each of them) to construct a new form. In the context of rural Tanzania, neither rights nor patronage serve as catchall idioms of accountability. It is the very flexibility of claims-making—and its essential rootedness in core values of *both* rights *and* relationships—that allows poor rural people to capture as much of the state and subsistence as they do.

The Politics of Safety-First: Symbolic, Practical, and Structural Terms of Patronage

Many scholars of political rhetoric have noted the way in which state actors deploy the "cultural intimacy" of domestic images to extract loyalty from citizens and consolidate power (Herzfeld 1997; also Lakoff 2002; Askew 2002; Glassman 1995; and Herzfeld 1997). In a similar vein Cole and Durham have argued that "age and generational symbolism" have long "been used to naturalize situations of conquest and rule" (2006, 7). In Tanzania, to be sure, the idioms of kinship, fatherhood, and eldership have long been politically useful for conceptualizing and organizing the relationship between the government and its citizens and the relations of hierarchy, dependency, and power that they entail.

A central pillar and propagator of this political symbolism in Tanzania has been the mainland political party TANU (the Tanganyika African National Union) that ushered in independence and later came to be known as Chama cha Mapinduzi, or CCM. Until 1965 a number of parties vied for leadership in independent Tanzania, but by 1965, President Nyerere had pronounced Tanzania a one-party state. An independent Tanzania, Nyerere argued, had no need for multiple parties that would divide and fracture. The whole of the Tanzanian people could and should cease all argument, and speak with one voice—that of the party.[1] Nyerere's socialist vision, Ujamaa, centered on an idea of the "African Family" (Nyerere 1968). It is important to note that these politics of unity aimed for economic as well as political convergence throughout the 1960s and 70s. Nyerere himself was called the "father of the nation," and after his retirement from politics, CCM seemed to intensify its use of this reference to secure its own legitimacy (Schatzberg 2001). For if Nyerere was father of the nation-family, then CCM could pronounce itself the father of the government.

The need for CCM to jockey for party dominance increased as the socialist and one-party era drew to a close. By 1990 the Soviet Union had collapsed; the Western powers were using donor money to promote multipartyism; and Tanzania's African neighbors were moving toward multiparty democracies. A reform movement began voicing its dissent about the one-party state, and Nyerere himself, sensing a shift in the political winds, began a strong campaign for multipartyism inside CCM. The government convened a group to examine popular opinion about the matter. In the Nyalali Commission's historic referendum, only 21 percent of people surveyed supported a multiparty system, with

78 percent in favor of the current single-party approach. Despite this pervasive popular ambivalence about multipartyism, the commission supported the re-introduction of multipartyism, noting that it was in the country's "best interests." On May 7, 1992, Parliament approved a bill to make Tanzania a multiparty state. In the first multiparty general elections in 1995, CCM's Benjamin Mkapa was elected union president with 61.8 percent of the popular vote.

For the next ten years Mkapa presided over the continued liberalization of the Tanzanian economy. But CCM's continued insistence on a culture of political unity was challenged by the economic divergence that liberalization produced by the turn of the millennium. Cartoonist FeDë depicts the sense of jarring historical disjuncture that these shifts induced in Tanzania despite elite attempts to mask it. In the cartoon, "the period of Nyerere" is drawn with Nyerere as a father feeding a bottle to the suckling Tanzanian citizenry. This era represents a sharp contrast to the period of colonialism before it—depicted as a white farmer merrily drinking a bottle as he is pulled in a wagon by Tanzania, personified as a child in chains who is also hoeing the earth. It also contrasts with the contemporary moment—depicted as a well-fed "Leader" urinating on the child Tanzania who is kneeling in a puddle of urine as the "Leader" spouts socialist rhetoric: "Let's continue to join together so that we uphold peace, love, and unity." Though the relationship between government and citizenry shows sharp fissures between these three eras, consistencies in political discourse—"peace, love, and unity"— elide these discontinuities.[2]

And yet, despite increasing wealth disparities around the turn of the millennium, electoral support for the ruling party seemed to remain strong. After nearly two decades of economic liberalization, an Afrobarometer report based on surveys with over 2000 people found that in 2001 Tanzanians were highly politicized but not highly organized (Chaligha et al. 2002). They had high levels of dissatisfaction with the national economy (in fact they were some of the most dissatisfied citizens in Africa) and yet they were also extremely supportive of the economic reforms their government was making. The report also found that Tanzanians widely perceived corruption in the government, at the same time as they placed extremely high levels of trust in it. In fact, some Tanzanians seemed to trust the government more than the citizenry itself: 60 percent of respondents agreed that "People are like children; the government should take care of them like a parent" (Afrobarometer 2004; 2006; Ekman 2009).

In this idiom of political relations—narrated as a story of the happy nation-family—the Tanzanian state is "father" to its citizens. This idea of the nation as family implies a set of political norms—that is, ideas about how Tanzanians think others should act in the political sphere (even if people regularly transgress, contest, or criticize such norms) (see Brennan 2012; Ivaska 2005; Lal 2015; Phillips 2010; 2011; Schneider 2014). "Political children," this narrative goes, owe their

Figure 6.1. Singidans await Kikwete in Namfua Stadium in Singida Town.
Photo by author, 2005.

father allegiance, labor, and respect. The "father" in turn will provide, develop, care, guide, and discipline. A glimpse of this political narrative in use during my fieldwork in 2005 is illustrative.

On September 22, 2005, the people of Singida welcomed ruling party presidential candidate Jakaya Kikwete to the soccer stadium in Singida Town. A tattered CCM flag whipped atop a tall tree pole; the day was windy and hot. By three in the afternoon, Singidans streamed into the stadium. It was a river of yellow and green, with people sporting CCM baseball hats, scarves, khangas, and t-shirts that party touts had been doling out for weeks (see fig. 6.2). Kikwete's eyes were literally everywhere—his face peering out from the chests of jeering adolescents, from the foreheads of party officials, from the backsides of the dancing women. Kikwete posters lining the stadium were emblazoned with the CCM seal—its golden hammer and axe glinting in the unrelenting dry season sun.

Kikwete was late. The Master of Ceremonies explained that supporters on his route from Manyoni district had prevented him from passing—that in the hopes of receiving a few words from the soon-to-be president, they had laid down in the road to block his passage. In the meantime in Singida stadium,

Figure 6.2. CCM supporters sport campaign swag in Namfua Stadium, Singida. Photo by author, 2005.

a band from Dar es Salaam played music and people danced to CCM and Nyerere praise songs, *Bongo Flava* (Tanzanian hip hop), and *Mawindi*, the local Nyaturu dance. As the sun drew near the horizon, word reached the stadium that Kikwete's caravan of sports-utility vehicles was drawing near. The MC worked the crowd into a cheering frenzy. Reminding them of the gifts distributed freely for the rally, he ordered, "When he arrives, wave your hats and scarves. He who does not wave them and wears the hat of CCM, take it from him, for it is CCM who has clothed him." The next day, Senge, a 26-year-old young man from urban Singida recalled the scene: "People felt bad to have their presents taken, so they did as he requested, and said, '*Karibu, Mheshimiwa!*' (Welcome, your Honorable!), waving their hats and scarves. Kikwete arrived with so many people and presents to give out. He didn't talk many policies, like his opponents. He just made a lot of promises—to build roads, and hospitals, to bring water, and secondary schools. He didn't explain why these things are so late in coming or where the money for our minerals has gone. He spoke only good words, and people were happy."

Kikwete was not the first presidential candidate to come to Singida that election season. But he put on by far the best show. In contrast, his greatest rival for the region in 2005, the Civic United Front's (CUF) Professor Ibrahim Lipumba had stirred the crowd with his sharp critique of CCM rule. He fired up his audience with the substance of his speech—challenging the people of Singida to confront the political and economic disparities exacerbated by the current leadership—but put on neither paternal airs nor costly bells and whistles. Kikwete had been welcomed into the town's largest venue—the soccer stadium—and from seated up on high was entertained by CCM performance troupes bused in from Dar es Salaam. Lipumba was welcomed onto an empty lot across from the stadium, where his audience waited soberly beneath trees, listening to the diatribe of a local CUF leader for hours before Lipumba's arrival. CCM parliamentary candidates and ward councilor candidates, dressed in *kitenge* shirts (tailored cotton print shirts of the style worn by wealthy government officials) of the CCM colors of gold and green, already looked official. They arrived in the long caravan of sports-utility vehicles with Kikwete, where they had the honor of being introduced and sanctioned by "the future president of Tanzania." Meanwhile their local CUF opponents emerged from the ranks of the audience beneath the trees to be introduced in the *mitumba* (second-hand clothes) that were their everyday wear.

For many voters in Singida, the sharp contrast between these two brief campaign visits supported a dominant discourse of electoral politics—one that asserts that the Tanzanian government is "father" to its citizen-children, and that only CCM possesses the qualities, resources, accumulated wisdom, and descent from Nyerere to be that father. Ruling party candidates at campaign rallies argued that opposition parties were still "too young" and "hungry" (see chap. 4). Extravagant spending on ruling party campaign events, *takrima* (gifts from candidates to potential voters), and candidates' own expensive clothing made it clear that it is only CCM who can provide for its nation-family. And the hierarchies suggested by these apparent wealth differences as well as the minimal substantive engagement in political issues by CCM candidates suggested to voters that their guardianship would remain peaceable and the nation's unity preserved.

But this promised patronage and implied clientelism consisted of more than just rhetoric in rural Singida. It is important to note the resources and protection that patronage promised to rural citizens in 2005, and what was expected of them in exchange. Political candidates, as we saw from Kikwete's visit to Singida, use their money not only to put on a good show, but also for takrima, the gift economy of elections in Tanzania. Those who defend the practice argue that takrima is a form of hospitality intended to thank those who help with election campaigns, though most agree that its practice is abused when extended to offering gifts to voters, which has often been the case. In 2005, voters jokingly referred to campaign season as "harvesting season"—the season of exchanging votes for gifts of money, beer, meals, and party apparel referred to colloquially as "food," "soda," "sugar" or "tea." Despite the fact that election "harvests" are unequally distributed and not all partake, takrima and CCM's public displays of wealth were powerful cues in a context where the primary political platform is poverty reduction and a primary means of economic security is patronage.

But voters seeking patronage in an elected official are not lured simply by the short-term reward of takrima. Takrima, for many rural Tanzanians, is also a political mobilization of the notion of *relationship*, of the idea of the state as father and the nation as a family in which people take care of those with whom they are historically connected. In accepting takrima, many seek assurance that—when the harvest fails or disaster strikes—it is certain, or probable, or even just a remote possibility that a lifeline will be tossed. For distribution in patronage politics is unapologetically directed by *relationships* rather than by disinterested notions of equality and impartiality. And indeed, between 2005 and 2015, elected officials and political candidates in Singida delivered food aid to some villages more than others during times of dearth; provided small sums of money in response to personal requests; and offered sporadic access to the pipeline of resources and political influence that constituted the CCM machinery. These reciprocal relations of patronage promised nothing in the way of equality, mobility, prosperity, or even a fair share. But they did assure an entitlement to subsistence, to a *living* out of village life (cf. Scott 1976). And so long as subsistence succeeded for most of the population, people tolerated patrons who "ate" more than their share. Rather than confronting inequality, people preferred to focus on the struggles of their daily lives, mirroring the forbearance of villagers sketched in Chinua Achebe's fourth novel, *Man of the People*:

> "Let them eat," was the people's opinion, "after all when white men used to do all the eating did we commit suicide?" Of course not. And where is the all-powerful white man today? He came, he ate and he went. But we are still around. The important thing then is to stay alive; if you do you will outlive your present annoyance. The great thing, as the old people have told us, is reminiscence; and only those who survive can have it. Besides, if you survive, who knows? It may be your turn to eat tomorrow. Your son may bring home your share ([1967] 2016, 161–2).

In affirming this system of patronage in the 2005 election with votes for CCM, many people saw themselves as securing the possibility of development that patronage offered, regardless of the political cost. One opposition candidate from the Civic United Front told me that people were reluctant to vote for the opposition, who might represent them more fairly, but who would likely prove ineffective in bringing them resources for development. The general perception was that those who choose opposition politicians for local leaders forfeit development because the opposition will be denied funding for projects from upper levels of bureaucracy where CCM is entrenched, or that they will be refused popular support from some groups of constituents below. Many villagers were wary of the tensions that multipartyism introduced into the rural government structure and the functions of communication, arbitration, labor mobilization, and taxation that the party had historically overseen through the ten-house cell system (Phillips 2014). This is easier to understand with a closer look at the rural state in Singida, where wards are divided into villages, villages into hamlets, and hamlets into ten-house cells.[3] Although officials at most of these levels could conceivably be elected from any political party, ten-cell leaders could not, because the office itself is a party structure. In Singida, as in other African countries where patronage and paternalism prevail, power must be "eaten whole," held exclusively rather than shared or balanced (Schatzberg 2001).

In the implicit political contract that governed these relations, it was understood that more was required of Singidans than simply their vote. They needed to submit to, and were often called to publicly perform, what Emma Hunter (2013) has called "good citizenship," conceptualized in domestic terms. This family metaphor suggested to Singidans that their labor is a resource of the national household: if the father is to bring food to the table (or if the government is to bring development to Singida), then the children must help to labor for it. "Building the nation," a phrase generally associated with Nyerere's political project of socialist development, was used specifically in contemporary Singida to refer to michango, or the contributions of labor and money to development projects described in chapter 5.

Yet building the nation required not only labor and money but a unified political voice. As Achebe wrote (of an unnamed African country) in *A Man of the People*,

> We had all been in the rain together until yesterday. Then a handful of us—the smart and the lucky and hardly ever the best—had scrambled for the one shelter our former rulers left, and had taken it over and barricaded themselves in. And from within they sought to persuade the rest through numerous loud-speakers, that the first phase of the struggle had been won and that the next phase—the extension of our new house—was even more important and called for new and original tactics; it required that all argument should cease and the whole people speak with one voice and that any more dissent and argument outside the door of the shelter would subvert and bring down the whole house. ([1967] 2016, 37)

The role of the political children in this relationship was to cease critique and to cede decision-making and the "need to know" to political elders. For Tanzanians this has entailed a tolerance of half-truths, acceptance of a general lack of trans-parency and the suppression of conflicting ideas by keeping arguments "inside the family" (i.e., inside CCM).

The marked difference in rhetorical strategies used by CCM's Jakaya Kikwete and CUF's Ibrahim Lipumba in their 2005 visits to Singida is illustrative of these political norms and (in the case of CUF) their transgression. Kikwete spoke *"maneno mazuri tu"* ("only good words") in his Singida speech, and "made lots of promises." CCM supporters noted that Kikwete's "good words" indicated his commitment to peace and security and symbolized continuity in years to come. Kikwete's critics however emphasized the emptiness of his words and famous smile, his avoidance of assuming any CCM responsibility for what many rural Tanzanians perceived as stalled development. Lipumba's speech is indicative of what is often understood to be an alternative idiom of citizenship: that of opposi-tion and advocacy associated with rights-based politics. Lipumba and his fellow CUF candidates satisfied those Singida residents thirsty for a more substantive message in 2005 by sharply critiquing CCM for its role in corruption and its development of the few rather than the many.

In general, candidates from the ruling party have tended to avoid engaging in substantive issues at campaign rallies. Even as its candidates made promise after promise in 2010, CCM barred all its candidates from participating in tele-vised campaign debates, rationalizing this move by stating that the party knows best how to present its policies to the public through campaign rallies.[4] This refusal to engage in substantive debate with political opponents and the reliance on a one-way flow of propaganda neutralizes opportunities for public criticism and preserves the idea of political leaders as figures whose authority and knowl-edge cannot be questioned.

So why, for so many years, did rural Singidans consent to the terms of governance for which patronage calls? What is in it for them? One answer lies in Singidans' historically driven political analytic and its key principle (most of the time) of "safety-first." In voting for particular candidates for public office, most Singidans sought, above all, a *relationship*. And they sought relationships with *people who had relationships* that could secure access to the resources so dearly needed for subsistence and development. Even takrima (which in a certain light is little more than vote-buying) signaled connection, affiliation, and a certain level of proximity to authority and resources that still holds sway in contexts of scarcity. And consenting to michango (which might otherwise be perceived simply as a violent form of taxation) constituted a favor that might later be reciprocated. As the Nyaturu say "A debt is wealth." For even a sliver of promise that one might benefit from this network—absent other alternatives—it was worth offering one's political support. Engaging in more politically fraught rights-based politics entailed the risk not only that one's choice might prove an ineffective patron or leader, but that one might find oneself entirely excluded from the network of relationships that was undeniably in control of the power and resources of the state. The risk of political change or deviation might at times be worth taking, but only at the threshold of subsistence, when there was nothing left to lose.

"Where the Sharp Edge of the State Machinery Meets the Rural Folk": Michango and the Shift to Rights in the 2010 Singida East Parliamentary Elections

Hunger in 2006 and an unprecedented escalation of michango disrupted the seeming political stasis following the 2005 elections. As I noted in chapter 5, in 2006—a food-scarce year when the majority of villagers were skipping meals to get by—the total mandated financial contributions to development exceeded 35 dollars.[5] In a context where the average per capita income was (at that time) between 120 and 240 dollars per year and 70 percent of one's income was estimated to be spent on food, such claims on rural people's resources were beyond excessive. Singidans had reached a tipping point at which they experienced government demands as persistent threats to subsistence. The political contract and the "safety-first" principle that had long privileged CCM seemed to be breaking down. Enter Tundu Lissu on the Singida political scene.

Born in 1968 in Singida, Tundu Antiphas Mughwai Lissu went on to study Law at the University of Dar es Salaam, finishing in 1994. In 1995, during the very first multiparty parliamentary elections in Tanzania, Lissu contested as a candidate for the NCCR-Mageuzi party ("I have never been part of the political establishment!"). By 1997 he had earned a Master of Law degree (LLM) at the University of Warwick in the United Kingdom. As a lawyer, Lissu sees himself as a rural community organizer, with a history of taking on class action suits around land rights, mining rights, and natural conservation. In a 2012 interview he noted these issues lay on the boundary where "the sharp end of the state machinery meets the rural folk." So contesting the 2010 elections on the platform of resisting michango, he observed, was an extension of those politics. He acknowledged the effectiveness of that choice: "I think if there is one single issue that got me elected, it was michango."

Rights-based approaches to development and politics tend to distinguish between two groups of people: those who *bear rights* but whose rights are not yet realized and *duty bearers*, the institutions who are obliged to fulfill those rights. Advocates try to strengthen the capacity of the duty bearers and enable the rights holders to claim their rights. Such tactics tend to rely on persistent advocacy and legal expertise to align the distribution of resources with human rights law, the rhetoric of development policy, and approved national budgets. In comparison with the aforementioned discourse of patronage that had predominated in Singida since independence, Lissu offered a rather different way of understanding Tanzanian politics:

> I have a very ambivalent attitude toward the state. I don't dismiss it. It's this monstrous reality we have to contend with. Contending with it, in my view, means resisting it. It's seeking to change it by resisting it, by mobilizing its victims to resist, to force changes through resistance, and essentially to democratize it. I believe in democracy. I believe in the capacity to change the state by building the capacity to resist. So I don't share the ideologies that seem to seek to consign the state to the dustbin of history. It's too soon, it's too soon for that. The reality we have to contend with is that the state is still very much alive in its modern form and it is very violent ... vis-a-vis the poor. And I don't think I have joined it. I don't like that. It is not joining. There are institutions in the state, and parliament is a modern institution of the state. I look at parliament as a very good forum for mobilizing resistance. That's how I see it: it is a dung heap, which you don't kiss, but you stand on it and tell whoever is willing to listen how stinky it is! ([*laughs*] I have gained some notoriety).

The premises of Lissu's rights-based approach to politics and its rhetorical divergence from CCM's politics of patronage stand out in this statement. The operative political metaphor in Lissu's imagery is not the state as father and the nation as family, but the state as parasite, and the nation an assemblage of diverse and competing groups with varying capacities to deflect state encroachment. In this view, the state is hardly benevolent; at best it is self-interested and self-serving, at worst, violent and exploitative. Improving it and bettering one's own terms of existence requires either keeping it at bay, or outright resisting it. In this project a diversity of opinion, the freedom to express dissent, and public debate are fundamental. Power must be shared, balanced, and kept in check, not "eaten whole." In the following pages my analysis of Lissu's political platform of michango in 2010 highlights both the distinctions and also the shared attributes between rights and patronage as discourses of political practice and claims-making in a context of precarity and food insecurity.

Seeing Michango through a Discourse of Rights

Lissu's focus on the politics of participation, he told me in a 2012 interview, is rooted in his experience with the Tanzanian state of his childhood, when as a six-year old child, he watched schoolchildren, teachers, and the local militia demolishing homes to force people to relocate for villagization. People's homes, he remembered, "were razed to the ground, by their own children who were told to do so by their teachers, who were told to tell their [students] by these tyrants in their areas. And, of course the orders came from high up.... So that is my first test really with the violence of the state. And not just the violence of the state, but the stupidity of the state—the arrogance of the state in its *ignorance* of rural conditions." Among Lissu's other childhood memories, the specter of forced contributions looms large: "They call them contributions, but really it's a tax. And they are unlegislated; they are completely obligatory; and they are extortionist. They are collected in the most brutal way." He remembers the forced contributions of 1978 and 1979 to build the CCM party regional office. In 1982, in Class 7, he remembers michango for the Namfua [soccer] Stadium in Singida Town, far from the village where he lived with his parents. And in 1986 he remembers the collections for the district secondary schools: "People were meant to pay through their noses with whatever little they had. And then after that, they began with the ward schools. So, the villagers have paid with their sweat and blood and tears and everything for 30 years. A whole generation has been brought up on this violence of the state and these extortionist practices of the government. And of course it is all done in the name of development. And so to understand my politics, you have to understand that history."

As I described previously, the word "michango" refers to a wide range of contributions by individuals and households to community development projects; the operation of schools, churches, and the local government; weddings, funerals, and other ceremonies and special events—some more voluntary and socially sanctioned than others. Some of these requests are consistently seen to be legitimate: the funding of weddings, funerals, and other social life events is accepted in good years and in bad and households take them in stride and consistently donate what they can. But the legitimacy of requests for contributions for development and other social projects often waxes and wanes with the annual and multi-year cycles of scarcity and bounty.

For many Singidans, understanding some michango as oppressive and coercive, rather than voluntary and beneficent, was neither new nor far-fetched. The oppressive and coercive nature of government mandates for community contributions of labor and resources even in circumstances of severe hardship (described in chap. 5) had certainly become clear to me during my field research in Tanzania between 2004 and 2007, before I had ever heard Tundu Lissu's name (Lissu would not launch his campaign for the 2010 elections until 2008). Singidans had long grumbled and at times protested about the terms of michango. But Lissu's campaign—launched widely in 2008 and 2009—represented the first public acknowledgement by a government official or political candidate that michango represented anything other than good faith government efforts to mobilize communities to help themselves. He brought the issue of michango into *public* debate, naming aloud the repressive terms of its conditions, rather than seeking to negotiate michango "within the family" and behind closed doors, as a favor or demand in a larger system of reciprocal but unequal relations.

For the people I lived among and visited during the period of my research, the legitimacy of michango depended on timing, as it related to the citizenry's state of subsistence, but also on the extent to which communities were engaged in decision-making about projects—that is, the extent to which *majighana* (Ny. "voluntary action") and *witegheyi* (Ny. "listening to each other") had taken place during planning (see chap. 5). This was a nuance that Lissu acknowledged whole-heartedly. Different than the way some Singidans later interpreted his stance, Lissu did not campaign in 2010 against all types of michango. He protested only those that functioned as a violent form of state taxation on rural people. He argued that if one looked at Singida's history, one would find many examples of communities who—of their own volition—came up with plans to build schools or pool their resources to improve their lives. These, he urged, should continue.

Lissu introduced an additional criterion to debates about the legitimacy of michango: whether or not funding from the government or other institutions for particular projects was supposed to already exist. In doing so, he pushed the issue of michango into a legal realm by tying the practice directly to corruption, which is illegal in Tanzania and is regulated (not always successfully) by a complex of laws and oversight institutions. Lissu's argument was that michango collected through the violence of the state were a mask for systemic government corruption that hides the predation of the state on rural people and their labor.

> You have a government that is pretty much predatory, at all levels. It's a parasitic, rent-seeking state … a state that literally sucks the blood of the people. And money is eaten at the top, a lot.… The government throws billions of shillings into schools every year. And you know what happens, the *mkurugenzi* (the district executive director) who is the accounting officer for finances never gets what she signs for. She will sign for a billion shillings but the district will probably only get 500 million. So mkurugenzi signs and her bosses tell her, OK, here is the money, you will know what to do. If the bosses have taken

their cut, the mkurugenzi's people take their cut and it goes down to the ward level, and they take their cut. It never reaches the villages. So between the mkurugenzi and the peasant at the bottom, how do you make up for the short-fall? Michango. Michango. So michango is the answer for this stealing that goes on. We need michango because we need to show for the money we have taken and stolen. And then michango also becomes an end in itself because you also steal the michango. So the villagers are forced to contribute to make up for the stolen money and then their contribution is also stolen. So nothing gets done.[6]

That such "eating" had occurred was hardly news to rural Singidans. What was new was embedding government "eating" in a political narrative that saw all corruption as illegitimate and that invited consistent indignation rather than a resignation to "Let them eat."

Showing evidence of the discrepancy between budgeting and disbursement was key to Lissu's political tactics in Singida. Unlike CCM's patronage politics which relied on the explicit curating of the public's access to information, in the opposition's rights-based politics, transparency was (ostensibly at least) the name of the game. In contrast to many parliamentary representatives whose visits to constituents were largely ceremonial, Lissu carried financial books and budgets with him wherever he went.

> It requires a lot of work. You have to know where the money is. I always carry the budget books ... to my villages. [The villagers] know, "Bunge [MP Lissu] always comes with documents." I say ... "This is the money they say is set aside for your schools. Have you seen it?" They say, "no way!!" "So if you changa [contribute], this is how they get rich." This forced contribution thing has the potential to change the political face of this country, if it is articulated by someone who knows what it is all about.

Political entitlements to development were embedded in laws, policies, and budgets, not in vague political contracts or promises to "care for" one's clients.

This analysis of michango politics resonated with Singidans during Lissu's campaign, but many expressed doubt that they could effectively resist it. Lissu recalled the dialogue surrounding the relatively simple and effective plan he proposed. He told the villagers,

> "We cannot hope to democratize the state any time soon. So since we're not going to see the money if we give it, don't give it!" The villagers would ask: "If they come with the militia, what do we do Mr. Lissu?" And I asked them, "How many usually come, a hundred?" And they would laugh and say "No, just five or ten." And they would look at themselves, they are hundreds. And I would tell them "Just say no! You are not arresting anyone! You are not taking anybody's chicken! Just rebel!" And when villagers would express concern about being taken to court, I told them "Go to court and ask the judge what

law allows these people to collect money from [you]. There's never been any law; the whole thing has been an illegal act. And if that doesn't work, give me a call!"

Such advice recast the government's role from being an institution that imposed the will of the state onto the people to one that might protect them from it.

Lissu brought these rights tactics to bear on his campaign as well. This involved shedding public light on the shadowy dimensions of rural elections and coordinating all the opposition parties to monitor and immediately communicate results. In the face of fears by supporters that polling station attendants would be bought by the ruling party (as many speculated had been done in earlier elections), Lissu organized one polling attendant from each of the six opposition parties to monitor the results at each station. Upon completion of vote-counting, each station sent a text message and votes were tallied by ten o'clock that evening.

> So at 10 on Monday we go to the addition center in town, where they now bring in all votes from everywhere, and we had our results, and our forms. We were unbeatable. And we did it on a shoestring. Every polling agent cost me 800 shillings [around 50 cents]: 300 for a bottle of water, 200 for some biscuits, and 300 for some juice—the cheapest on the market. So we beat [CCM] with their millions! And why? We had been fighting for 3 years! And I'm completely broke! And I would say, "You are going to sell me because I don't have money to bribe you the way these people bribe you? Go ahead! I don't pay michango, you do!" And people fought to become polling agents. And so—that's Singida for you.

Whereas prior to 2010, preferential relationships were seen to be necessary for—indeed constitutive of—politics, Lissu convinced his supporters that such clientelism would be devastating to effective government. And most importantly, they would be the ones to suffer. This ability to *persuade* his supporters was critical to Lissu's campaign since he was not equipped to lure them with takrima or other forms of resource transfer. It highlights a crucial aspect of rights-based politics—that words are as important as money. If in the case of takrima, transfers of money or other material goods established a relationship that promised some degree of obligation, then Lissu used *words* to communicate and confirm the existence of a legal framework that seemed to promise a similar degree of commitment. As one parliamentary candidate for CUF in Singida Town observed to me, "[CUF] can't rely on takrima. Our words are that which pulls people to us. For us, our words are the money that will attract people to us."

And with these tactics, Lissu beat CCM, and he beat michango as well. With so much hype around michango during the election period, it did not take much effort by rural Singidans after the elections for michango to just go away. Most Singidans saw the 2010 elections as a referendum on michango, and the village leaders I spoke with said they did not dare announce michango, for fear of the public reaction (particularly by the younger village men) who had found Lissu's platform so compelling.

What is important to note is that Lissu's campaign did not introduce an entirely new way of thinking, but rather a shift in what could be said aloud. It changed practice by pushing into the village space words, ideas, and proposed action that no longer needed to be grumbled or muttered only behind closed doors or between friends, or spoken loudly in the city but whispered in the village. Critique and opposition could now more easily be shouted from village rooftops, without the threat or expectation of retribution. If Lissu's campaign changed Singidans' thinking at all, it was not with a novel concept of rights. As we have seen, an idea of obligation and entitlement had long pre-existed Tundu Lissu: the notion of "right" was right there all along. Rather Lissu's campaign sanctioned new ideas about what constituted a rural political environment that would foster "development"—which under Nyerere had required that (in Achebe's words) "all argument should cease and the whole people speak with one voice," a voice that came from above and outside, not from within communities themselves. Now, that voice from below could no longer be so easily dismissed as a trouble-maker, or (as a Nyaturu proverb goes) as "an ankle-bell" that "makes only meaningless noise." That ankle-bell, it turned out, was essential to subsistence in these precarious times.

Weighing Rights versus Patronage: Post-2010 Reactions and Reverberations

Upon returning to Singida in 2012, I found a mixed response to Lissu's time in office. The incessant—and at times violent—claims by local government officials on rural households in Singida slowed, leaving residents more able to use their scarce resources for subsistence needs, small business endeavors, household development, or school tuition for children. Moreover, Lissu's national-scale opposition politics helped to place Singida Region squarely on Tanzania's political map.[7] But some of the same interlocutors who had expressed hope and jubilation, were now disillusioned—both with Lissu and their fellow Singidans. Many complained that now that michango were prohibited and a parliamentary representative had confirmed the level of corruption many rural Singidans had suspected, people's willingness to oblige their leaders by participating in development projects at all was at an all-time low. Many noted, "Lissu says the money should be there—let the government do its work." While many families felt a sense of relief from the pressure of contributions, they also noted it was not clear how the village's progress would continue. A woman serving on the village council observed that the system was still leaking money: "There are holes at the level of our administrators. Lissu was elected to follow up on those holes. But the way I see it, the problems are still there. Still, we haven't seen the money we are supposed to be seeing. Still there are problems with the implementation. Still there are many holes." Refusing the michango, people noted, did not actually aid the money, goods, or services in getting to Singida. Rather, it just made its failure to arrive that much more visible because community efforts were not happening either.

Lissu acknowledged the limitations of his anti-michango politics. On one hand, coercive extraction had ceased and citizens were more aware of the corruption that michango had hid. But without the arrival of aid committed to digging wells, building clinics, improving roads, and supplying schools, the everyday conditions of their existence and their challenges to subsistence remained the same. Lissu blamed this on the lack of oppositional oversight of district financial affairs.

> But the challenges ... where do we get water? The money goes to the district. In our district council, a council of 69 members, there are only 6 from the opposition, including myself. So the challenges of providing services, of making sure the money that we get from the government is spent wisely, are immense.... Nowadays I sit on the finance committee that reviews the budget. So I am now on a junction where all the financial traffic passes through. I watch everything that's going on because I get the documents and these are supposed to be secrets. And they are open secrets to my villagers. Whenever I go to meetings, I say this is our money, this is how it is being eaten. And I can't stop it. There's a huge amount of awareness about how the government operates, about how resources are spent or misspent. And that has given people an acute awareness of the limitations of the political changes that they have accomplished with their own hands. We have an MP, yes, we don't contribute, yes, but still things are not getting done because this MP doesn't have much of a say about how resources are allocated within the council and how they are spent.

The answers, he went on to note, lay with the electorate: "And I don't have answers for that ... we have to change how they see things." With the larger government continuing to operate as a party network, the rights strategies of advocacy, participation, and transparency had limited effect.

Village leaders and council members lamented the renewed difficulty of their work. "We are very squeezed now" (*tumebanwa sana*). Caught between a results-driven national and international development regime with unfunded mandates on the one side, and a rural populace fed up with state demands on the other, village leaders had lost a sense of efficacy and community respect. One leader talked of giving up his unpaid elected role, noting that: "In the constituency, there are no contributions, and it's become very hard to lead people. Each person knows now how the world is going. People see the debates in parliament, and what politicians have done. And they expect that harsh steps (*hatua kali*) will be taken. But without a strong principle in the [national] government, it's too difficult [for us local leaders] to lead. But if money is brought, and people are informed and they see the work happening, then they don't have any quarrels.

But if not then they cannot understand." The government's crisis in legitimacy made leadership of an unfunded rural state too difficult.

This sense of a loss of political obligation applied not only to the leadership, but also to the relationships between villagers. The political contract had shifted. Rights-based politics called on Singidans to actively engage in the political process, advocate, and hold the government accountable in return for specific entitlements named in laws, policies, and budgets. Under patronage, in contrast, people had consented to give freely of their labor and resources in return for the general guarantee of a living. They had agreed to listen to the government and be taught by it about their own needs. Through refusing michango and CCM's monopoly, they seemed to have neutralized the political contract of patronage. But they also, some complained, had undermined the collective obligation of community members to engage in development for the benefit of the community as a whole. In the absence of a sense of obligation to financially mobilize to build schools, clinics, and cattle watering places, people wondered, what would obligate or connect them? And without michango in these far corners of Tanzania, where in the world would development come from now?

Religious leaders complained that not only were people refusing to contribute to government projects for which funding existed, but they also had stopped giving to unfunded school projects, and even to their churches, mosques, and other community self-help initiatives. One acknowledged government corruption as a fact of life, but directed his fury at Lissu:

> The child of Tundu Lissu studies in Europe. The child of Tundu Lissu studies in America. And he says, "don't contribute"? *Hii ndiyo nguvu yake!* [This is his power!] But my child if I want him to study, I must build him a school. The government is corrupt ... so what?!? [*He shrugged his shoulders as if to say that this was old news*]. You have to use your power to build a school so that your child studies, and his grandchild and his grandchild and so on.... Better that we have something ... *hata kwa machozi*, even if it's through tears!

The stakes, he argued, were ones' own children, and villagers did not have the privilege of simply paying fees to a school—they had to build one. Another noted: "There may be government corruption, but there's still not enough money to fix all the schools, so civic participation is necessary. Those complaints about CCM [corruption] have nothing to do with us. What concerns us is that our children don't have desks and chairs."

Both praise for and complaints about Lissu were generally framed in terms of his approach to politics which was characterized by his incessant demands for rights and transparency and his unwillingness (or inability) to engage in the patron-client relations so embedded in the Tanzanian parliamentary system. That which appealed to some clearly alienated others. A retired minister and theologian living in town defended Lissu and criticized those who claimed that he had banned *all* contributions and that Lissu himself had personally stunted development:

> Lissu is not saying that no one should give michango. He's saying that it should be officialized and legalized. Receipts should be given. It's not constitutional to make these demands, and it should be put into the legal system so that it is regulated. Right now, no reports are given. If you don't give reports, then I have no idea how this money is used or if it is misappropriated. But people don't understand the democratic principle. No one here knows the constitution. When we were under Great Britain, we learned the entire constitution at school. I knew my rights. Now it is just like in George Orwell. The pigs are running the show and they're calling all the shots!

But another leader complained that Lissu had debilitated village governments and other community leaders, because "participation cannot happen without a command."

> If he's taken away the command, he has taken away everything. People don't have the habit of going to volunteer for something. They must be supervised [*kusimamiwa*]. People have become used to being pursued [*kufuatwa*]. It's the work of the leader to come and ask for contributions. You don't go and give them to him. But if the leader comes and you don't have the money, then it's your turn to go and find him. But to go to him in the first round ... never. We don't have that habit! [*Tabia ile hamna!*]. You still have to do the work of persuading them. You call them. You say, "*Changie mawazo. Changie maneno. Mnsemaje?*" [Contribute your thoughts. Contribute your words. What do you think?'] You persuade them.

Critics of Lissu often compared him with CCM representatives who during elections and at various points in their terms brought small gifts and money to their constituents or made large contributions to development projects. One frequent comparison was with Mohammed Dewji—a young and very wealthy CCM parliamentarian for Singida Urban constituency between 2005 and 2015 (Forbes magazine placed Dewji at #31 on their 2015 list of the wealthiest people in Africa; his net worth was estimated to be 1.3 billion dollars; he was 41 years old at the time). After his election in 2005 Dewji was known to attend few parliamentary sessions and to speak little when he was there, but he tapped into his personal wealth to build schools and dig wells through an NGO he had funded in Singida Town. Comparing him with Dewji, one elder said of Lissu: "Better for [Lissu] to be quiet and bring development, than to have so many words but bring nothing!" But one urban constituent complained the opposite about Dewji. "He's done nothing. In the newspaper last year they counted the number of times people contributed in Parliament. Dewji has never said anything. He's done nothing for us."[8]

Those who for a variety of reasons opposed Lissu's politics used this lack of patronage as the key way to dismiss him. "Tundu Lissu has never given money to anyone. Not during hunger. Not for any project. He refuses the relationship! At least Dewji builds things!" Another person noted, "Missanga [another CCM parliamentarian in Singida] promised 1,056,000 to his constituency. But Lissu has not even spent 10 shillings to buy tea leaves!" Another village government representative noted: "Lissu doesn't work through action, he only works through making people angry." And a religious leader admonished him: "to have faith without action [without giving his own money], the spirit dies." An elder taxi driver praised Dewji's bequests to Singida Town and criticized Lissu's political activity at the national level, "Law and politics are two different things. But Lissu mixes the two. So he has brought nothing. We hear he is all over the place. One day Kigoma, another Arusha. But he doesn't come to see his own people. So five years has brought nothing. But Dewji has brought wheelchairs and sponsored women's groups."

Another civil society leader offered a more nuanced comparison between the two leaders who, though not competing for the same constituency, occupy the same discursive realm in politics because Singidans so often compare them.

> That's interesting because if the question is, "who is defending the interests of the wananchi to the national state?" then you would say Tundu Lissu. But if the question is, "who is delivering the goodies to the village?" then it's Dewji. It would be very interesting to see ... who people want to vote for next time. They are in different constituencies, but imagine if they are running against each other! Dewji very proudly talks about the percentage by which he won. It was one of the top landslides.... I've spoken with him quite a few times, and he speaks quite passionately: "I've been blessed with funds, and I really want to bring development" and he rattles off statistics, like how many wells and how many schools he has built.... And he has done it. And that's how he describes himself as a politician. In fact he says, "I don't like siasa [politics]" ... meaning bunge, party politics, and so on ... "I care about my people and I want to bring development to them" and he rattles off the very large amounts he has given. But if Tip O'Neil is right and all politics is local, you could argue that the guy who delivers, no matter how ill- or well-gotten his wealth, may be the best.... Of course what you want to do is to make sure the government is fulfilling its responsibilities and uses the resources it collects properly and is not substituting its poor performance with what citizens need to give ... [Tundu Lissu's] narrative is very clear: "It's the government's responsibility. The government is taxing people. It should be paying for these things, period." And there's another thing I also agree with. The prohibition against the Draconian forced michango.... Because it's so rough; it's so crude, and it doesn't at all take into account [the conditions of people's lives].... It's so laced with the threat of violence. And so with those things I'm completely with Tundu."

By 2014 Lissu was more optimistic about the results of the movement, noting that more district development money was making it to the village. "Now that the people are not coughing up the money that has been eaten, where are you going to hide?" Two large water projects had started in the district and Lissu noted: "No one has paid a penny! No one has been asked to contribute labor! Those who dig the trenches are paid!" He also noted the effects of the Constituency Development Fund, launched by the national government in 2008. Singida East now receives 36 million shillings (approximately US$17,000 in 2015) each year to seed small projects in the constituency: "We meet and divide it up to build a classroom here, a classroom there. We give it to community groups for development projects. It's very little money. In terms of changing people's lives, it's a drop in the sea. But the change in people's attitude! 'It's possible to get money from the government!' These are things that we didn't know existed. We've always been preached on the gospel of '*bajeti ndogo bajeti ndogo … changa changa changa!*' ('small budget small budget … contribute contribute contribute!'). So we are moving."

Debates about CCM politics were clearly heating up again in May 2014, with the 2015 parliamentary and presidential elections looming ahead. During an early campaign visit to Singida East constituency by CCM Secretary General Abdulrahman Kinana, CCM supporters in Singida region drew national attention to Lissu's michango politics. Speeches reported in many Swahili-speaking newspapers highlighted some constituents' concerns that Lissu's ban on michango had stopped development in its tracks. An article in the newspaper *Habari* quoted a highly performative complaint to Kinana from a resident of the Singida East village of Unyaghumpi: "*Ndugu* Kinana, we ask you to help us because since we elected our parliamentarian, Tundu Lissu, he has not continued with the projects that the former parliamentarian from CCM had done, after he made us refuse to contribute any contributions required by the council for the purpose of development, we have continued in our condition of poverty."[9] The article reported that, in response, Kinana asked Lissu to "stop gossiping on stage and to return to his citizens to fulfill the promises he had given, because he should have all the money he is given in parliament." This admonishment of Lissu for not using his parliamentary salary to support development in his constituency served to highlight Lissu's lack of involvement in patron-client relations and to shame him for it in front of his constituents.

Lissu acknowledged the difficulty of the expectations that he will provide personal support to his constituents in Singida, where a day of farm labor (when it is available) earns them barely more than a dollar per day.

> You can be sure that if someone dies in my constituency, or even if they die outside the constituency but they are from Singida East, I am probably the first to know [because they ask him for condolence or funeral money]. And these are my people! These are people who suffered with me for three years [during

the 2010 campaign] before I became an MP! They never asked for a thing! You know? And how do you tell them, "Look, I am not your mobile ATM?!" How do you tell them that? How do you say no? And they hear these stories ... you are paid 300,000 shillings [approximately US$140 in 2014] per day ... that you are flush with cash!! The demands are just enough to send you crazy. *Kabisa. Kabisa. Kabisa* [Completely. Completely. Completely].

As Daniel Jordan Smith has so eloquently written of Nigeria, Singidans inhabit a world where "politicians must prove, or pretend, that they are both good democrats and good patrons ... [where] common folk simultaneously condemn the corruption of politicians and cultivate corruption in their own patrons as the only means by which their interests are served" (2007, 171).

No one I spoke with doubted Lissu's own integrity (I never once heard a charge of corruption or "eating" against him—all the more significant in this context in which corruption is also an idiom of political critique, as well as a charge of wrongdoing). Yet his resistance approach was criticized for disrupting social and political consensus without offering an alternative path to social progress. And no doubt the sense of hope he introduced for rural Singidans during the 2010 elections created a bubble of expectation that was difficult to sustain in the face of current politics. Indeed, when I asked Lissu in 2012 what was most difficult in his work of representing rural people in parliament, his answer was frank: "The frightful fear that you just cannot meet the expectations. People expect the world out of this movement ... and it really frightens me. I've unleashed monsters of expectations. And ... I don't know.... I do my best. I'm completely open with my people. No secrets. Absolutely no secrets. They know everything. They know how much money I get paid. And that helps. The relationship is very easy. But the expectations are just sky-high. And who can blame them? Who can blame them?"

Capturing Subsistence

Lissu was re-elected for another term in 2015, despite an influx of CCM resources to defeat him (he has caused even more headaches for the ruling party at the national level than he has for them in Singida!). Thus, far from reading Singidans, renewed longing for patronage as a verdict on Lissu's performance as MP, we should understand it as an effort to rehabilitate social and economic relations of reciprocity in what Ferguson calls a global context of *"asocial* inequality" (emphasis added). Singidans are not rejecting rights-based approaches outright, they are simply acknowledging the *inadequacy* of a depersonalized and disinterested notion of rights as a discourse of redistribution on its own in the contemporary political and economic context of rural Tanzania.

It is perhaps not surprising then, that some of the same people who have celebrated Lissu's victories also criticize him for his lack of engagement in patron-client relations. I know from personal experience with requests for money that saying "I can't this time" is a very different type of refusal (and far more locally legitimate) than saying "I won't," even for the best and most principled of reasons. In the first, the obligation is at least acknowledged, even if left unfulfilled. In the latter, the obligation is denied, or in Singidans' terms, the relationship is refused ("*anakataa uhusiano*"): the prior being a prime example of a *social* inequality; the latter being a perfect example of an *asocial* one. In their current context of precarity, Singidans are not ready to "reject relationships" straightaway. They use complaints about Lissu's refusal to engage in patron-client relations both to pressure him to engage economically with them, and to court favor with the political establishment.

It is clear that Singidans' analyses of their material circumstances drive their political subjectivities in critical (and not illogical) ways, for "it is perfectly reasonable that the peasant who each season courts hunger and all its consequences should hold a somewhat different opinion of risk-taking than the investor who is gambling 'off the top'" (Scott 1976, 15). But what is also clear from the events related above, is that it is not that Singidans want the most just or the most fruitful political relationship on offer, but that they actually want *both*. Neither rights nor patronage serve as catchall idioms of accountability. It is the very flexibility of claims-making, and its essential rootedness in *both* rights and relationships, that allows poor rural people to capture as much of the state as they do.

While democratic forms have certainly taken on momentum in millennial Tanzania with well-funded activism by Tanzanian civil society organizations, this is not a teleological shift. It is not that a patron-client system is gradually being replaced by a more evolved rights-based one, but rather that the two are coeval, and being patch-worked together in innovative, sometimes surprising, and often contradictory new ways. Singidans seem to code-switch between these two ostensibly distinct modalities of membership in the nation in relation to the political opportunities that are on offer, and the presence and shortage of their means to achieve subsistence.

But, to be clear, Singidans are not just reacting to material stimuli, aiming to bring in the goods through whatever it takes. They don't just have *experiences* with inequality with which they react to political stimuli; they have analyses of them as well. That is, they have theories about how rights are part and parcel of a relationship-based politics. And neither their concept of *rights*, nor their ideas about *what is right*, center on the impartial or disinterested modes of distribution and redistribution that seem to drive contemporary notions of universal human rights. Rather Singidans' notions of rights (and rightness) are deeply and inextricably embedded in relationships between people. Thus, Singidans code-mix as much as they code-switch, as they work toward a relationship-based politics that incorporates a notion of rights—one that holds the values of *both* relationships *and* rights as useful and essential for claims-making. Subsistence citizenship in rural central Tanzania entails fusing these two cognatic idioms, as well as swinging between them.

So where does this leave Singidans in this second decade of the new millennium? The successful resistance to michango by Singida East constituents is certainly testament to the power of effective community organizing in the face of exploitation. But the ongoing struggle to secure funds allocated for the purposes of development in their constituency also speaks to the marginal status of economic human rights in a neoliberal age. Lissu, for his part, still holds faith in solidarity and struggle:

> Like all other rights throughout history, like all other concessions from the state, our rights will always be fought for. Always. You will get schools if you fight for them. What is taken for granted in the Western world now—universal education, this is a project of decades of generation of struggle by civil society, by the working class movement. Brown vs the Board of Education did not bring desegregation. Demonstrations did that. So the universal language of rights is misleading. It creates an unnecessary ideological fog in my view. These are only realizable through struggle, through fight. If the organized people are strong enough to compel the state to provide free universal care, it will be done. If you are too weak to do that, you will never get it. It is true of Tanzania. It is true of the United States. It is true of every country in the world.

Lissu, in spite of whatever failings people attribute to him, gives credit to the people he represents for their own capacity to discipline the state, calling it to serve them rather than a global elite. Yet, as I have described here, resisting state predation is far more feasible than obligating national and international political bodies to honor global commitments to economic rights like food, housing, or education. But with "sky-high" expectations and mounting frustrations, there is a new impetus for change among Singidans. And as Lissu notes, "Who can blame them? Who can blame them?"

Notes

1. In 1974, Nyerere declared TANU's supremacy over all government and societal institutions. Parliament, under the party constitution, became a "committee of the party" (Mmuya 1996, 3). By 1976 newspaper and radio media were brought under government control. Even the country's development blueprint—the Arusha Declaration—was passed to parliament only for a cursory ratification, never for serious deliberation. By 1977 the mainland's TANU party and the isles' Afro-Shirazi party had merged to form a sole ruling party for the union, renamed the "the Party of the Revolution," the *Chama Cha Mapinduzi* (CCM).

2. Cartoon by Nestory Fedeliko ("FeDë"), downloaded February 13, 2014, https://www.facebook.com/artistfede.

3. President Nyerere's TANU government established the cell system in 1963 as the smallest party unit of the single-party state to eradicate rural isolation (ten houses was the minimum unit that could form a cell) by setting up a system for communication, tax collection, and security. The system also linked rural households to the village development committee, charged with implementing Nyerere's grand schemes to deliver electricity, water, and schooling. Even after the 1992 turn to multipartyism, the CCM (formerly TANU) cell remains the basic unit of government in many parts of rural Tanzania.

4. J. Mwakisyala,"Tanzanians tired of promises," *East African Business Week*, September 13, 2010.

5. These included mandatory contributions of 13,000 TSH for the water project; 1000 TSH for supplies for the old division secondary school; 24,000 TSH for the new ward secondary school; 300 TSH for the Mwenge parade; 700 TSH for the salaries of the school cooks and guards; and additional small contributions to the CCM party and the Committee for the Children from the Most Vulnerable Environments.

6. The mass firings of district and regional officials that occurred during Kikwete's term in office suggest that this "eating" of government resources was indeed occurring during the period of this research.

7. In addition to Tundu Lissu, other high-profile Tanzanians have recently constituted Singida's political leadership. Prominent Tanzanian businessman Mohammed Dewji was MP of Singida Urban 2005 to 2015. Singida's MP for Singida North constituency, Lazaro Nyalandu, became the Minister for Natural Resources and Tourism in January 2014.

8. Dewji won again with a landslide in 2010, but decided not to contend in 2015.

9. "CCM Singida Wamlipua Lissu Kwa Kinana." *Habari*, May 23, 2014. Author translation of quote.

Conclusion

The Seasons of Subsistence and Citizenship

> If we yield to our anguish over their anguish, we may all too readily rush to Judgment, imposing our solutions on their situations, and dismissing the ways in which they deal with their adversity as something that would become unnecessary if they could share a life like ours. Perhaps, however, in our preoccupation with controlling the forces of life and death and insulating ourselves against baleful influences, we have lost our capacity to be open to the world and depleted our resources to cope with unpredictable hardship. In which case, the situation of the other may be seen not simply as one we might want to save them from, making them more like us, but as one we might learn from, even if this means greater acceptance of the suffering in this world, less bellicose or concerned talk about how we may set the world to rights, and a place for silence.
>
> Michael Jackson, "The Prose of Suffering"

> Life in the bush is only possible with assistance.
>
> Man dictating letter in Abderrahmane Sissako's film *Life on Earth*

WITH HIS LYRICAL 1998 film, *La Vie sur Terre* ("Life on Earth"), Abderrahmane Sissako captures a slice of rural west African life from Sokolo, a small town comprised of seventeen villages in southcentral Mali, on the cusp of the new millennium.[1] Sokolo is an out-of-the-way place by any estimation, and the visual poem that is Sissako's work renders both its remoteness and its resilience achingly human. The sun's position is a constant point of reference. Throughout the film a group of men listening to the radio outside a house crowds into an ever-shrinking patch of shade, until finally the sun forces them to disperse. Drought has eclipsed most of the year's crop, and birds threaten to destroy the rest of it, leaving the town's young to fight the monotonous and demoralizing battle of constantly defending the fields. Birds flee the stick of a man whipping a synthetic rice bag in one field and then re-settle in another until a young boy waves them along again. In this desperate project to make them leave, one's own effort is meaningless without others. A man dictates a letter to be sent abroad: "Life in the bush is only possible with assistance." In the background Salif Keita intones his poignant "Folon," a melodic meditation on social and political participation in the past and present.

Everyone in *La Vie sur Terre* is on the move—in action, or in connection (in 2008 Sissako noted "it was not my intention to make a film where everyone is in motion, but it happened and I became aware of it only afterward"[2]). A passenger truck lurches by lined with layers of people, and then cargo, and then still more people. A migrant Dramane—the filmmaker himself—returns home; his father awaits, fingering prayer beads. A small boy paddles a boat, carrying the man and his bicycle across the river. A woman heads to the well with her plastic bucket as the cattle amble from their watering place. A young woman, who we come to know as Nana, patiently traverses the bumps in the road on her bicycle, stopping to resuscitate a flat tire with a pump she carries. A tailor works his sewing machine. A photographer helps people to fashion the selves they imagine.

People come to the post office to make telephone calls to other towns, to France, to all kinds of places. The postal worker at the heart of this human-technological interface tries every secret he knows to get the calls through, absorbing the personal details of people's lives and their discreet desperation into his quiet persistence. Sometimes he succeeds. In one scene the disabled postmaster shuffles laboriously across the village to tell the filmmaker his call has finally connected. The quiet, humble solidarity in these scenes is excruciating in its pace and profound in its power. The technological crudeness of the government post office contrasts with the snippets of news we hear from France and reports of its millennial celebrations. Ultimately, we have a sense of both muted connection and audible disconnection. Sissako's voiceover with the words of Aimé Césaire could not be more apt: "My ear to the ground / I hear tomorrow pass."

The reality of communication in the bush—and indeed life itself—relies on these small favors, this rustic apparatus of people, these karmic contributions amid the hustle, bustle, and anxieties of village life. There is no clearer evidence of what Abdoumaliq Simone has asserted: "people are infrastructure" (2004). In the end, the people in this film are not waiting for help from the outside. As the postmaster tells Dramane, "It's hard to reach people. It's a question of luck."

I begin the ending of this book with these scenes from Sissako to return us to the notion of subsistence citizenship which, like *La Vie sur Terre*, tracks and traverses the relationships between poor and rich; village and city; colony and metropole; women and men; society and government; son and father; past, present, and future. Organizing the relations between these spaces, times, classes, spheres, genders, and generations, postcolonial citizenship is the ongoing project of re-structuring inclusions, exclusions, entitlements, and obligations, and of recasting the narratives used to explain, support, contest, and legitimize them. Colonialism and the contemporary global economy, to be sure, construct some of the political and economic realities that condition rural Singidans' life experiences today: the market as foremost determinant of value; the extractive nature of statecraft, the paternalistic character of government, and the disproportionate ratio of obligations to entitlements all bear echoes of colonial governance, if they do not nearly replicate them. And people in Singida go about their daily lives partly in reference to this historical experience of the state and to a global political economy that frames their everyday wants and needs.

But the story of the Nyaturu of Singida has also shown that people come to their engagement with the government and the nation bearing political baggage from home as well. That is, they bring ideas, expectations, and strategies related to belonging, membership, entitlement, obligation, and patterns of interaction and distribution from the mode and context of their livelihood to their political preferences and practices. These ideas and expectations constitute and condition—though never absolutely—rural peoples' interactions in the political realm. Let me be clear: this political subjectivity, which I describe is not deficient, unsuccessful, or ineffective, but is rather a particular relationship between smallholder farmers and the twenty-first century state that is both constituted and constrained by the banality of hunger and the everyday project of meeting basic needs.

Understanding the terms of this relationship sheds new light on the ethnographic conundra I have presented in this book: Why did villagers go on strike *against* development? Why so much support for the ruling party in 2005 amid deteriorating conditions? Why sell grain at its lowest price and purchase it back at its highest? Why did a rights-talking opposition candidate suddenly win the 2010 parliamentary election in Singida East? Why did some people become so disillusioned with him? And why, amid all this struggle and labor and sacrifice for "building the nation," did rural people so often accept and reproduce narratives of rural dependency?

Common answers from Western social scientists to these types of questions tend—as Jean and John Comaroff have noted—to "deal in stereotypes, to reduce [Africa's] politics to typefying adjectives—communalist, clientalist, patriarchal, paternalist, and the like. Which is far too simple. Not to say pejorative" (1997, 129). Certainly in the Tanzanian context the puzzles of rural politics have all too often been boiled down to explanations of "rural culture"—the stubborn peasant's adherence to tradition and unwillingness to change in the face of a drastically transformed political and economic environment. Yet the resonance of this explanation is considerably undermined by the evidence offered here: that rural people are all-too-ready to adopt new technologies, techniques, and political strategies when these are deemed not to put their subsistence at stake.

Much more robust answers to these questions lie in the notion of subsistence citizenship. The citizenship of those who, year after year, live at or near the threshold of subsistence bears the same distinctive temporal and spatial attributes that their livelihoods do. People's political practice is shaped, at least in part, by their experiences of and insights into the conditions of their rural lives: seasonality in relation to water and food supply; ebbs and flows of political attention and engagement in relation to election cycles and dearth; and unpredictability in terms of the climate, market, and government aid. As the food supply has its seasons in so much of rural Africa, so does citizenship.

Subsistence citizenship is also marked by the character and condition of government agents' own authority and practice: political opportunism in the face of disaster, the high stakes of rural dependency on food aid, and the invisibility of rural governance and rural suffering that permits coercion without repercussion and, at times, neglect without shame. Rural people in Singida have a keen grasp of the palpable and embodied constraints on political agency that these conditions present, and of a national political culture that refuses (and vilifies) claims-making on behalf of sub-national groups. Thus, they have tended to employ an advocacy with a softer edge, one that embeds an idea of rights within a relationship-based politics. They engage the widely circulating moral idioms of age, family, and food as they simultaneously, and increasingly, individualize their efforts for material improvement and resist demands on their labor, time, and resources for development initiatives.

Understanding subsistence citizenship also helps untangle puzzles about rural Singidans' concepts of political legitimacy, corruption, and distribution of wealth. In a life centered on subsistence agriculture, the rightful share is not an equal share. One's share of the nation (like one's share of the harvest) is gradated by the proximity of one's identity and one's networks to the core of the nation (as it is to the household). Entitlements from the nation, like entitlements from one's family or neighbors, require face-to-face interactions that confirm or construct the relation and provide the opportunity to press moral and political obligations. Moreover, to access one's entitlements, these relationships are never to be taken for granted; rather relationships themselves must be *fed* with material transactions. It is no wonder then that political analysts like Chaligha et al. note that in Tanzania they see that "widespread perceptions of corruption co-exist with even more widespread expressions of trust" (2002, 2).

Though rights-based claims certainly have their season in Singida, it is clear that rural Singidans perceive a risk of rights-talk in relation to the power of paternalistic entreaties as modes of claims-making from those more well-off. Singidans see the concept of rights as risky because it all too often disentangles claims from ideas about mutual obligation and a relationship-based politics that has been forged and tended over time. In contrast, patronage has been more effective at capturing the state and its resources—at least for subsistence, if not for development—by nurturing more persistent moral connections to those in power. As the cases of the 2006 hunger and Lissu's election underscore, an oppositional approach to claims-making through rights discourses seems to become most viable in rural Singida at the threshold of subsistence, when there is little left to lose.

It is important to note that despite the differences described between these two discourses of distribution—rights and patronage—some of their tactics are much the same: each leverages labor, political support, and moral, social, and political pressure against the resources of the government, its representatives, and its sponsors. But for rural Singidans, the charge and the tone of these two forms of claims-making is fundamentally different: just as a smile or a tear differs from a scowl, as a subjunctive contrasts with an imperative, as an outstretched hand clashes with a fist. Patronage claims reference a history of mutual aid and hint at future interdependence. But when claims on patronage relationships fail and a refusal suggests that the relationship is being denied or abdicated, then Singidans turn to an asocial or legal notion of rights as a last resort. Such recourse to a notion of disinterested membership (like national citizenship or belonging to the human species) renders *social* relationships beside the point, even inappropriate. Rights thus imply, as I noted above, *asocial equalities*, normative assertions about equal opportunity and distribution that, in the village at least, are cast adrift from the relationships through which they might actually be realized.

So, while an asocial notion of rights has its time and place in subsistence agriculture contexts—that is, at the threshold of subsistence—it is somewhat counter-intuitive in a political space in which distribution is governed on a daily basis by relationships and their social work. Yet it is essential to note that neither rights nor patronage alone suffice as idioms of accountability. It is the code-switching and code-mixing of these two forms that allow poor rural people to capture as much of the state as they do. In the context of an extractive state-building project, rural Tanzanians resist total depletion by insisting that food is not *just* a commodity or aid, but *also* an entitlement and a gift. They are creating and maintaining relationships that simultaneously connect them to resources beyond the village even as they limit the state's incursion into their daily lives.

Both rights and patronage present alternative discourses of distribution to that of the market, the latter being all too often taken for granted in today's world. Yet one must ask if the difference between rights and patronage is so very great—that is, if they are not two of a kind, or one a subset of the other. Are rights-based claims simply one form of a broader category of patronage—that depends precariously on the capricious beneficence of, not wealthy patrons, but institutions, parties, or polities to press claims through legislation, adjudication, or advocacy? Or are patron-based claims merely one form of rights practice that use narratives of crisis, shame, and moral obligation to press claims on individuals, rather than on institutions, in settings where institutions are entirely unfunded—where they consist quite conspicuously of nothing more than people? Further exploration of when rights language is used, by whom, and to what ends will shed useful light on these questions. Meanwhile, it is no surprise that Singidans code-mix across these two idioms of claims-making as much as they code-switch, working toward a relationship-based politics that incorporates a notion of rights—one that holds the values of *both* relationships *and* rights as useful and essential for claims-making.

Finally, we must recognize that the scholarly and state preoccupation with quantifying food deprivation, measuring hunger, and declaring famine is a *political* concern as much as it is a scientific or a moral one. Identifying where on the sliding scale of deprivation a market discourse of the distribution of food becomes morally and politically unjustifiable, and when a new discourse of distribution should kick in, are questions that are never debated outside the interests, agendas, and capacities of individuals and institutions. When it comes to the issue of food aid, development, and redistribution, perhaps we should concern ourselves less with defining which type and level of food deprivation is biologically, socially, and politically tolerable and pay more attention to what type of distribution is *fair*. Not "what is *a right*?" but "what is *right*"? If we take our cue from rural Singidans, then such questions can only be reasoned *through relationships*, not in denial of them. Until then, as Sissako suggests, Singidans will rely neither on the unpredictable grace of the sun, nor on that of their government, but on the far more predictable grace of their neighbors.

Notes

1. Abderrahmane Sissako, *La Vie Sur Terre* (France, 1998). *La Vie sur Terre* was commissioned by a French/Swiss television channel as part of a series titled "The Year 2000 Seen by ..." Films were commissioned to be set in ten different countries on December 31, 1999, and directed by young filmmakers. Sissako was the only African filmmaker selected.

2. Abderrahmane Sissako, "Abderrahmane Sissako on *Life on Earth* (1998)," translation by Alison Levine (Virginia Film Festival, Charlottesville, VA, 1 November 2008), https://www.youtube.com/watch?v=9tMvVl_dWao.

Bibliography

Abélès, Marc, and Chantal Collard. 1985. *Age, Pouvoir et Société en Afrique Noire.* [*Age, Power, and Society in Black Africa*]. Paris: Karthala & Montreal, PUM (Presses Universitaires de Montréal).

Abrams, Philip "Notes on the Difficulty of Studying the State." *Journal of Historical Sociology* no. 1, (1977): 58–89.

Abu-Sada, Caroline. *In the Eyes of Others: How People in Crises Perceive Humanitarian Aid.* Paris: Médecins sans Frontières, 2012.

Achebe, Chinua. *A Man of the People.* New York: Anchor Books, 2016 [1967].

Adichie, Chimamanda Ngozi. 2009. The Danger of a Single Story. TED Talk. https://www.ted.com/talks/chimamanda_adichie_the_danger_of_a_single_story.

Adunbi, Omolade. *Oil Wealth and Insurgency in Nigeria.* Bloomington: Indiana University Press, 2015.

Afrobarometer. 2009. Popular Attitudes toward Democracy in Tanzania: A Summary of Afrobarometer Indicators, 2001–2008. *Briefing Papers.* Afrobarometer.

———. 2009. Tanzanians and their MPs: What the People Want, and What They Don't Always Get. In *Briefing Papers.* Afrobarometer.

Agar, Michael. *The Professional Stranger: An Informal Introduction to Ethnography.* Bingley: Emerald Group Publishing, 2008.

Aminzade, Ronald. *Race, Nation, and Citizenship in Post-Colonial Africa: The Case of Tanzania.* New York: Cambridge University Press, 2013.

Ansell, Aaron. *Zero Hunger: Political Culture and Antipoverty Policy in Northeast Brazil.* Chapel Hill: University of North Carolina Press, 2014.

Appadurai, Arjun. "Gastro-Politics in Hindu South Asia." *American Ethnologist* no. 8 (1981): 494–511.

———. *The Social Life of Things: Commodities in Cultural Perspective.* Cambridge: Cambridge University Press, 1986.

———. "Dead Certainty: Ethnic Violence in the Era of Globalization." *Development and Change* no. 29 (1998): 905–925.

Apple, Michael. *Ideology and Curriculum.* London: Routledge, 1979.

Arrighi, Giovanni, and John S. Saul. *Essays on the Political Economy of Rural Africa.* New York: Monthly Review Press, 1973.

Askew, Kelly Michelle. *Performing the Nation: Swahili Music and Cultural Politics in Tanzania.* Chicago: University of Chicago Press, 2002.

Balile, Deodatus. 2013, Jan. 23. Mtwara Residents at Odds with Tanzanian Govt over Gas Plant." *Sabahi.*

Baro, Mamadou, and Tara F. Deubel. "Persistent Hunger: Perspectives on Vulnerability, Famine and Food Security in Sub-Saharan Africa." *Annual Review of Anthropology* no. 35 (2006): 521–538.

Bayart, Jean-François. 1993. *The State in Africa: The Politics of the Belly.* New York: Longman.

Becker, Felicitas. 2013. "Remembering Nyerere: Political Rhetoric and Dissent in Contemporary Tanzania." *African Affairs* no. 112 (447):1–24.

Berman, Bruce, and John Lonsdale. 1992. *Unhappy Valley: Conflict in Kenya and Africa.* London: James Currey.

Bernstein, Henry. 1981. "Notes on State and Peasantry in Tanzania." *Review of African Political Economy* (21).

Bernstein, Henry, and Terence J. Byrnes. 2001. "From Peasant Studies to Agrarian Change." *Journal of Agrarian Change* no. 1 (1):1–56.

Berry, Sara. 1984. "The Food Crisis and Agrarian Change in Africa: A Review Essay." *African Studies Review* no. 27 (2):59–112.

———. 1993. *No Condition is Permanent: The Social Dynamics of Agrarian Change in Sub-Saharan Africa.* Madison: University of Wisconsin Press.

Bienen, Henry. 1967. *Tanzania: Party Transformation and Economic Development.* Princeton: Princeton University Press.

Bigman, David. 2011. *Poverty, Hunger, and Democracy in Africa: Potential and Limitations of Democracy in Cementing Multiethnic Societies.* New York: Palgrave MacMillan.

Bjerk, Paul. 2005. "'Building a New Eden': Lutheran Church Youth Choir Performances in Tanzania." *Journal of Religion in Africa* no. 35 (3):324–361.

———. 2010. "Sovereignty and Socialism in Tanzania: The Historiography of an African State." *History in Africa* no. 37:275–319.

———. 2013. "Remembering Villagisation in Tanzania: National Consciousness Amidst Economic Failure." In *Africa after Fifty Years: Retrospections and Reflections,* edited by Toyin Falola, Maurice Amutabi and Sylvester Gundona. New Jersey: Africa World Press.

———. 2015. *Building a Peaceful Nation: Julius Nyerere and the Establishment of Sovereignty in Tanzania, 1960–1964.* Rochester: University of Rochester Press.

Bornstein, Erica. 2005. *The Spirit of Development: Protestant NGOs, Morality, and Economics in Zimbabwe.* Palo Alto: Stanford University Press.

Bourdieu, Pierre. 1984. *Distinction: A Social Critique of the Judgment of Taste.* Cambridge: Harvard University Press.

———. 1996. *State Nobility: Elite Schools in the Field of Power.* Cambridge: Polity Press.

Bourdieu, Pierre with Jean-Claude Passeron. 1990. *Reproduction in Education, Society and Culture* London: Sage.

Bourdon, Natalie J. 2013. "Opening Pandora's Box: Human Rights, Customary Law, and the "Communal Liberal Self" in Tanzania." In *Gender Justice and Legal Pluralities: Latin American and African Perspectives,* edited by Rachel Seider and John Andrew NcNeish. New York: Routledge.

Bowie, Katherine. 1998. "The Alchemy of Charity: Of Class and Buddhism in Northern Thailand." *American Anthropologist* no. 100 (2).

Branco, Manuel Couret. 2009. *Economics Versus Human Rights.* New York: Routledge.

Brennan, James R. 2006. "Blood Enemies: Exploitation and Urban Citizenship in the Nationalist Political Thought of Tanzania, 1958–75." *The Journal of African History* no. 47 (3):389–413.

———. 2012. *Taifa: Making Nation and Race in Urban Tanzania.* Athens, OH: Ohio University Press.

———. 2014. "Julius Rex: Nyerere through the Eyes of his Critics, 1953–2013." *Journal of Eastern African Studies* no. 8 (3):459–477.

Brennan, L. 1984. "The Development of the Indian Famine Codes: Personalities, Politics, and Policies." *Famine* no. 1:91–111.

Brooke, Clark. 1967. "The Heritage of Famine in Central Tanzania." *Tanzania Notes and Records* no. 66 (20).

Bryceson, D.F. 1978. Peasant Food Production and Food Supply in Relation to the Historical Development of Commodity Production in Pre-Colonial and Colonial Tanganyika, Service Paper. Bureau of Resource Assessment and Land Use Planning, University of Dar es Salaam.

Buchert, Lene. 1994. *Education in the Development of Tanzania: 1919–1990*. London: James Currey Press.

Butler, Judith. 1993. *Bodies that Matter: On the Discursive Limits of 'Sex.'* New York: Routledge.

Butterly, John R., and Jack Shepherd. 2010. *Hunger: The Biology and Politics of Starvation*. Lebanon: University Press of New England.

Chabal, Patrick, and Jean-Pascal Daloz. 1999. *Africa Works: Disorder as Political Instrument*. Oxford: James Currey.

Chadema Diaspora. Uploaded 28 October 2013. Tangazo la Chadema: WaTanzania Wanataka Mabadiliko, Mwalimu Nyerere.

Chaīanov, A. V. 1986. *A.V. Chayanov on the Theory of Peasant Economy*. Madison: University of Wisconsin Press.

Chakrabarty, D. 2000. *Provincializing Europe: Postcolonial Thought and Historical Difference*. Princeton: Princeton University Press.

Chaligha, Amon, Robert Mattes, Michael Bratton, and Yul Derek Davids. 2002. Uncritical Citizens or Patient Trustees? Tanzanians' Views of Political and Economic Reform. In *Afrobarometer: A Comparative Series of National Public Attitude Surveys on Democracy, Markets, and Civil Society in Africa*.

Chambers, Robert. 1983. *Rural Development: Putting the Last First*. London: Longman.

———. 1994. "The Origins and Practice of Participatory Rural Appraisal." *World Development* no. 22 (7):953–69.

———. 1995. "Poverty and Livelihoods: Whose Reality Counts?" *Environment and Urbanization* no. 7 (1):173–204.

———. 2002. *Participatory Workshops: A Sourcebook of 21 Sets of Ideas and Activities*. New York: Earthscan.

———. 2008. *Revolutions in Development Inquiry*. London: Earthscan.

Chambers, Robert, and G.R. Conway. 1991. *Sustainable Rural Livelihoods: Practical Concepts for the 21st Century*. Sussex: Institute of Development Studies.

Chastre, Claire, and Heather Kindness. 2006. Access to Primary Health Care: Evidence from Singida Rural District. Save the Children.

Cheney, Kristen. 2007. *Pillars of the Nation: Child Citizens and Ugandan National Development*. Chicago: University of Chicago Press.

Chidzero, Bernard T. 1961. *Tanganyika and International Trusteeship*. Oxford: Oxford University Press.

Ching, Barbara, and Gerald W. Creed. 1997. *Knowing Your Place: Rural Identity and Cultural Hierarchy*. New York: Routledge.

Chipkin, Ivor. 2003. "'Functional' and 'Dysfunctional' Communities: The Making of National Citizens." *Journal of Southern African Studies* no. 29 (1):63–82.

Cliggett, Lisa. 2005. *Grains from Grass: Aging, Gender, and Famine in Rural Africa*. Ithaca: Cornell University Press.

Cohen, David, and E.S. Atieno Odhiambo. 1989. *Siaya: The Historical Anthropology of an African Landscape*. London: James Curry.

Cole, Jennifer, and Deborah Durham, eds. 2006. *Generations and Globalization: Youth, Age and Family in the New World Economy*. Bloomington: Indiana University Press.

Comaroff, John L., and Jean Comaroff, eds. 1996. *Civil Society and the Political Imagination in Africa*. Chicago: University of Chicago Press.

Comaroff, John L., and Jean Comaroff. 1997. "Postcolonial Politics and Discourses of Democracy in Southern Africa: An Anthropological Reflection on African Political Modernities." *Journal of Anthropological Research* no. 53 (2):123–146.

Condon, John C. 1967. "Nation Building and Image Building in the Tanzanian Press." *The Journal of Modern African Studies* no. 5 (3):335–54.

Consulate of the United Republic of Tanzania. 2015. *Symbols* [cited 8 August 2015 2015]. Available from http://www.tanzaniaconsul.com/symbols.html.

Cooke, B., and U. Kothari. 2001. *Participation: The New Tyranny?* London: Zed Books.

Cooper, Frederick. 2005. *Colonialism in Question: Theory, Knowledge, History*. Berkeley: University of California Press.

Cornwall, Andrea, and Nyamu-Musembi. 2004. "Putting the 'Rights-Based Approach' to Development into Perspective." *Third World Quarterly* no. 25 (8):1415–1437.

Cornwall, Andrea, Steven Robins, and Bettina Von Lieres. 2011. "States of Citizenship: Contexts and Cultures of Public Engagement and Citizen Action." *IDS Working Papers* no. 2011 (363):1–32.

Corrigan, Peter. 1997. *The Sociology of Consumption: An Introduction*. London: SAGE.

Cory, Hans. 1951. *Rimi Law and Custom*. Kampala: East African Institute of Social Research.

Coulson, Andrew. 1982. *Tanzania: A Political Economy*. New York: Oxford University Press.

Cowen, Michael, and Robert Shenton. 1996. *Doctrines of Development*. London: Routledge.

Crais, Clifton C. 2011. *Poverty, War, and Violence in South Africa*. Cambridge: Cambridge University Press.

Dangaremga, Tsitsi. 1988. *Nervous Conditions*. London: The Women's Press.

Das, Veena, and Deborah Poole, eds. 2004. *Anthropology in the Margins of the State*. Santa Fe, NM: School of American Research Press.

Dawes, James. 2007. *That the World May Know: Bearing Witness to Atrocities*. Cambridge: Harvard University Press.

d'Azevedo, Warren. 1962. "Common Principles and Variant Kinship Structures among the Gola of Western Liberia." *American Anthropologist* no. 64 (3):404–20.

de Castro, Josué. 1952. *The Geography of Hunger*. Boston: Little, Brown.

de Lame, Danielle. 2005. *A Hill among Thousand: Transformations and Ruptures in Rural Rwanda*. Madison: University of Wisconsin Press.

de Waal, Alexander. 1989. *Famine that Kills: Darfur, Sudan, 1984–1985*. Oxford: Clarendon Press.

———. 1996. "Social Contract and Deterring Famine: First Thoughts." *Disasters* no. 20 (3):194–205.

———. 1997. *Famine Crimes: Politics and the Disaster Relief Industry in Africa*. Oxford: James Currey.

———. 2000. Democratic Process and the Fight against Famine. In *IDS Working Paper Series*. Sussex: Institute of Development Studies.

Dean, Erin. 2010. "The Paradox of Power: Connection, Inequality, and Energy Development on Tumbatu Island, Zanzibar." *Ethnology* no. 49 (3):185–206.

Devereux, Stephen. 2001. "Sen's Entitlement Approach: Critiques and Counter-critiques." *Oxford Development Studies* no. 29 (3):245–263.

Drèze, Jean, and Amartya Sen, eds. 1990. *The Political Economy of Hunger*. Vol. 2: Famine Prevention. Oxford: Clarendon Press.

Dulani, Boniface, Robert Mattes, and Carolyn Logan. 2013. After a Decade of Growth in Africa, Little Change in Poverty at the Grassroots. In *Policy Brief*: Afrobarometer.

Durkheim, E. 1956. "Education: Its Nature and Role." In *Education and Sociology*. Glencoe: Free Press.

Edelman, Murray. 1988. *Constructing the Political Spectacle*. Chicago. University of Chicago Press.

———. 2005. "Bringing the Moral Economy Back in … to the Study of 21st-Century Transnational Peasant Movements." *American Anthropologist* no. 107 (3):331–345.

———. 2013. What is a Peasant? What are Peasantries? A Briefing Paper on Issues of Definition. Paper read at Intergovernmental Working Group on a United Nations Declaration on the Rights of Peasants and Other People Working in Rural Areas, 15–19 July, Geneva.

Edelman, Marc, and Angelique Haugerud, eds. 2005. *The Anthropology of Development and Globalization: From Classical Political Economy to Contemporary Neoliberalism*. Malden, MA: Blackwell.

Edmondson, Laura. 2007. *Performance and Politics in Tanzania: The Nation on Stage*. Bloomington: Indiana University Press.

Eisenstadt, S.N., and Rene Lemarchand, eds. 1981. *Political Clientelism, Patronage and Development*. London: SAGE.

Ekman, Joakim. 2009. "Political Participation and Regime Stability: A Framework for Analyzing Hybrid Regimes." *International Political Science Review* no. 30 (1):7–31.

Ellis, Stephen. 2011. *Season of Rains: Africa in the World*. Chicago: Chicago University Press.

Englund, Harri. 2006. *Prisoners of Freedom: Human Rights and the African Poor*. Berkeley: University of California Press.

———. 2011. *Human Rights and African Airwaves: Mediating Equality on the Chichewa Radio*. Bloomington: Indiana University Press.

Eyakuze, Aidan, and Ben Taylor. April 2015. "Four Bills Later: Is Blogging with Statistics in Tanzania Now Only for Adrenalin Junkies?" In *Mtega*, edited by Ben Taylor.

Fabian, Johannes. 1983. *Time and the Other*. New York: Columbia University Press.

Fanon, Franz. 1963. *Wretched of the Earth*. Translated by Constance Farrington. New York: Grove Press.

Farmer, Paul, and Nicole Gastineau. 2009. "Re-Thinking Health and Human Rights: Time for a Paradigm Shift." In *Human Rights: An Anthropological Reader*, edited by Mark Goodale. Malden, MA: Wiley-Blackwell.

Fassin, Didier. 2012. *Humanitarian Reason: A Moral History of the Present*. Berkeley: University of California Press.

Feierman, Steven. 1990. *Peasant Intellectuals: Anthropology and History in Tanzania*. Madison: University of Wisconsin Press.

Ferguson, James. 1992. "The Country and the City on the Copperbelt." *Cultural Anthropology* no. 7 (1):80–92.

———. 1994. *The Anti-Politics Machine: Development, Depoliticization, and Bureaucratic Power in Lesotho.* Minneapolis: University of Minnesota Press.

———. 1999. *Expectations of Modernity: Myths and Meanings of Urban Life on the Zambian Copperbelt.* Berkeley: University of California Press.

———. 2006. *Global Shadows: Africa in the Neoliberal World Order.* Durham: Duke University Press.

———. 2010. "The Uses of Neoliberalism." *Antipode* no. 41:166–184.

———. 2015. *Give a Man a Fish: Reflections on the New Politics of Distribution.* Durham: Duke University Press.

Ferguson, James, and Akhil Gupta. 2002. "Spatializing States: Toward an Ethnography of Neoliberal Governmentality." *American Ethnologist* no. 29 (4):981–1002.

Ferme, Mariane. 2001. *The Underneath of Things: Violence, History, and the Everyday in Sierra Leone.* Berkeley: University of California Press.

Fjeldstad, Odd-Helge. 1995. Taxation and Tax Reforms in Tanzania: A Survey. In *Working Paper.* Bergen: Chr. Michelsen Institute.

———. 2001. "Taxation, Coercion and Donors: Local Government Tax Enforcement in Tanzania." *The Journal of Modern African Studies* no. 39 (2):289–306.

Food and Agriculture Organization of the United Nations. 2008. *About the Right to Food.* http://www.fao.org/righttofood.

Fortes, M., and E.E. Evans-Pritchard, eds. 1940. *African Political Systems.* Oxford: Oxford University Press.

Foucault, Michel. 1977. "Discipline and Punish: The Birth of a Prison." New York: Random House.

Fouéré, Marie-Aude. 2009. "J. K. Nyerere entre Mythe et Histoire: Analyse de la Production d'un Culture Nationale en Tanzanie Post-Socialiste" [J.K. Nyerere Between Myth and History: Analysis of the Production of a National Culture in Post-Socialist Tanzania." *Les Cahier d'Afrique de l'Est* no. 4:197–224.

———. 2011. "L'Imaginaire National à l'Épreuve du Post-Socialisme." *Politique Africaine* no. 121 (69–85).

———. 2014. "Julius Nyerere, Ujamaa, and Political Morality in Contemporary Tanzania." *African Studies Review* no. 57 (1):1–24.

Fouéré, Marie-Aude, ed. 2015. *Remembering Nyerere in Tanzania: History, Memory, Legacy.* Dar es Salaam: Mkuki na Nyota.

Freire, Paolo. 1970. *Pedagogy of the Oppressed.* New York: Continuum.

Galemba, Rebecca. 2012. ""Corn is Food, Not Contraband": The Right to "Free Trade" at the Mexico-Guatemala Border." *American Ethnologist* no. 39 (4):716–734.

Geertz, Clifford. 1973. *The Interpretation of Culture.* New York: Basic Books.

Geschiere, Peter. 2009. *The Perils of Belonging: Autochthony, Citizenship, and Exclusion in Africa & Europe.* Chicago: University of Chicago Press.

Geschiere, Peter, and J. Gugler. 1998. "The Urban-Rural Connection: Changing Issues of Belonging and Identification." *Africa* no. 68 (3):309–20.

Giblin, James. 1986. "Famine and Social Change during the Transition to Colonial Rule in Northeastern Tanzania, 1880–1896." *African Economic History* (15):85–105.

———. 2005. *A History of the Excluded: Making Family a Refuge from State in Twentieth-Century Tanzania.* Oxford: James Currey.

Giblin, James, and Jamie Monson, eds. 2010. *Maji Maji: Lifting the Fog of War.* Leiden: Brill.

Gieringer, Franz. 1990. "To Praise the Sun." A Traditional Nyaturu Hymn of Praising God and Asking for His Blessings." *Anthropos* no. 85 (4/6):518–523.

Glassman, Jonathon. 1995. *Feasts and Riot: Revelry, Rebellion, and Popular Consciousness on the Swahili Coast, 1856–1888.* Portsmouth, NH: Heinemann.

Gore, Charles. 1993. "Entitlement Relations and 'Unruly' Social Practice: A Commentary on the Work of Amartya Sen." *The Journal of Development Studies* no. 29 (3):429–460.

Graeber, David. 2001. *Toward an Anthropological Theory of Value: The False Coin of Our Own Dreams.* New York: Palgrave.

Graham, Aubrey. 2014. "One Hundred Years of Suffering? "Humanitarian Crisis Photography" and Self-Representation in the Democratic Republic of the Congo." *Social Dynamics: A Journal of African Studies* no. 40 (1):140–163.

Gramsci, Antonio. 1971. *Selections from the Prison Notebooks.* New York: International Publishers.

Green, Maia. 2000. "Participatory Development and the Appropriation of Agency in Southern Tanzania." *Critique of Anthropology* no. 20 (1).

———. 2014. *The Development State: Aid, Culture, & Civil Society in Tanzania.* London: James Currey.

Gupta, Akhil. 1998. *Postcolonial Developments: Agriculture in the Making of Modern India.* Durham: Duke University Press.

———. 2012. *Red Tape: Bureaucracy, Structural Violence, and Poverty in India.* Durham: Duke University Press.

Hadley, Craig, and CL Patil. 2006. "Food Insecurity in Rural Tanzania is Associated with Maternal Anxiety and Depression." *American Journal of Human Biology* no. 18 (3):359–368.

Hall-Matthews, David. 2007. "Historical Roots of Famine Relief Paradigms: Ideas on Dependency and Free Trade in India in the 1870s." *Disasters* no. 20 (3):216–230.

Harvey, David. 2006. *Spaces of Global Capitalism: Towards a Theory of Uneven Geographical Development.* London: Verso.

Haugerud, Angelique. 1995. *The Culture of Politics in Modern Kenya.* Cambridge: Cambridge University Press.

Heilman, Bruce E., and Paul J. Kaiser. 2002. "Religion, Identity and Politics in Tanzania." *Third World Quarterly* no. 23 (4):691–709.

Herzfeld, Michael. 1993. *The Social Production of Indifference: Exploring the Symbolic Roots of Western Bureaucracy.* Chicago: University of Chicago Press.

———. 1997. *Cultural Intimacy: Social Poetics in the Nation-State.* New York: Routledge.

Hewitt, K. 1983. "The Idea of Calamity in a Technocratic Age." In *Interpretations of Calamity, from the Viewpoint of Human Ecology,* edited by K. Hewitt. Boston: Allen & Unwin.

Hickel, Jason. 2015. *Democracy as Death: The Moral Order of Anti-Liberal Politics in South Africa.* Berkeley: University of California Press.

Hinnebusch, Thomas J., and Sarah M. Mirza. 1998. *Kiswahili: Msingi wa Kusema, Kusoma na Kuandika [Swahili: A Foundation for Speaking, Reading, and Writing]* Lanham, MD: University Press of America.

Hochschild, Adam. 1998. *King Leopold's Ghost: A Story of Greed, Terror and Heroism in Africa.* New York: Houghton Mifflin.

Hodgson, Dorothy Louise. 2001. *Once Intrepid Warriors: Gender, Ethnicity, and the Cultural Politics of Maasai Development.* Bloomington: Indiana University Press.

———. 2011. *Being Maasai, Becoming Indigenous: Postcolonial Politics in a Neoliberal World.* Bloomington: Indiana University Press.

———. 2017. *Gender Justice and the Problem of Culture: From Customary Law to Human Rights in Tanzania.* Bloomington: Indiana University Press.

Holston, James. 2008. *Insurgent Citizenship: Disjunctions of Democracy and Modernity in Brazil.* Princeton: Princeton University Press.

Holston, James, and Arjun Appaduari. 1996. "Cities and Citizenship." *Public Culture* no. 8:187–204.

Howard, Mary, and Ann V. Millard, eds. 1997. *Hunger and Shame: Poverty and Child Malnutrition on Mount Kilimanjaro.* New York: Routledge.

Hunter, Emma. 2013. "Dutiful Subjects, Patriotic Citizens, and the Concept of 'Good Citizenship' in Twentieth-Century Tanzania." *The Historical Journal* no. 56 (1):257–277.

———. 2015. *Political Thought and the Public Sphere in Tanzania.* Cambridge: Cambridge University Press.

Hutchinson, Sharon. 1996. *Nuer Dilemmas: Coping with Money, War, and the State.* Berkeley: University of California Press.

Hyden, Goran. 1969. *Political Development in Rural Tanzania.* Nairobi: East African Publishing House.

———. 1980. *Beyond Ujamaa in Tanzania: Underdevelopment and an Uncaptured Peasantry.* Berkeley: University of California Press.

Igoe, James. 2006. "Becoming Indigenous Peoples: Difference, Inequality, and the Globalization of East African Identity Politics." *African Affairs* no. 105 (420):399–420.

Iliffe, John. 1969. *Tanganyika Under German Rule, 1905–1912.* Nairobi: East African Publishing House.

———. 1979. *A Modern History of Tanganyika.* Cambridge: Cambridge University Press.

———. 1987. *The African Poor: A History.* Edited by Raymond Danowski and Library Raymond Danowski Poetry. Cambridge: Cambridge University Press.

———. 1990. *Famine in Zimbabwe: 1890–1960.* Gweru: Mambo Press.

Ingle, Clyde R. 1972. *From Village to State in Tanzania: The Politics of Rural Development.* Ithaca: Cornell University Press.

Institute for Security Studies. 2012. "Tanzania's CCM: Is the Benign Hegemony Crumbling?" *ISS Today*, 12 July 2014.

International Monetary Fund and International Development Association. 1999. "Tanzania: Preliminary Document on the Initiative for the Heavily Indebted Poor Countries."

Isaacman, Allen F. 1993. "Peasants and Rural Social Protest in Africa." In *Confronting Historical Paradigms: Peasants, Labor, and the Capitalist World System in Africa and Latin America*, edited by Frederick Cooper, Allen F. Isaacman, Florencia E. Mallon, William Roseberry and Steve J. Stern. Madison: University of Wisconsin Press.

Ivaska, Andrew. 2005. "Of Students, 'Nizers,' and a Struggle over Youth: Tanzania's 1966 National Service Crisis." *Africa Today* no. 51 (3):83–107.

———. 2011. *Cultured States: Youth, Gender, and Modern Style in 1960s Dar es Salaam.* Durham: Duke University Press.

Jackson, Michael. 2011. *Life Within Limits: Well-Being in a World of Want.* Durham: Duke University Press.

———. 2013. "The Prose of Suffering." In *Lifeworlds: Essays in Existential Anthropology*, edited by Michael Jackson. Chicago: University of Chicago Press.

James, Deborah. 2013. "Citizenship and Land in South Africa: From Rights to Responsibilities." *Critique of Anthropology* no. 33 (1):26–46.

Jellicoe, Marguerite. 1969. "The Turu Resistance Movement." *Tanzania Notes and Records* no. LXX:1–12.

———. 1978. *The Long Path: A Case Study of Social Change in Wahi, Singida District, Tanzania.* Nairobi: East African Publishing House.

Jellicoe, Marguerite, Philip Puja, and Jeremiah Sombi. 1967. "Praising the Sun." *Transition* no. 31:27–31.

Jennings, Michael. 2003. "'We Must Run While Others Walk': Popular Participation and Development Crisis in Tanzania, 1961–9." *The Journal of Modern African Studies* no. 41 (2):163–187.

———. 2008. *Surrogates of the State: NGOs, Development, and Ujamaa in Tanzania.* Bloomfield, CT: Kumarian Press.

Kahn, Hilary E., ed. 2014. *Framing the Global: Entry Points for Research.* Bloomington: Indiana University Press.

Kahn, Miriam. 1986. *Always Hungry, Never Greedy: Food and the Expression of Gender in a Melanesian Society.* Prospect Heights, IL: Waveland Press.

Kaiser, Paul J. 1996. "Structural Adjustment and the Fragile Nation: The Demise of Social Unity in Tanzania." *The Journal of Modern African Studies* no. 39 (2):227–37.

Kearney, Michael. 1996. *Reconceptualizing the Peasantry: Anthropology in Global Perspective.* Boulder: Westview Press.

Kelsall, Tim. 2004. Contentious Politics, Local Governance, and the Self: A Tanzanian Case Study. Uppsala: Nordiska Afrikainstitutet.

———. 2007. "Notes on Recent Elections: The Presidential and Parliamentary Elections in Tanzania, October and December 2005." *Electoral Studies* no. 26 (2):525–529.

———. 2012. "Neo-Patrimonialism, Rent-Seeking and Development: Going with the Grain?" *New Political Economy* no. 17 (5):677–682.

Kendall, Nancy. 2007. "Education for All Meets Political Democratization: Free Primary Education and the Neoliberalization of the Malawian School and State." *Comparative Education Review* no. 51 (3):281–305.

Kijanga, Peter A.S. 1977. *Ujamaa and the Role of the Church in Tanzania*, Aquinas Institute of Theology, St. Louis.

———. Unpublished manuscript. *Ukuta Ryuva/Yuva.* Singida, Tanzania.

Kimambo, I.N., and A.J. Temu. 1969. *A History of Tanzania.* Chicago: Northwestern University Press.

Kipnis, Andrew. 2007. "Neoliberalism Reified: Suzhi Discourse and Tropes of Neoliberalism in the People's Republic of China." *Journal of the Royal Anthropological Institute* no. 13 (2):383–400.

Kissi, Edward. 2005. "Beneath International Famine Relief in Ethiopia: The United States, Ethiopia, and the Debate over Relief Aid, Development Assistance, and Human Rights." *African Studies Review* no. 48 (2):111–132.

Kleemeier, E. 2000. "The Impact of Participation on Sustainability: An Analysis of the Malawi Rural Piped Scheme Program." *World Development* no. 29 (5):929–944.

Klein, Naomi. 2007. *The Shock Doctrine: The Rise of Disaster Capitalism.* New York: Picador.

Krantz, Lasse. 2001. The Sustainable Livelihood Approach to Poverty Reduction: An Introduction. Stockholm: SIDA.

Kwayu, Aikande. 2014, May 19. Politics of Image or Can We call it the Image Strategy? #CCM vs #Opposition. In *ByGrace*. Dar es Salaam.

———. 2015. "Different 'Uses of Nyerere' in the Constitutional Review Debates: A Touchstone for Legitimacy in Tanzania." In *Remembering Nyerere: History, Memory, Legacy*, edited by Marie-Aude Fouéré. Dar es Salaam: Mkuki na Nyota.

Kymlicka, Will, and Wayne Norman. 1994. "Return of the Citizen: A Survey of Recent Work on Citizenship Theory." *Ethics* no. 104:352–381.

Lakoff, George. 2002. *Moral Politics, How Liberals and Conservatives Think*. Chicago: University of Chicago Press.

Lal, Priya. 2012. "Self-Reliance and the State: The Multiple Meanings of Development in Early Post-Colonial Tanzania." *Africa* no. 82 (2):212–34.

———. 2015. *African Socialism in Postcolonial Tanzania: Between the Village and the World*. Cambridge: Cambridge University Press.

Langwick, Stacey Ann. 2011. *Bodies, Politics, and African Healing: The Matter of Maladies in Tanzania*. Bloomington: Indiana University Press.

Latour, Bruno. 2005. *Reassembling the Social: An Introduction to Actor-Network Theory*. Oxford: Oxford University Press.

Leach, Melissa, Robin Mearns, and Ian Scoones. 1999. "Environmental Entitlements: Dynamics and Institutions in Community-Based Natural Resource Management." *World Development* no. 27 (2):225–247.

Lemarchand, Rene. 1989. "African Peasantries, Reciprocity and the Market: The Economy of Affection Reconsidered." *Cahiers d'Etudes Africaines* no. 29 (113):33–67.

Leys, Colin. 2005. "The Rise and Fall of Development Theory." In *The Anthropology of Development and Globalization*, edited by Marc Edelman and Angelique Haugerud. Malden, MA: Blackwell.

Li, Tania Murray. 2001. "Masyarakat Adat, Difference, and the Limits of Recognition in Indonesia's Forest Zone." *Modern Asian Studies* no. 35 (3):645–676.

———. 2007. *The Will to Improve: Governmentality, Development, and the Practice of Politics*. Durham: Duke University Press.

———. 2014. *Land's End: Capitalist Relations on an Indigenous Frontier*. Durham: Duke University Press.

Lipton, Michael. 1975. "Urban Bias and Food Policy in Poor Countries." *Food Policy* (1):41–52.

———. 1977. *Why Poor People Stay Poor: Urban Bias in World Development*. Cambridge: Harvard University Press.

Little, Peter D. 1992. *The Elusive Granary: Herder, Farmer, and State in Northern Kenya*. Cambridge: Cambridge University Press.

———. 2013. *Economic and Political Reform in Africa: Anthropological Perspectives*. Bloomington: Indiana University Press.

Lofchie, Michael F. 2014. *The Political Economy of Tanzania: Decline and Recovery*. Philadelphia: University of Pennsylvania Press.

Lonsdale, John. 1981. "States and Social Processes in Africa: A Historiographical Survey." *African Studies Review* no. 24 (2/3):139–225.

Low, Setha, ed. 1999. *Theorizing the City: The New Urban Anthropology Reader*. New Brunswick, NJ: Rutgers University Press.

Lugongo, Bernard. 2012. "Graft pulls down Kikwete's Approval Rate by 20pc" *The East African*.

Maddox, Gregory. 1990. "Mtunya: Famine in Central Tanzania, 1917–20." no. 31 (2):181–197.

———. 1996. "Gender and Famine in Central Tanzania: 1916–1961." *African Studies Review* no. 39 (1):83–101.

Maddox, Gregory, and James Leonard Giblin, eds. 2005. *In Search of a Nation: Histories of Authority and Dissidence in Tanzania*. Oxford: James Currey.

Magubane, Zine. 2008. "The (Product) Red Man's Burden: Charity, Celebrity, and the Contradictions of Coevalness." *Journal of Pan African Studies* no. 2 (6).

Makhulu, Anne-Maria, Beth A. Buggenhagen, Stephen Jackson, eds. 2010. *Hard Work, Hard Times: Global Volatility and African Subjectivities*. Berkeley: University of California Press.

Makinda, Kidua O.H. 1992. *The Educational Aspects of Nyaturu Dance Songs*, University of Dar es Salaam, Dar es Salaam.

Makulilo, Alexander Boniface. 2012. "Unleveled Playfield and Democracy in Tanzania." *Journal of Politics and Law* no. 5 (2).

———. 2014. Why the CCM is Still in Power in Tanzania? A Reply. *Social Science Research Network*, http://papers.ssrn.com/so13/papers.cfm?abstract_id=2458778.

Malkki, Lisa H. 1995. *Purity and Exile: Violence, Memory and National Cosmology among Hutu Refugees in Tanzania*. Chicago: University of Chicago Press.

———. 2015. *The Need to Help: The Domestic Arts of International Humanitarianism*. Durham: Duke University Press.

Mamdani, Mahmood. 1996. *Citizen and Subject: Contemporary Africa and the Legacy of Late Colonialism*. Princeton: Princeton University Press.

Mampilly, Zachariah. August 2013. "Accursed by Man, Not God: The Fight for Tanzania's Gas Lands." *Warscapes*.

Markandaya, Kamala. 1954. *Nectar in a Sieve*. New York: Signet/New American Library.

Marx, Karl. 2008 [1995]. *Capital: A New Abridgement*. Oxford: Oxford University Press.

Mathews, Gordon, Carolina Izquierdo, and Gōdon Mashūzu, eds. 2009. *Pursuits of Happiness: Well-Being in Anthropological Perspective*. New York: Berghahn Books.

Mauss, Marcel. 1967. *The Gift: Forms and Functions of Exchange in Archaic Societies*. New York: W.W. Norton & Company.

Mbembé, J. A. 2001. *On the Postcolony*. Berkeley: University of California Press.

Mbilinyi, Marjorie. 1990. "Struggles over the Labor of Women Peasants and Farm Workers." *TAAMULI* no. 1 (1/2).

McGovern, Mike. 2011. *Making War in Côte d'Ivoire*. Chicago: University of Chicago Press.

———. 2013. *Unmasking the State: Making Guinea Modern*. Chicago: University of Chicago Press.

Mdachi, Patrick. 1991. *WaNyaturu wa Singida: Mila na Desturi Zao*. Ndanda, Tanzania: Ndanda Mission Press.

Mesaki, Simeon, and Edmund Matotay. 2014. "Levels, Causes and Consequences of the Fear Phenomena: Findings from a Pilot Study in Tanzania." *Global Journal of Human-Social Science: Political Science* no. 14 (1):1–13.

Meskell, Lynn, ed. 2005. *Archaeologies of Materiality*. Malden, MA: Wiley-Blackwell.

Michener, Victoria. 1998. "The Participatory Approach: Contradiction and Co-option in Burkina Faso." *World Development* no. 26 (12):2105–2118.

Mintz, Sidney. 1985. *Sweetness and Power: The Place of Sugar in Modern History*. New York: Penguin Books.

Mitchell, Timothy. 2002. *Rule of Experts: Egypt, Techno-Politics, Modernity*. Berkeley: University of California Press.

———. 2011. *Carbon Democracy: Political Power in the Age of Oil*. London: Verso.

Mmuya, Max. 1996. *Government and Political Parties in Tanzania (after the 1995 Election): Facts and Figures*. Dar es Salaam: Friedrich-Ebert Stiftung.

———. 1998. *Political Reform in Eclipse: Crises and Cleavages in Political Parties*. Dar es Salaam: Friedrich-Ebert Stiftung.

Mmuya, Max, and Amon Chaligha. 1992. *Towards Multiparty Politics in Tanzania*. Dar es Salaam: Dar es Salaam University Press.

———. 1994. *Political Parties and Democracy in Tanzania*. Dar es Salaam: Dar es Salaam University Press.

Monga, Celestin. 1996. *The Anthropology of Anger: Civil Society and Democracy in Africa*. Boulder, CO: Lynne Rienner.

Moore, Barrington. 1966. *Social Origins of Dictatorship and Democracy: Lord and Peasant in the Making of the Modern World*. Boston: Beacon Press.

Moore, Mick. 2001. "Empowerment at Last?" *Journal of International Development* no. 13:321–329.

Morley, David. 1992. *Television Audiences and Cultural Studies*. New York: Routledge.

Mosse, David. 1994. "Authority, Gender and Knowledge: Theoretical Reflections on the Practice of Participatory Rural Appraisal." *Development and Change* no. 25:497–526.

———. 2001. "'People's Knowledge,' Participation, and Patronage: Operations and Representations in Rural Development." In *Participation: The New Tyranny?* edited by B. Cooke and U. Kothari. London: Zed Books.

———. 2005. *Cultivating Development: An Ethnography of Aid Policy and Practice*. Ann Arbor: Pluto Press.

Mwakikagile, G. 2006. *Tanzania Under Mwalimu Nyerere: Reflections on an African Statesman*. Dar es Salaam: New Africa Press.

Mwakyembe, H.G. 1993. "The Parliament and the Electoral Process." In *The State and the Working People in Tanzania*, edited by Issa G. Shivji. Dakar: Codesria.

Mwapachu, Juma V. 1979. "Operation Planned Villages in Rural Tanzania: A Revolutionary Strategy for Development." In *African Socialism in Practice*, edited by Andrew Coulson. Nottingham: Spokesman.

———. 2005. *Confronting New Realities: Reflections on Tanzania's Radical Transformation*. Dar es Salaam: E & D Limited.

Nadasdy, Paul. 2003. *Hunters and Bureaucrats: Power, Knowledge, and Aboriginal-State Relations in the Southwest Yukon*. Vancouver: UBC Press.

Narayan, Deepa. 1995. Contribution of People's Participation: Evidence from 121 Rural Water Supply Projects. Washington DC: The International Bank for Reconstruction and Development/The World Bank.

National Bureau of Statistics and ICF Macro. 2011. Tanzania: Demographic and Health Survey, 2010. Dar es Salaam: National Bureau of Statistics and ICF Macro.

National Bureau of Statistics and ORC Macro. 2005. Tanzania Demographic and Health Survey, 2004–2005. Dar es Salaam: National Bureau of Statistics and ORC Macro.

Nord, Roger, Yuri Sobolev, David Dunn, Alejandro Hajdenberg, Niko Hobdarl, Samar Mazlad, and Stephane Roudet. 2009. Tanzania: Story of an African Transition. Washington, DC: International Monetary Fund.

Ntuah, R.R. 1985. *Community Participation in Planning for Basic Education in Tanzania: A Case Study for Dodoma and Singida Regions*, Ph.D. Thesis, School of Education, Stanford University, Palo Alto.

Nugent, David, ed. 2002. *Locating Capitalism in Time and Space: Global Restructurings, Politics, and Identity*. Palo Alto: Stanford University Press.

Nyamnjoh, Francis. 2002. "'A Child is One Person's Only in the Womb': Domestication, Agency and Subjectivity in the Cameroonian Grassfields." In *Postcolonial Subjectivities in Africa*, edited by Richard Werbner. London: Zed Books.

Nyerere, Julius K. 1967. The Arusha Declaration. Dar es Salaam: United Republic of Tanzania.

———. 1968. *Freedom and Socialism: A Selection from Writings and Speeches, 1965–67*. Dar es Salaam: Oxford University Press.

———. 1968. *Ujamaa: Essays on Socialism*. London: Oxford University Press.

———. 1975. "Education for Liberation in Africa." *Prospects: Quarterly Review of Education* no. V (I).

O'Gorman, Melanie. 2012. "Why the CCM Won't Lose: The Roots of Single-Party Dominance in Tanzania." *Journal of Contemporary African Studies* no. 30 (2):313–333.

Okri, Ben. 1993. *The Famished Road*. New York: Anchor Books.

Oliech, Yohana K. C. 1975. *Rural Spatial Organization: The Case of Singida District*, M.A. Thesis. University of Dar es Salaam.

Olivier de Sardan, Jean-Pierre. 2005. *Anthropology and Development: Understanding Contemporary Social Change*. London: Zed Books.

Olson, Howard. 1964. "Rimi Proverbs." *Tanganyika Notes and Records* no. 62 (March).

———. 2002. *Footprints: Memoirs of Howard S. Olson*: Howard S. Olson.

———. 1964. *The Phonology and Morphology of Rimi*. Hartford, CT: Hartford Seminary Foundation.

Pallotti, Arrigo. 2008. "Tanzania: Decentralising Power or Spreading Poverty." *Review of African Political Economy* no. 116:221–235.

Pateman, Carole. 1983. "Feminist Critiques of the Public/Private Dichotomy." In *Public and Private in Social Life*, edited by S.I. Benn and G.F. Gaus, 281–303. New York: St. Martin's Press.

Perullo, Alex. 2011. *Live from Dar es Salaam: Popular Music and Tanzania's Music Economy*. Bloomington: Indiana University Press.

Peters, Pauline E. 2004. "Inequality and Social Conflict Over Land in Africa." *Journal of Agrarian Change* no. 4 (3):269–314.

Phillips, Kristin D. 2009. "Hunger, Healing, and Citizenship in Central Tanzania." *African Studies Review* no. 52 (1).

———. 2010. "Pater Rules Best: Political Kinship and Party Politics in Tanzania's Presidential Elections." *PoLAR: Political and Legal Anthropology Review* no. 33 (1):109–132.

———. 2011. "Educational Policymaking in the Tanzanian Postcolony: Authenticity, Accountability, and the Politics of Culture." *Critical Studies in Education* no. 52 (3):235–250.

———. 2013. "Dividing the Labor of Development: Education and Participation in Rural Tanzania." *Comparative Education Review* no. 57 (4):637–661.

———. 2014. Nyumba Kumi (the Ten-House Cell): Politics, Infrastructure, and the Grid of Governance in Rural Tanzania. Paper presented at the Annual Meetings of the American Anthropological Association. Washington DC.

———. 2015. "Nyerere's Ghost: Political Filiation, Paternal Discipline, and the Construction of Legitimacy in Multiparty Tanzania." In *Remembering Nyerere: History, Memory, Legacy*, edited by Marie-Aude Fouéré. Dar es Salaam: Mkuki na Nyota.

———. Unpublished manuscript. "Secrets, Lions, and Revelations: Women's Rites and the Politics of Knowledge in Tanzania."

Phillips, Kristin D., and Amy Stambach. 2008. "Cultivating Choice: The Invisible Hands of Educational Opportunity in Tanzania." In *The Globalisation of School Choice?* edited by M. Forsey, S. Davies and G. Walford. Oxford: Symposium Books.

Pigg, Stacy Leigh. 1992. "Inventing Social Categories through Place: Social Representations and Development in Nepal." *Comparative Studies in Society and History* no. 34 (3):491–513.

Piot, Charles. 1999. *Remotely Global: Village Modernity in West Africa*. Chicago: University of Chicago Press.

———. 2010. *Nostalgia for the Future: West Africa after the Cold War*. Chicago: University of Chicago Press.

Polanyi, Karl. 2001 [1944]. *The Great Transformation: The Political and Economic Origins of Our Time*. Boston: Beacon Press.

Policy Forum. *Growth in Tanzania: Is it Reducing Poverty?* 2009. Available from http://www.policyforum-tz.org/growth-tanzania-it-reducing-poverty.

Ponte, Stefano. 2001. "Policy Reforms, Market Failures and Input Use in African Smallholder Agriculture." *European Journal of Development Research* no. 13 (1):1–29.

———. 2002. *Farmers and Markets in Tanzania: How Policy Reforms Affect Rural Livelihoods in Africa*. Oxford: James Currey.

Popkin, Samuel L. 1979. *The Rational Peasant: The Political Economy of Rural Society in Vietnam*. Berkeley: University of California Press.

Pottier, Johan. 1999. *Anthropology of Food: The Social Dynamics of Food Security*. Cambridge: Polity Press.

Pritchett, James Anthony. 2007. *Friends for Life, Friends for Death: Cohorts and Consciousness among the Lunda-Ndembu*. Charlottesville: University of Virginia Press.

Redfield, Peter. 2013. *Life in Crisis: The Ethical Journey of Doctors without Borders*. Berkeley: University of California Press.

Redfield, Peter, and Erica Bornstein, eds. 2010. *Forces of Compassion: Humanitarianism between Ethics and Politics*. Santa Fe: School of American Research.

REPOA. 2006. Local Government Reform in Tanzania, 2002–2005: Summary of Research Findings on Governance. Dar es Salaam: REPOA.

REPOA and Afrobarometer. 2012. Press Release: Progress on Poverty Indicators. Dar es Salaam: REPOA.

Richards, Audrey. 1932. *Hunger and Work in a Savage Tribe: A Functional Study of Nutrition among the Southern Bantu*. London: Routledge.

———. 1939. *Land, Labour, and Diet in Northern Rhodesia: An Economic Study of the Bemba Tribe*. Oxford: Oxford University Press.

Romero, Simon, and Sara Shahriari. 2011. "Quinoa's Global Success Creates Quandary at Home." *New York Times*, March 19, 2011.

Roncoli, Carla, Benjamin S. Orlove, Merit Kabugo, and Milton Waiswa. 2011. "Cultural Styles of Participation in Farmers' Discussions of Seasonal Climate Forecasts in Uganda." no. 28:123–138.

Rosaldo, Renato, ed. 2003. *Cultural Citizenship in Southeast Asia: Nation and Belonging in the Hinterlands*. Berkeley: University of California Press.

Rostow, W.W. 1960. *The Stages of Economic Growth: A Non-Communist Manifesto*. Cambridge: Cambridge University Press.

Samoff, Joel. 1974. *Tanzania: Local Politics and the Structure of Power*. Madison: University of Wisconsin Press.

Sanders, Todd. 2008. *Beyond Bodies: Rainmaking and Sense Making in Tanzania*. Toronto: University of Toronto Press.

Sara, Jennifer, and Travis Katz. 1998. Making Rural Water Sustainable: Report on the Impact of Project Rules. Washington DC: World Bank, UNDP-World Bank Water and Sanitation Program.

Sassen, Saskia. 2014. "Foreword." In *Framing the Global: Entry Points for Research*, edited by Hilary E. Kahn. Bloomington: Indiana University Press.

Schatzberg, Michael G. 2001. *Political Legitimacy in Middle Africa: Father, Family, Food*. Bloomington: Indiana University Press.

Scheper-Hughes, Nancy. 1992. *Death without Weeping: The Violence of Everyday Life in Brazil*. Berkeley: University of California Press.

Scherz, China. 2014. *Having People, Having Heart: Charity, Sustainable Development, and Problems of Dependence in Central Uganda*. Chicago: University of Chicago Press.

Schneider, Harold K. 1970. *The Wahi Wanyaturu: Economics in an African Society*. New York: Wenner-Gren Foundation for Anthropological Research.

———. 1974. *Economic Man: The Anthropology of Economics*. New York: Free Press.

———. 1982. "Male-Female Conflict and Lion Men of Singida." In *African Religious Groups and Beliefs: Papers in Honor of William R. Bascom*, edited by Simon Ottenberg. Meerut, India: Archana Publications for the Folklore Institute.

Schneider, Leander. 2006. "Colonial Legacies and Postcolonial Authoritarianism: Connects and Disconnects." *African Studies Review* no. 49 (1):93–118.

———. 2006. "The Maasai's New Clothes: A Developmentalist Modernity and its Exclusions." *Africa Today* no. 53 (1):101–29.

———. 2011. "Bearing Risk is Hard to Do: Crop Price Risk Transfer for Poor Farmers and Low-Income Countries." *Development in Practice* no. 21 (4&5):536–549.

———. 2014. *Government of Development: Peasants and Politicians in Postcolonial Tanzania*. Bloomington: Indiana University Press.

Scott, James C. 1976. *The Moral Economy of the Peasant: Rebellion and Subsistence in Southeast Asia*. New Haven: Yale University Press.

———. 1985. *Weapons of the Weak: Everyday Forms of Peasant Resistance*. New Haven: Yale University Press.

———. 1990. *Domination and the Arts of Resistance: Hidden Transcripts*. New Haven: Yale University Press.

———. 1998. *Seeing Like a State: How Certain Schemes to Improve the Human Condition Have Failed*. New Haven: Yale University Press.

———. 2009. *The Art of Not Being Governed: An Anarchist History of Upland Southeast Asia*. New Haven: Yale University Press.

Scotton, Carol M. 1965. "Some Swahili Political Words." *The Journal of Modern African Studies* no. 3:527–41.

Sen, Amartya. 1981. *Poverty and Famines: An Essay on Entitlement and Deprivation*. Oxford: Clarendon Press.

———. 1990. "Food, Economics, and Entitlements." In *The Political Economy of Hunger*, edited by Jean Dreze and Amartya Sen. Oxford: Clarendon Press.

———. 1999a. *Commodities and Capabilities*. Delhi: Oxford University Press.

———. 1999b. *Development as Freedom*. New York: Knopf.

———. 2009. *The Idea of Justice*. Cambridge, MA: Belknap Press of Harvard University Press.

Shayo, Rose. 1995. Parties and Political Development in Tanzania. Auckland Park, South Africa: Electoral Institute for Sustainable Democracy in Africa.

Shipton, Parker. 1990. "African Famines and Food Security: Anthropological Perspectives." *Annual Review of Anthropology* no. 19:353–94.

———. 2007. *The Nature of Entrustment: Intimacy, Exchange, and the Sacred in Africa*. New Haven: Yale University Press.

Shivji, Issa G. 1989. *The Concept of Human Rights in Africa*. Dakar: Codesria Book Series.

———. 1996. "Constructing a New Rights Regime: Promises, Problems, and Prospects." *UTAFITI (New Series)* no. 3 (1):1–46.

Silverstone, Roger. 1994. *Television and Everyday Life*. New York: Routledge.

Simmel, Georg. 1978. *The Philosophy of Money*. New York: Routledge.

Simone, AbdouMaliq. 2004. "People as Infrastructure: Intersecting Fragments in Johannesburg." *Public Culture* no. 16 (3):407–429.

Singh, K.S. 1993. "The Famine Code: The Context and Continuity." In *Famine and Society*, edited by J. Floud and A. Rangasami. New Delhi.

Sissako, Abderrahmane. 1 November 2008. Abderrahmane Sissako on 'Life on Earth' (1998). In *Virginia Film Festival*. Charlottesville, VA: YouTube.

———. 1998. La Vie sur Terre. France: California Newsreel.

Slater, D. 1977. "Colonialism and the Spatial Structure of Underdevelopment: Outlines of an Alternative Approach with Special Reference to Tanzania." In *Third World Urbanization*, edited by Janet Abu-Lughod and Richard Hay, 165–175. Chicago: Maaroufa Press.

Smith, Daniel Jordan. 2007. *A Culture of Corruption: Everyday Deception and Popular Discontent in Nigeria*. Princeton: Princeton University Press.

Smith, James. 2008. *Bewitching Development: Witchcraft and the Reinvention of Development in Neoliberal Kenya*. Chicago: University of Chicago Press.

Snyder, Katherine A. 2005. *The Iraqw of Tanzania: Negotiating Rural Development*. Boulder: Westview Press.

Southall, R. 2005. "The 'Dominant Party Debate' and the South African Party System." *AfricaSpectrum* no. 40 (1):61–82.

Stambach, Amy. 2000. *Lessons from Mount Kilimanjaro: Schooling, Community, and Gender in East Africa*. New York: Routledge.

———. 2010. *Faith in Schools: Religion, Education, and American Evangelicals in East Africa*. Palo Alto: Stanford University Press.

Stiglitz, Joseph. 2003. *Globalization and its Discontents*. New York: W.W. Norton.

Strathern, Marilyn. 1988. *The Gender of the Gift: Problems with Women and Problems with Society in Melanesia*. Berkeley: University of California Press.

Stroeken, Koen. 2005. "Immunizing Strategies: Hip-Hop and Critique in Tanzania." *Africa* no. 75 (4):488–509.

Sumbai, Gasiano Gaspary Ntandu. 2015. *History of Food Security and Coping Strategies Against Famines: A Case of Iramba District, 1880–1961*, Ph.D. Thesis, Department of History, University of Dar es Salaam, Dar es Salaam, Tanzania.

Swarup, Anita. 2007. Famine a Visible Result of Climate Change in Eastern Africa. International Federation of Red Cross and Red Crescent Societies (IFRC).

Tanzania Food and Nutrition Centre, and TAHEA Iringa. 2013. Household Food and Nutrition Security Baseline Survey for Dodoma, Iringa, Njombe and Singida. Iringa: TAHEA-Iringa.

Tawney, R. H. 1966. *Land and Labor in China*. Boston: Beacon Press.

Taylor, Ben. 22 June 2015. Hard at Work in Green and Gold: Kinana's Politics of Image. In *Mtega*.

TEMCO. 2011. The Report of the 2010 General Elections in Tanzania. Dar es Salaam: University of Dar es Salaam.

Thompson, E. P. 1971. "The Moral Economy of the English Crowd in the Eighteenth Century." *Past & Present* no. 50 (1):76–136.

———. 1978. "Eighteenth-Century English Society: Class Struggle without Class." *Social History* no. 3 (2):133–165.

———. 1991. *Customs in Common*. New York: The New Press.

Thompson, Katrina Daly. 2006. "The Stereotype in Tanzania[n] Comics: Swahili and the Ethnic Other." *International Journal of Comic Art* no. 8 (2):228–247.

Tripp, Aili Mari. 1997. *Changing the Rules: The Politics of Liberalization and the Urban Informal Economy in Tanzania*. Berkeley: University of California Press.

Trouillot, Michel-Rolph. 1995. *Silencing the Past: Power and the Production of History*. Boston: Beacon Press.

Tsing, Anna. 1993. *In the Realm of the Diamond Queen: Marginality in an Out-of-the-Way Place*. Princeton: Princeton University Press.

Turnbull, Colin. 1972. *The Mountain People*. New York: Simon & Schuster.

Twaweza. 2015. *Rapid Analysis and Key Questions on Tanzania's Statistics Act* 15 April 2015 [downloaded 15 May 2015]. Available from http://twaweza.org/go/stats-act-analysis.

United Nations. 1966. International Covenant on Economic, Social, and Cultural Rights. Geneva: Office of the High Commissioner for Human Rights.

United Republic of Tanzania. 2010. Trends in Food Insecurity in Tanzania: Food Security and Nutrition Analysis of Tanzania Household Budget Surveys 2000/01 and 2007. Dar es Salaam: United Republic of Tanzania.

———. 2012. Tanzania National Panel Survey Report: Wave 2, 2010–2011. Dar es Salaam: National Bureau of Statistics & Ministry of Finance.

———. 2013a. Key Findings: 2011/12 Household Budget Survey, Tanzania Mainland. Dar es Salaam: National Bureau of Statistics.

———. 2013b. Tanzania in Figures, 2012. Dar es Salaam: National Bureau of Statistics.

———. 2015. Housing Condition, Household Amenities and Assets Monograph: 2012 Population and Housing Census. Dar es Salaam: National Bureau of Statistics.

Vaughan, Megan. 2007. *The Story of an African Famine: Gender and Famine in Twentieth-Century Malawi*. Cambridge: Cambridge University Press.

Vavrus, Frances. 2003. *Desire and Decline: Schooling Amid Crisis in Tanzania*. New York: Peter Lang.

———. 2005. "Adjusting Inequality: Education and Structural Adjustment Policies in Tanzania." *Harvard Educational Review* no. 75 (2):174–201.

Verdery, Katherine, and Caroline Humphrey, eds. 2004. *Property in Question: Value Transformation in the Global Economy, Wenner-Gren International Series*. Oxford: Berg.

Von Sick, Eberhard. 1915. *Die Waniaturu (Walimi): Ethnographische Skizze Eines Bantustammes*. Translated by Sister Rosemarie Steinbach. Berlin: Baessler Archiv.

Wainaina, Binyavanga. 2005. "How to Write about Africa." *Granta* no. 92.

———. 2010. "How to Write about Africa II: The Revenge." *Bidoun* no. II.

Waters, Tony. 1992. "A Cultural Analysis of the Economy of Affection and the Uncaptured Peasantry in Tanzania." *The Journal of Modern African Studies* no. 30 (1):163–175.

Watts, Michael. 1983. *Silent Violence: Food, Famine, and Peasantry in Northern Nigeria*. Berkeley: University of California Press.

Weiner, Annette. 1985. "Inalienable Wealth." *American Ethnologist* no. 12 (1):210–227.

———. 1992. *Inalieable Possessions: The Paradox of Keeping While Giving*. Berkeley: University of California Press.

Weinstein, Laura. 2011. "The Politics of Government Expenditures in Tanzania, 1999–2007." *African Studies Review* no. 54 (1):33–57.

Weiss, Brad. 1996. *The Making and Unmaking of the Haya Lived World: Consumption, Commoditization, and Everyday Practice*. Durham: Duke University Press.

———. 2009. *Street Dreams and Hip Hop Barbershops: Global Fantasy in Urban Tanzania*. Bloomington: Indiana University Press.

Werbner, Richard, ed. 2002. *Postcolonial Subjectivities in Africa*. London: Zed Books.

White Fathers. 1915. *The Rimi or Turu*. Dar es Salaam: Missionaries of Africa.

Whitehead, Ann. 1990. "Rural Women and Food Production in Sub-Saharan Africa." In *The Political Economy of Hunger*, edited by Jean Dreze and Amartya Sen. Oxford: Clarendon Press.

Whitehead, Neil. 2003. *Histories and Historicities in Amazonia*. Lincoln: University of Nebraska Press.

Wilk, Richard, and Lisa Cliggett. 2007. *Economies and Cultures: Foundations of Economic Anthropology*. Boulder: Westview Press.

Williams, Raymond. 1973. *The Country and the City*. New York: Oxford University Press.

Willis, Paul. 1977. *Learning to Labour: How Working Class Kids Get Working Class Jobs*. New York: Columbia University Press.

Wilson, Richard Ashby. 2006. "Afterword to "Anthropology and Human Rights in a New Key: The Social Life of Human Rights." *American Anthropologist* no. 108 (1):77–83.

Wolf, Eric R. 1966. *Peasants*. Englewood Cliffs, N.J.: Englewood Cliffs, N.J.: Prentice-Hall.

———. 1999. *Envisioning Power: Ideologies of Dominance and Crisis*. Berkeley: University of California Press.

———. 2001. *Pathways of Power: Building an Anthropology of the Modern World*. Berkeley: University of California Press.

World Bank. 2006. Local Government Taxation Reform in Tanzania: A Poverty and Social Impact Analysis (PSIA). Social Development Department: Economic and Work Sector.

World Food Programme. 2013. Tanzania 2012: Comprehensive Food Security and Vulnerability Analysis. Rome: World Food Programme.

Ziegler, Jean. 2011. *Betting on Famine: Why the World Still Goes Hungry*. New York: The New Press.

Index

KRISTIN D. PHILLIPS is Senior Lecturer in Anthropology at Emory University. Her research and teaching focus on the themes of citizenship, development, and social change in East Africa. She has published in *African Studies Review, PoLAR: Political and Legal Anthropology Review, Comparative Education Review, Critical Studies in Education*, and several edited volumes.

CPSIA information can be obtained
at www.ICGtesting.com
Printed in the USA
LVHW012352290919
632646LV00019B/153/P